Simon David Stein
The Phonetics of Derived Words in English

Linguistische Arbeiten

Edited by
Klaus von Heusinger, Agnes Jäger,
Gereon Müller, Ingo Plag,
Elisabeth Stark and Richard Wiese

Volume 585

Simon David Stein

The Phonetics of Derived Words in English

Tracing Morphology in Speech Production

DE GRUYTER

D61

ISBN 978-3-11-153683-5
e-ISBN (PDF) 978-3-11-102547-6
e-ISBN (EPUB) 978-3-11-102578-0
ISSN 0344-6727

Library of Congress Control Number: 2022946827

Bibliographic information published by the Deutsche Nationalbibliothek
The Deutsche Nationalbibliothek lists this publication in the Deutsche Nationalbibliografie; detailed bibliographic data are available on the internet at http://dnb.dnb.de.

© 2024 Walter de Gruyter GmbH, Berlin/Boston
This volume is text- and page-identical with the hardback published in 2023.

www.degruyter.com

Contents

Acknowledgements —— VII

List of figures —— IX

List of tables —— XI

1	**Introduction** —— 1	
2	**Storing and processing derived words** —— 8	
2.1	The decompositional perspective —— 9	
2.1.1	Base frequency as against word frequency —— 17	
2.1.2	Morphological segmentability —— 24	
2.1.3	Prosodic word integration —— 31	
2.1.4	Affix informativeness —— 39	
2.2	The non-decompositional perspective —— 47	
2.2.1	Discriminative learning —— 51	
2.3	Summary of hypotheses and questions —— 58	
3	**General method** —— 62	
3.1	Selection of morphological categories —— 63	
3.2	Building the datasets —— 66	
3.2.1	Description of the corpora —— 67	
3.2.2	Data extraction and cleaning —— 68	
3.3	Variables —— 73	
3.3.1	Response variable —— 73	
3.3.2	Predictor variables —— 76	
3.4	General modeling procedure —— 81	
4	**Frequency measures** —— 85	
4.1	Method —— 85	
4.2	Results —— 88	
4.2.1	Category-internal analyses —— 88	
4.2.2	Across-category analysis —— 96	
4.3	Discussion —— 97	
5	**Prosodic word integration** —— 105	
5.1	Method —— 105	

| 5.2 | Results —— 108 |
| 5.3 | Discussion —— 118 |

6	**Affix informativeness —— 125**
6.1	Method —— 125
6.2	Results —— 130
6.2.1	Conditional affix probability —— 130
6.2.2	Semantic information load —— 142
6.3	Discussion —— 150

7	**Linear discriminative learning —— 157**
7.1	Method —— 157
7.1.1	Dataset —— 157
7.1.2	Training data —— 159
7.1.3	Matrices for form and meaning —— 160
7.1.4	Comprehension and production mapping —— 164
7.1.5	LDL variables —— 166
7.1.6	Modeling word durations —— 170
7.2	Results —— 172
7.2.1	General comparison of the networks —— 172
7.2.2	Predicting durations with LDL variables —— 173
7.2.2.1	Mean word support and path entropies —— 179
7.2.2.2	Semantic density and semantic vector length —— 181
7.3	Discussion —— 185

| 8 | **General discussion —— 192** |

| 9 | **Conclusion —— 205** |

References —— 207

Index —— 225

Acknowledgements

This book is a slightly altered version of my doctoral dissertation. Even though it is my name that appears on the cover page, a dissertation is always the product of more than a single person's contribution. Without the help of many awesome people, I would not have been able to complete it, and I owe these people my thanks.

I thank my supervisor, Ingo Plag, for giving me the opportunity to engage in this project, and for the many, many things I have learned from him during those three and a half years. Ingo is gifted with that special sixth sense: he always knows when his students need the freedom to work independently, and when they need encouragement, supervision, and guidance (even when they themselves don't realize which one it is that they need). I could not have wished for a better supervisor.

Thank you to my mentor, Arne Lohmann, for everything that he has taught me and the many interesting and fun conversations we had during his time in Düsseldorf. I thank him especially for helping me in my first steps of navigating the scary world of statistical analysis. I also thank the members of my examining board, Tania Kouteva, Heidrun Dorgeloh, Kevin Tang, and Hana Filip.

I thank all the members in the DFG research unit FOR2373 *Spoken Morphology* for their valuable insights, their many helpful tips for my project, and their never-ending intellectual input during all the colloquium discussions and beyond. Thanks especially to Yu-Ying Chuang and Harald Baayen for their advice on the intricacies of linear discriminative learning.

I am grateful to the *Deutsche Forschungsgemeinschaft* (DFG, German Research Foundation) for funding this research (Project Morpho-Phonetic Variation in English, PL 151/7-2 and PL 151/8-2), which allowed me to fully concentrate on this dissertation for more than three years.

Thank you to everyone at the *New Zealand Institute of Language, Brain and Behaviour* (NZILBB) in Christchurch, for their generous support during my research stay in Aotearoa. You are an amazing team and I felt welcomed and supported from my first explorations of LaBB-CAT to the full hard drive of data I left with. Thanks especially to Jennifer Hay, James Brand, Dan Villarreal, Jacq Jones, Simon Todd, Emma Parnell, and, last but certainly not least, Robert Fromont for his incredible LaBB-CAT support.

Thank you to all my past lecturers from the department of English Studies at Heinrich Heine University Düsseldorf – both linguistics and literary studies – who have shaped my path in one way or another and made my studies an unforgettable journey. A special thanks is due to Sabine Arndt-Lappe, not just for her valuable input on prosodic boundaries during my dissertation project, but also for giving me the opportunity to work in the English Linguistics department as a student assistant back when I attended her undergraduate seminar on phonetics. Without this opportunity, I may not have had the chance to write this dissertation.

I thank the audiences of the many conferences and workshops I attended during these three years, especially the audiences of MMM 12, P&P 15, MoProc 2019, LingSoc 2019, IMM 19, WoW 2020, Interfaces of Phonetics 2021, PaPE 4, AIMM 5, and Holger Mitterer for his input on the comparison of frequency effects. I also thank the reviewers for *Frontiers in Psychology* and *Laboratory Phonology*, including Kevin Tang, Christina Manouilidou, Jessie S. Nixon, Valeria Caruso, and two anonymous reviewers. These people's comments contributed to making this dissertation better than other potential versions of it would have been.

Thank you to the Ang 3 team at Heinrich Heine University Düsseldorf. All of you have made writing this dissertation far more enjoyable than writing a dissertation should have any right to be. Special thanks to Marie Engemann, Ghattas Eid, Viktoria Schneider and Dominic Schmitz for sharing this journey with me, to Sonia Ben Hedia for her guidance, advice, and helpful resources when I was starting to follow in her footsteps, and to Ulrike Kayser for working her magic and always being there for us. Thank you to the student assistants Ann-Sophie Haan, Jennifer Keller, Maximilian Kempen, Sally Kolasa, Lisa-Marie Schmitz, Adiseu Slaviu, and Julika Weber for their help with segmentation and data cleaning. Special thanks to Lukas Ostrowski for proofreading the final version.

I thank my mother for continuously supporting me throughout my studies. Without her support, I would not have been able to complete them in the way that I did. Finally, I thank Sebastian Sabas for never failing to believe in me. Despite his reluctance to acknowledge how interesting the content of this book is, Wusel's critical comments, his academic passion – and compassion –, and his friendship made me keep going all these years, and I am still convinced that he will one day realize that he does, in fact, love linguistics.

List of figures

Fig. 2.1: Schematic illustration of a sign-based view of morphemes —— 10
Fig. 2.2: The prosodic hierarchy —— 32
Fig. 2.3: Three types of prosodic word integration for affixes —— 34
Fig. 2.4: Schematic illustration of a discriminative view —— 52
Fig. 3.1: Example of a token of *happiness* —— 70
Fig. 3.2: Example of a token of *sadness* —— 71
Fig. 3.3: Comparison of duration variables —— 75
Fig. 4.1: Overview of frequency effects in the Audio BNC —— 89
Fig. 4.2: Overview of frequency effects in the QuakeBox corpus —— 90
Fig. 4.3: Overview of frequency effects in the ONZE corpus —— 91
Fig. 5.1: Interaction of TYPE OF MORPHEME with RELATIVE FREQUENCY —— 112
Fig. 5.2: Interaction effects between PROSODIC CATEGORY and TYPE OF MORPHEME —— 114
Fig. 6.1: Distribution of CONDITIONAL AFFIX PROBABILITY by type of affix —— 133
Fig. 6.2: Effects of CONDITIONAL AFFIX PROBABILITY for prefixes —— 137
Fig. 6.3: Effects of CONDITIONAL AFFIX PROBABILITY for suffixes —— 141
Fig. 6.4: Effects of SEMANTIC INFORMATION LOAD in the three corpora —— 145
Fig. 6.5: Effects of SEMANTIC INFORMATION LOAD as a categorical variable —— 149
Fig. 7.1: Comprehension and production mapping —— 165
Fig. 7.2: Toy example of an articulatory path for the word *lawless* —— 167
Fig. 7.3: Effects on WORD DURATION DIFFERENCE in the linear regression LDL models —— 177
Fig. 7.4: Effects on WORD DURATION DIFFERENCE in the mixed-effects LDL models —— 178
Fig. 7.5: Density distributions of variables by derivational function —— 179
Fig. 7.6: Type count of top 8 neighbors by network and morphological function —— 185

List of tables

Tab. 2.1: Summary of predictions for prosodic category effects —— 39
Tab. 2.2: Example cases for the measurement of conditional affix probability —— 45
Tab. 3.1: Investigated affixes in the three corpora —— 64
Tab. 3.2: Overview of initial types and tokens —— 72
Tab. 4.1: Overview of category-internal frequency effects —— 94
Tab. 4.2: Overview of across-category frequency effects —— 96
Tab. 5.1: Review: Investigated affixes in the three corpora —— 106
Tab. 5.2: Overview of types and tokens, at least three observations per type —— 107
Tab. 5.3: ANOVA p-values for prosodic integration models —— 109
Tab. 5.4: BIC approximation to the Bayes Factor (BF) —— 109
Tab. 5.5: Final prosodic integration models —— 111
Tab. 5.6: Overview of prosodic category effects in the different conditions —— 117
Tab. 6.1: Review: Example cases for the measurement of *conditional affix probability* —— 125
Tab. 6.2: Criteria for the classification of affixes —— 127
Tab. 6.3: Hierarchy of affixes according to the semantic information load score —— 127
Tab. 6.4: Overview of category-internal effects of CONDITIONAL AFFIX PROBABILITY —— 131
Tab. 6.5: Audio BNC models with CONDITIONAL AFFIX PROBABILITY (prefixes only) —— 134
Tab. 6.6: QuakeBox models with CONDITIONAL AFFIX PROBABILITY (prefixes only) —— 135
Tab. 6.7: ONZE models with CONDITIONAL AFFIX PROBABILITY (prefixes only) —— 136
Tab. 6.8: Audio BNC models with CONDITIONAL AFFIX PROBABILITY (suffixes only) —— 138
Tab. 6.9: QuakeBox models with CONDITIONAL AFFIX PROBABILITY (suffixes only) —— 139
Tab. 6.10: ONZE models with CONDITIONAL AFFIX PROBABILITY (suffixes only) —— 140
Tab. 6.11: Audio BNC models with SEMANTIC INFORMATION LOAD —— 142
Tab. 6.12: QuakeBox models with SEMANTIC INFORMATION LOAD —— 143
Tab. 6.13: ONZE models with SEMANTIC INFORMATION LOAD —— 144
Tab. 6.14: Audio BNC models with categorical SEMANTIC INFORMATION LOAD —— 146
Tab. 6.15: QuakeBox models with categorical SEMANTIC INFORMATION LOAD —— 147
Tab. 6.16: ONZE models with categorical SEMANTIC INFORMATION LOAD —— 148
Tab. 7.1: Overview of tokens and types per morphological category for LDL —— 158
Tab. 7.2: Schematic examples of a cue matrix C (left) and a semantic matrix S (right) —— 160
Tab. 7.3: Final standard regression LDL models —— 173
Tab. 7.4: Final mixed-effects LDL models —— 173
Tab. 7.5: Traditional models with non-LDL predictors —— 175
Tab. 7.6: Relative importance of variables —— 176
Tab. 7.7: Extract from the closest semantic neighbors of DIS words —— 183

1 Introduction

Humans have the astonishing ability to transmit thoughts from the mind of one person to the mind of another via sound, yet to this day do not understand how exactly they are able to do that. What happens on the way from a thought to an acoustic signal, and from an acoustic signal to a thought? How is linguistic information structured and processed, and what units of form and units of meaning do these processes operate on?

It turns out that the properties of an acoustic signal provide a window through which researchers can infer what happens in speech processing. Complex words in particular (such as *happiness*) seem to leave traces of their structure in their phonetic realization. Over the past years, evidence has been accumulating that the phonetic detail of complex words can vary as a function of morphological structure (see, e.g., Schmitz et al. 2021a; Engemann & Plag 2021; Plag et al. 2020; Bell et al. 2020; Zuraw et al. 2020; Tomaschek et al. 2019; Ben Hedia 2019; Plag & Ben Hedia 2018; Plag et al. 2017; Seyfarth et al. 2017; Zimmermann 2016; Blazej & Cohen-Goldberg 2015; Lee-Kim et al. 2013; Cohen-Goldberg 2013; Sugahara & Turk 2009; Hay 2007, 2003; Cho 2001). We can use these morphological traces in the signal to gain valuable insights into how such words are stored in and retrieved from the brain, and how they are processed and produced.

However, researchers interested in morpho-phonetic effects continue to face two unresolved problems. The first one is primarily empirical in nature, the second one is primarily theoretical in nature. The first problem is that some of these morphological effects on phonetic detail are notoriously inconsistent. For example, effects of morphological segmentability on acoustic duration emerge in some studies under some conditions for some affixes (Plag & Ben Hedia 2018; Hay 2007, 2003), but research has also yielded many null effects (Plag & Ben Hedia 2018; Ben Hedia & Plag 2017; Zimmerer et al. 2014; Schuppler et al. 2012; Pluymaekers et al. 2005b). It is unclear which factors govern the interplay between morphology and phonetic realization, and under which conditions effects can emerge or not emerge.

The second problem is that – when we do observe morphological effects on pho-netic detail – it is unclear why these effects exist, and where they come from. Do they originate from correlates of morphemic structure (e.g., Selkirk 1982)? That is, can we trace back the phonetic variation we find to symbolic morphemes – units of form and meaning, or "signs," which humans use to structure their world? Under this perspective, morphological effects on phonetic detail are usually explained with reference to morphemic units like affixes (such as -*ness*) and bases (such as *happy*), to their independent storage in the mental lexicon and their computation in speech processing, and to the boundaries between these morphemes in complex words (*happi | ness*). Language processing is viewed as a staged, feed-forward process which passes on the output of hierarchically organized representations (morphemes, syllables, phonemes) to the respective next level. In speech production, words are composed from morphemes, and in speech comprehension, words are decomposed into morphemes, and this organization will then leave traces of these morphemes and their boundaries in articulation. I will subsume such interpretations of morphological effects on phonetic realization under the term *decompositional perspective*. One major problem with this perspective is that it is currently unclear how morphemes can pass on their structural information to articulation, given that many models assume that morphemic idiosyncrasies or boundaries should not be accessible postlexically (e.g., Levelt et al. 1999; Kiparsky 1982). Sticking to a decompositional perspective, we would thus have to assume that while words are indeed being decomposed and morphemes do have ontological reality, it is the speech production models and theories of the morphology-phonology interaction that fail to accurately capture how these units are processed.

The alternative option is to assume that morphological effects on phonetic detail effects originate from nonmorphemic structure and do not require decomposition in the first place. For example, more recent approaches suggest that such effects can also originate from dynamic patterns of shared association strengths of forms and meanings (e.g., Baayen et al. 2019b; Baayen et al. 2011; Ramscar et al. 2010). In these approaches, morphological effects on phonetic realization are explained with reference to words (*happiness*), their relations to each other, and to their sublexical and collocational properties. Words are not computed from stored morphemes and so do not feature internal boundaries, but instead simply share similarities of form and meaning which can emerge in a dynamic, associative learning process. Morphemes do not have independent ontological status. I will subsume such interpretations of morphological effects on phonetic realization under the term *non-decompositional perspective*. One problem with this perspective is that, since some of its computational implementations are more recent, much less research has been conducted that puts the pertinent models to the test, or that explicitly addresses how known effects could be reinterpreted in this view. It is thus necessary to investigate if, how well, and which properties of the form-meaning associations in these approaches explain the phonetic variation that we find in complex words.

At this point, we have identified two overarching objectives in this field. The first is to further test for effects of correlates of morphological structure in phonetic detail. It is necessary, on the one hand, to attempt to replicate effects that have previously been inconsistent, and, on the other, to expand on past research with different methods, new data, and more morphological categories considered. The second objective is to investigate where these morphological effects can originate from. It is therefore necessary to examine both traditional morpho-phonetic variables whose effects could be interpreted from a decompositional perspective, as well as more recent measures which can be derived from a non-decompositional approach. Of course, there are many researcher degrees of freedom in choosing from both the set of morphological parameters and the set of potential phonetic parameters to investigate.

One of the phonetic parameters that have received attention in morpho-phonetic research is acoustic duration. Morphological structure seems to affect how long segments, groups of segments, or words are pronounced. For example, the duration of English word-final [s] and [z] differs depending on morphological status and inflectional function (Plag et al. 2020; Tomaschek et al. 2019; Seyfarth et al. 2017; Plag et al. 2017). For the purposes of the present book, we can broadly categorize morphological effects on acoustic duration into the two groups outlined above – those effects that have been interpreted from a decompositional perspective, and those effects that have been found using a non-decompositional approach.

On the one hand, there are those effects that have been interpreted from a decompositional perspective. One of the most well-known diagnostics of morphemic computation and storage in the lexicon is frequency. While *word frequency* effects on duration have been taken as evidence for the storage of morphologically unanalyzed whole words, *base frequency* effects have been taken as evidence for the storage of bases (e.g., Caselli et al. 2016). If bases are stored, then multimorphemic words may be compositionally assembled during production and disassembled during comprehension. Moreover, some studies have observed acoustic reduction in various domains as a function of the frequency of the word relative to the frequency of its base. This so-called *relative frequency* supposedly reflects morphological segmentability, i.e., how easily speakers can decompose a complex word into its constituents (e.g., Zuraw et al. 2020; Plag & Ben Hedia 2018; Hay 2007, 2003). In this case, both whole words and morphemes could be stored, with segmentability governing which entries are accessed and processed more quickly. However, as referenced earlier, evidence for segmentability effects has been inconsistent. Moreover, morphological effects are assumed to be interconnected with or modulated by *prosodic word status*. Prosody may not only influence duration itself, but how integrated an affix is into its prosodic host word (Raffelsiefen 1999) may also dictate under which conditions segmentability influences duration (as speculated by Plag & Ben Hedia 2018). In addition, some research suggests that it may be equally important to look at predictors which capture morphological *affix informativeness*, i.e., at how semantically informative an affix is or how predictable it is in its context (e.g., Ben Hedia 2019; Hanique & Ernestus 2012).

On the other hand, there are those effects that have been found using a non-decompositional approach. Compared to the predictors that have been developed with a decompositional perspective in mind, we do not yet find as much of an established canon of predictors in non-decompositional approaches. However, several studies indicate that a number of measures derived from discriminative approaches are able to model acoustic duration, such as different operationalizations of certainty and activation diversity (e.g., Schmitz et al. 2021b; Chuang et al. 2020; Tomaschek et al. 2019; Tucker et al. 2019a). It is necessary to explore how well these newly generated measures can deal with durational data, and how to interpret their potential effects conceptually.

The present book modeled acoustic duration under both perspectives, in four different exploratory studies. Under the decompositional perspective, I investigated frequency measures (base frequency as against word frequency, relative frequency as a measure of morphological segmentability), prosodic word integration (and its interaction with relative frequency), and affix informativeness measures (conditional affix probability and semantic information load). Under the non-decompositional perspective, I investigated measures derived from linear discriminative learning networks (Baayen et al. 2019b). I examined how well each of these predictors, or sets of predictors, explains the durational variation in large datasets of complex words with a wide range of morphological categories. I will discuss the results with regard to the two overarching objectives – first, which morphological effects on phonetic realization we can find, and second, where these effects possibly originate from and what they tell us about speech production.

The need for larger datasets and the need to investigate more morphological categories naturally narrow down the potential research materials to languages for which large databases are available, and to domains which feature a variety of morphological categories. English derivational morphology fulfills these criteria. Morpho-phonetic effects in English and other languages have been observed for both inflection and derivation, but due to their distributional and frequential properties, English derivational functions lend themselves easily as categories of investigation. In addition, the derivatives and affixes associated with these derivational functions differ in interesting parameters, such as semantic transparency, morphological productivity, or position with reference to the base word. English derivational morphology thus provides the perfect testing grounds to investigate which morphological features may affect phonetic detail in which way. It is also necessary to extend previous findings for inflectional morphology (see, e.g., Caselli et al. 2016 for frequency measures in the decompositional perspective, or Tomaschek et al. 2019 for certainty measures in the non-decompositional perspective) to derivational data.

The studies in the present book used three different corpora from two varieties of English, and eight different morphological categories each. The frequency measures, types of prosodic word integration, and affix informativeness measures were tested on durational data from the morphological categories NESS, LESS, PRE, IZE, ATION, DIS, UN, and IN in British English varieties from the Audio BNC (Coleman et al. 2012), and from the categories NESS, ATION, DIS, UN, ABLE, ITY, MENT, and RE in New Zealand English varieties from the QuakeBox corpus (Walsh et al. 2013) and the ONZE corpus (Gordon et al. 2007). The categories to test these predictors from the decompositional perspective were selected in such a way that different types of prosodic integration (Raffelsiefen 2007, 1999) are represented, making it possible to test for effects of prosodic structure. The measures derived from the linear discriminative learning networks, on the other hand, were tested on durational data from the morphological categories DIS, NESS, LESS, ATION, and IZE in British English varieties from the Audio BNC (Coleman et al. 2012). To predict acoustic duration, I used multiple linear regression models and mixed-effects regression models, controlling for important covariates like speech rate, expected segment duration, number of syllables, biphone probability, and bigram frequency.[1]

To preview the results, the first study finds that the three frequency measures are not predictive for acoustic duration in a large-scale modeling approach within and across morphological categories. Neither base frequency, nor word frequency, nor relative frequency (segmentability) emerge as robust predictors of the data. The second study finds that the lack of relative frequency effects is not related to the type of prosodic word integration: prosodic structure is not a gatekeeper for effects of morphological segmentability. Neither does prosodic structure itself offer a convincing account of durational differences. The third study finds that the informativeness of an affix, when operationalized as conditional affix probability, yields mostly null effects as well as inconsistent effects when modeling duration. Similarly, when informativeness is operationalized as the semantic information load of the affix, its effects do not consistent-

---

[1] Open science statement: All data and code used for the studies reported here are available publicly at https://osf.io/4h5f3/. Several of the studies included in this book report null effects.

ly support the prediction that more informativeness should lead to less acoustic reduction. Together, the measures taking a decompositional approach are found to be highly unconvincing in their predictiveness for acoustic durations.

Finally, the fourth study explored the non-decompositional perspective as an alternative and finds that several measures derived from linear discriminative learning networks are predictive for acoustic duration. For example, words are lengthened when the semantic support of the word's predicted articulatory path is stronger (i.e., when the speaker is more certain in production). This study also finds that differences between morphological categories can emerge without explicitly encoding for each complex word the semantics of the derivational function that it shares with other words. This suggests that non-decompositional discriminative learning models are a promising alternative to the decompositional perspective, and that their measures are worth exploring in future research. Despite this finding, the present work cautions against uncritically adapting seemingly intuitive concepts like "certainty," "frequency," "probability," "predictability," "informativeness," or "entropy" as explanations for speech processing phenomena. Throughout the theoretical discussion of the results reported in this book, I emphasize that these notions are strongly interrelated and conceptually often inseparable. Only in acknowledging that the concepts we use in our exploration of the mechanisms of speech processing are merely metaphors can we advance in a critical and deconstructive understanding of language. I ultimately argue that this mindset offers a more honest way of conceptualizing how we investigate speech processing – namely, as a search for better metaphors.

The remainder of this book is structured as follows. Chapter 2 discusses how derived words can be assumed to be stored and processed. It introduces approaches associated with the decompositional and the non-decompositional perspective (Sections 2.1 and 2.2), explains and reviews previous research on the measures that I used in each study, deriving predictions and questions within each perspective (Sections 2.1.1 to 2.1.4 and Section 2.2.1), and summarizes the predictions and questions (Section 2.3). Chapter 3 presents the general method used in the corpus studies. It first introduces the morphological categories under investigation and the affixes associated with them, outlining their features and properties that are relevant for comparison (Section 3.1). It then describes the corpora (Section 3.2.1), explains how the datasets were extracted and cleaned (Section 3.2.2) as well as how the variables were generated (Section 3.3), and illustrates the general modeling procedure (Section 3.4). The methods specific to each of the four studies are described in their dedicated chapters, together with the results and discussion for each individual study. Chapter 4 focuses on the frequency measures, Chapter 5 on prosodic word integration, Chapter 6 on the affix informativeness measures, and Chapter 7 on the measures derived from the linear discriminative learning networks. In Chapter 8, I discuss these findings more generally in light of approaches associated with the decompositional and non-decompositional perspectives. Chapter 9 concludes this book.[2]

---

2 Earlier versions of the studies in Chapter 7 and Chapter 5 were published in Stein & Plag (2021) and Stein & Plag (2022), respectively. These chapters were only minimally altered for this book. The pertinent chapters will be identified by footnotes. Several smaller sections or paragraphs from these previously published studies have been incorporated in both altered and unaltered form throughout Chapters 2 and 3 (particularly Sections 2.1.2, 2.1.3, and 2.2.1), Section 4.3, and Chapter 8 of this book.

2 Storing and processing derived words

Starting from the observation that morphological structure seems to affect articulatory detail has important implications for the research process of the studies reported in the present book. Instead of testing a specific theory that may or may not explain a number of phenomena, much morpho-phonetic research is characterized by observing a phenomenon that may or may not be explained by a number of theories. In order to make sense of the observed phenomenon, the present studies thus need to consider a wide range of approaches from different disciplines. This need for theoretical eclecticism is inherent to research at the interfaces of morphology, phonology, and phonetics, but also to interdisciplinary research in general. Given that different disciplines often fail to communicate with each other, however, this in-between position may not only enrich, but also complicate the search for a unified theoretical understanding of the phenomenon in question.

The present book addresses this by broadly classifying the different approaches into two groups. There is a vast number of approaches to morphological analysis and language processing which make different assumptions about how derived words and other words are stored, accessed, and produced. These approaches can be categorized under various labels according to a variety of similarities, differences, and schools of thought (for example, syntagmatically oriented theories vs. paradigmatically oriented theories, models focusing on computation vs. models maximizing storage, full decomposition approaches vs. full-listing approaches, dual-mechanism approaches vs. usage-based approaches, morpheme-based approaches vs. word-based approaches, categorical vs. gradient approaches, feed-forward models vs. connectionist models, and more). For the purposes of the present book, let us group assumptions about morphological analysis and language processing under the two labels *decompositional perspective* and *non-decompositional perspective*.

Importantly, the binary grouping into decompositional and non-decompositional approaches is not to be taken as a definite classification. Certain approaches may feature some decompositional as well as non-decompositional elements. Instead, this grouping serves to simplify and bring order into the vast variety of theories and models whose orientation towards one direction or the other is relevant to morpho-phonetic questions, and to the mapping of form and meaning in speech processing. Nevertheless, the decompositional perspective and the non-decompositional perspective can be distinguished from each other based on several dimensions of classification: for example, whether they are generally oriented along the syntagmatic or paradigmatic axis, which units they assume speech processing to operate on, their degree of parsimony for storage in the mental lexicon, and the resulting structure of the speech production process. The following sections will describe the two perspectives and illustrate their alignment with these dimensions (Sections 2.1 and 2.2, respectively). I will review findings that have been gained under these perspectives, focusing especially on effects on acoustic duration. From these perspectives and previous findings I will then derive the predictions to be explored in the present corpus studies.

2.1 The decompositional perspective

Approaches which take a decompositional perspective in one way or another can be found both among linguistic theories concerned with morphological analysis and among psycholinguistic models of speech processing (e.g., Bermúdez-Otero 2018; Cohen-Goldberg 2013; Hay 2003, 2001; Marcus 2001; Levelt et al. 1999; Clahsen 1999; Pinker 1999; Marslen-Wilson & Tyler 1997; Wunderlich 1996; Halle & Marantz 1994; Prasada & Pinker 1993; Dell 1986; Selkirk 1982; Kiparsky 1982; Taft & Forster 1975; Halle 1973; Chomsky & Halle 1968). The basic assumptions and terminology of the decompositional perspective can be traced back to post-Bloomfieldian and Saussurean structuralism, and many of the core ideas were kept alive by generativism (as discussed in Pirrelli et al. 2020; Blevins et al. 2016). These ideas can still be found in most introductory linguistics textbooks nowadays. Common to decompositional approaches is the idea that language is a hierarchically organized semiotic system where words are decomposable into smaller morphological units. These units (like affixes, bases, stems) are fed into or combined with rules (e.g., a derivational process) that produce an outcome (e.g., a complex word). In speech processing models, this outcome may then be forwarded to other levels of this hierarchal system. In production, for example, an output of the morphological calculus could be forwarded to postlexical phonology and ultimately to phonetic realization.

Decompositional approaches are often, but not always, syntagmatically oriented (Milin et al. 2009). That is, they focus on the sequential organization and computation of linguistic units in a linear chain of speech, on these units' position in the surface structure, and on their syntactic co-occurrence. Word-internal structure is viewed similarly to syntax, complex words are concatenations of elements that can be analyzed in tree-like branching structures (Blevins et al. 2016). Paradigmatic relations, meanwhile, are often irrelevant or of minor importance in these approaches. That is, the connection of linguistic units to other related units in the language, the choice between them, and their allomorphic distribution are not the focus of analysis. This syntagmatic bias is evident in decompositional approaches of both formal morphological theories (e.g., item-and-arrangement theories, see Hockett 1954) and psycholinguistic models of speech production (e.g., Levelt et al. 1999). Most experimental studies on morphological processing, according to Milin et al. (2009: 214), have been inspired by syntagmatically oriented approaches.

So, what exactly are the units that are being computed and organized in such syntagmatic approaches to morphological processing? The decompositional perspective subsumes approaches that operate with specific morphological building blocks below the word level, like affixes and stems. These central units in morphological analysis are known as *morphemes*. Decompositional approaches assume that (complex) words can be decomposed into or analyzed as combinations of these morphemes. Traditional theories taking the decompositional perspective, such as item-and-arrangement theories (Hockett 1954), view morphemes as Saussurean signs (Saussure 1916). That is, morphemes are pairings of form and meaning, fixed semiotic symbols that have an independent existence from the grammar, like words. Figure 2.1 illustrates this view with a simple example from derivational morphology. A complex wordform like *happiness* /hæpinəs/ 'the quality or state of being happy' is analyzed as being composed of two form-meaning pairings, the base morpheme /hæpi/ 'happy' and the derivational suffix morpheme /nəs/ 'quality, state'.

SIGN-BASED VIEW

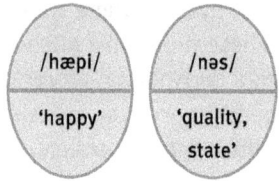

Fig. 2.1: Schematic illustration of a sign-based view of morphemes for the complex word *happiness*.

Since in a sign-based view, the morpheme is a morphosyntactic constituent, many decompositional approaches speak of *boundaries* between these constituents. Just as sentences are segmented into phrases with phrase boundaries, morphemic boundaries segment words into morphemes (*happi | ness*). It is generally acknowledged that these boundaries can vary in strength, even in traditional approaches (e.g., Kiparsky 1982; Chomsky & Halle 1968). These approaches, however, view boundary strength as categorical, while later approaches tend towards a gradient conception of boundary strength (e.g., Hay 2003, 2001). I will discuss boundary strength in more detail in Sections 2.1.2 and 2.1.3.

It is important to note that the sign-based view does not represent how a morpheme must necessarily be defined. For example, in an attempt to defend the morpheme against criticism from the non-decompositional perspective, Marantz (2013) points out that some theories which could be construed as decompositional (for example Distributed Morphology, Halle & Marantz 1994) do not define the morpheme as a sign. Rejecting this so-called *lexicalist* notion of morpheme (Marantz 2013), they instead define the morpheme as merely a morphophonological "spell-out" of morphosyntactic properties (see, e.g., Plag & Balling 2020 for discussion). Because this has important implications for the question of storage and the processing of derived words, let me briefly elaborate on the differences between these definitions.

The morpheme as a minimal sign in the Saussurean sense is an irreducible, atomic unit of form and meaning, the basic morphological building block out of which words are composed. Interpreting the morpheme in such a way brings along a number of problems (for an overview, see Plag & Balling 2020). For example, not every word is exhaustively analyzable into smaller units of form and meaning. There are zero morphs, empty morphs, and morphemes with the same form but different meanings. Thus, the morpheme as a sign cannot deal well with phenomena like non-concatenative morphology, polysemy, synonymy, and semantic opacity.

As a result, many approaches have rejected the definition of the morpheme as a sign. However, instead of abandoning the morpheme altogether, some of them have turned to the alternative definition of the morpheme as a morphophonological spell-out, or replaced the morpheme by such a spell-out (e.g., Marantz 2013; Halle & Marantz 1994; Beard 1995; Don 1993; Gussmann 1987; Szymanek 1985). Here, the morpheme is merely an abstract placeholder for morphosyntactic and morphophonological properties without independent lexical existence. In such a view, sometimes called *separationist*, form and meaning are separated. The morpheme acts as an anchor for phonological and semantic information, but this information does not constitute the morpheme. There is no longer a one-to-one mapping of form and meaning. For example, the same morpheme can be associated with multiple, different meanings and forms that are not tied to each other. The morpheme has a morphosyntactic side, which encompasses formal grammatical features like NOUN and may additionally contribute semantic information like 'the quality or state of', and a morphophonological exponent[1] side, i.e., potential phonological marking on the base which spells out the morphosyntactic information, like /nəs/ (Fábregas & Penke 2020; Harley 2012). These sides are dissociated from each other. So far, there has not been much research that directly tests the sign-based against the separationist view for derivational phenomena (see Plag & Balling 2020 for an overview).

Even though we must acknowledge the differences between a sign-based view and a separationist view of morphemes, it is important to remember that both views can still be categorized as belonging to the decompositional perspective. Even the separationist account decomposes complex words into lexical bases on the one hand, and grammatical exponents on the other (Blevins et al. 2016). The difference is that the sign-based view segments words into distinct morphological *symbols*, which carry form and meaning in a combined fashion and can be arranged morphosyntactically, while the separationist view segments words into form units and into abstract grammatical/semantic units that are then mapped onto each other (Plag & Balling 2020; Blevins et al. 2016). The sign-based view only goes the extra mile in pairing the forms and associated meanings (of bases as well as exponents) into fixed units and aligning these units syntagmatically (Blevins et al. 2016: 285). For the purposes of the present investigation, I will focus on the sign-based view and discuss differences to the separationist view whenever they are relevant.

Regarding words as a concatenation of morphemes has important implications for how humans store linguistic information in their mental lexicon. If we can analyze words into morphemes as minimal units of form and meaning, then morphemes might also be the units in our memory from which we build words during speech production, and the units into which we deconstruct words during speech comprehension. Memory, i.e., the "the ability to make what is learned persist through time," has been described with the commonly accepted metaphors of storage and retrieval (Divjak 2019: 99, 100). Morphemes could be the lexical access points to language, stored in our brains like files on a hard drive and ready to be retrieved and computed into words. This takes the Bloomfieldian idea of analyzing complex words into morphemic structure one step

---

[1] The term *exponent* can also be used generally for any recurrent chunks of form below the word level, even if it is not tied to a placeholder morpheme. For example, Baayen et al. (2018) use the term not only for the phonological spell-out of morphosyntactic and morphophonological properties, but also for any variation in form that discriminates between larger meaningful units. To avoid confusion, the studies reported in the present book do not use the term *exponent* for such discriminative approaches.

further by claiming that there is cognitive reality to this structure, and we make use of it in speech processing. This claim, sometimes called a *constructive* view of morphology, implies that we can reconstruct words from their separately stored building blocks, composing and decomposing them based on rules (Pirrelli et al. 2020).

The appeal of this view, especially in the 1950s, was that the mental lexicon could be conceptualized just as a small computer, such as a pocket calculator (Baayen 2007). Storage space was a major constraint on these devices, and so perhaps the human brain storage was likewise parsimonious, avoiding memorizing redundant information that could be derived from rules. It would store just the information that could not be derived from rules because it is not recurrent, rendering the lexicon what has been famously termed a "collection of the lawless" (Di Sciullo & Williams 1987: 4). In the post-Bloomfieldian and generative era, morphological theories would show their quality by finding rules that capture as many generalizations as possible in order to reduce redundancy (Blevins et al. 2016). This idea of parsimonious storage was thus quickly adapted also by psycholinguistic models of speech processing, such as Levelt et al. (1999). The lexicon would store only forms that could not be further reduced.

This view results in interesting consequences for speech processing, and for the steps that are assumed to occur in speech production and comprehension. Note that not all approaches grouped here under the decompositional umbrella make claims about such steps, as some of them are not concerned with speech processing but with formal morphological analysis. It is also important to remember that morphemes can be involved in speech processing without assuming strict compositionality and treating them as signs. However, the following assumptions about speech processing grouped in the decompositional perspective usually go hand in hand with those about sign-based morphological structure (Pirrelli et al. 2020).

In established psycholinguistic models of speech production such as Levelt et al. (1999) and subsequent versions, morphemes are an integral part of the speech production process. This process is generally characterized by a feed-forward structure. For example, Levelt et al. (1999) assume four main stages of production (activation of the lexical concept, lemma selection, morphological and phonological encoding, and phonetic encoding) where each stage feeds its output forward into the next one. These output representations include lexical concepts, lemmas, morphemes, phonological words, and phonetic gestural scores. As an example, let us briefly look at the stages of Levelt et al.'s (1999) model in chronological order.

First, at the stage of conceptual preparation, a lexical concept is activated. This is modulated by semantically related concepts, which are co-activated, as well as by pragmatics.[2] Second, when a lexical concept is activated, its activation then spreads to the next level, the level of lemma selection. The lemma node with the most activation support will be selected, and required syntactic features such as inflections can be checked. For derivation, already at this stage the model can be decompositional. This is because a complex word can be represented by separate lemmas, particularly in productive coinages. Third, the lemma must be passed on to morphological and phonological encoding. Crucially, for encoding, Levelt et al. (1999) assume stored morphemes as key units in the process. These morphemes are accessed separately (with some exceptions) and then provide their respective phonological templates. These templates merge into a single template corresponding to a prosodic word, which is then syllabified on the fly (i.e., syllabification is not stored beforehand). Fourth, and finally, the syllabic chunks of the syllabified word then activate phonetic syllable scores associated with those chunks. They are being selected from a repository of gestural scores stored for frequent syllables in a language. When all scores have been retrieved, articulation is initiated. As we can see, decompositional models of speech processing like Levelt et al. (1999) are largely characterized by hierarchically organized modules which compute the respective output units based on parts of decomposed words (morphemes, syllables). These are passed on in a feed-forward process.

A similar decompositional, feed-forward perspective can be found in theories of the morphology-phonology interface. Standard formal, structuralist or generative theories (Chomsky & Halle 1968; Kiparsky 1982) share the view on language as a system of hierarchically arranged modules, whose output units are passed on at their interfaces. For example, Lexical Phonology (Kiparsky 1982) posits that there are levels, or strata, which are associated with certain affixes and execute specific morphophonological rules to form a complex word. After a stem has been retrieved from the lexicon, it cycles through the first stratum. When all rules have been applied on this stratum, the output is passed on to the next one. From one stratum to the next, the morphological boundary between each affix and its base is erased, a process called *bracket erasure*. For example, there will no longer be a boundary between the affix *-ness* and its base

---

2 At this stage, Levelt et al. (1999) regard their model as semantically non-decompositional, since concepts are represented as wholes rather than as sets of semantic features connected to their hyperonyms. Note that this is a different notion of decompositionality than the one discussed in the present book.

happy. As soon as a word has passed all strata, it leaves the lexicon and undergoes the rules of postlexical phonology to determine subphonemic and contextual properties. That is, all phonological processes that follow, as well as the articulatory component, are considered to operate postlexically and have no longer access to morphological information. This is to account for the observation that some complex words behave like monomorphemic words (Chomsky & Halle 1968).

Again, we can see that similarly to psycholinguistic models of speech processing, these formal theories of the morphology-phonology interface operate with hierarchically organized modules and fixed units, like morphemes, which are transported through different levels in this hierarchy. This view is not restricted to traditional theories like Lexical Phonology, but is also adapted in newer iterations of stratal approaches, like Stratal Phonology or Stratal Optimality Theory (Bermúdez-Otero 2018). Combined with mechanisms from Optimality Theory (OT), here the stratal idea is modified such that in each of the cycles, different OT constraints apply. The core ideas of decomposition, modularity, and a feed-forward architecture, however, remain.

The present investigation is concerned with morpho-phonetic effects. Transferring the idea of decomposition from morphological description to theories and models which make claims about speech processing, however, brings along problems for the interpretation of such effects. As foreshadowed in the introduction, the observation that phonetic detail varies systematically with morphological properties (see again Schmitz et al. 2021a; Engemann & Plag 2021; Plag et al. 2020; Bell et al. 2020; Zuraw et al. 2020; Tomaschek et al. 2019; Ben Hedia 2019; Plag & Ben Hedia 2018; Plag et al. 2017; Seyfarth et al. 2017; Zimmermann 2016; Blazej & Cohen-Goldberg 2015; Lee-Kim et al. 2013; Cohen-Goldberg 2013; Sugahara & Turk 2009; Hay 2007, 2003; Cho 2001) is unaccounted for by both traditional and current models of the morphology-phonology interaction and of speech production (Roelofs & Ferreira 2019; Levelt et al. 1999; Dell 1986; Kiparsky 1982; Chomsky & Halle 1968). This is because these decompositional approaches do not allow articulation to access morphological information.

Starting with psycholinguistic models of speech production (Levelt et al. 1999), we have seen that these assume morphemes to select general phoneme templates which are eventually passed on to an articulator module to be realized phonetically. Semantic or lexical as well as phonological information is stored in the mental lexicon, but these representations do not vary in subphonemic detail according to morphological properties. In other words, the templates select ready-made, pre-programmed gestural scores which do not vary as a function of morphological structure. At the same time, the articulator module has no access to lexical information. There is no postlexical connection to previous stages. This means that a string of phonemes in a specific context will always be articulated independently of morphemic status. Variation in subphonemic detail would have to be accounted for by non-morphological factors alone, like speech rate (see discussion in Plag et al. 2017). However, morphophonetic studies generally control for such factors and show that there are morphological effects above and beyond phonetic predictors. Levelt et al. (1999: 3) do wonder to what extent their stages might "overlap," but it is unclear how much overlap we would need to explain effects of morphological structure in articulation. It is furthermore unclear if overlap could solve the problem in the first place, since the model would still operate on gestural scores.[3]

Regarding feed-forward theories of the morphology-phonology interface (Kiparsky 1982), we have seen that these theories assume morphological brackets around constituents to be erased in the process of passing on a word through morphological and phonological levels of processing. This means that no trace of morphological structure should be left at the level of phonetic realization. Similarly, Bermúdez-Otero (2018) makes it a design feature of Stratal Phonology that morphology and phonology are discrete modules separated by a strict boundary, where morphology has no influence on the phonological (and, presumably, phonetic) content of morphs. Consequently, such theories do not allow for a direct morpho-phonetic interface. At best, morphological information could be reflected in phonetic detail only indirectly, with potential effects being categorical in nature. For example, durational differences could be dependent on intermediate phonological steps like deletion. Yet, gradient morphological effects on the phonetic output have repeatedly been observed. For example, the observation that complex words are more acoustically reduced when they are less decomposable into their constituents (Zuraw et al. 2020; Plag & Ben Hedia 2018; Hay 2007, 2003) seems to suggest that information about gradient morphological boundaries must still be present at the phonetic level.

From the perspective of the speech production models and theories of the morphology-phonology interaction in the decompositional perspective, such effects are unexpected, and the mechanisms behind them are unclear. There are

---

[3] A more recent psycholinguistic model that operates on a template architecture in which abstract phonemes with no morphological information are inserted is Turk & Shattuck-Hufnagel's (2020) XT/3C-v1 model. However, this model focuses only on the lower-end parts of speech timing (starting with phonology). As the model is morphologically underspecified, it will not be discussed further in the present book.

two potential reactions to this insight. Either, we stick to the decompositional perspective. That is, we assume that the core decompositional ideas (morphemes as central units of both morphological analysis and cognition, and decomposed storage and rules instead of redundancy in the lexicon) are correct. In this case, we would conclude that what current approaches fail to capture is not the nature of units or representations, but the way in which these are handled in speech processing. Models like Levelt et al. (1999) and Kiparsky (1982) would have to be seriously modified to accommodate morpho-phonetic findings under the decompositional perspective.

The other potential reaction is that we do not stick to the decompositional perspective. Instead, we could take a radically different view that is decidedly non-compositional, examine how such a view conceptualizes morphological structure and the mapping of form and meaning in speech processing, and explore how it could explain morpho-phonetic effects. I will discuss this alternative perspective in Section 2.2. The purpose of the studies included in the present investigation is to explore measures from both the decompositional and the non-decompositional perspective. Before turning to the non-decompositional perspective, let us first proceed with a closer look at some of the most important measures that have been interpreted from the decompositional perspective.

While I will also consider evidence from other phonetic correlates that the present studies do not investigate, as well as from speech comprehension, the following discussion will be characterized by a special focus on effects on acoustic duration. It is well known that many words are massively reduced, especially in conversational speech (see, e.g., Johnson 2004). Large amounts of this durational variation are predicted by phonetic factors, such as speech rate. The present investigation, however, is interested in morphological predictors. In the following sections, I will focus on four of the most promising measures that have been used to explain durational variation from in a decompositional view, namely *base frequency* (as against *word frequency*) in Section 2.1.1, *morphological segmentability* in Section 2.1.2, *prosodic word integration* in Section 2.1.3., and *affix informativeness* in Section 2.1.4.

2.1.1 Base frequency as against word frequency

One of the most well-known diagnostics of morphemic computation and storage in the lexicon is lexical frequency. Lexical frequency is a property of linguistic units, such as morphemes or words, and describes how often these occur in a language. Here, *occurrence* refers to an instance of a linguistic unit being produced by a language user, such as a word being spoken or written. The more often a linguistic unit occurs in a language, the more often speakers will encounter and produce this unit. Importantly, humans seem to be able to pick up probabilistic information, including the frequency of occurrence of linguistic items, simply from what they experience (Divjak 2019: 75). It is assumed that the more frequent a linguistic unit is, the stronger it will be represented in the human mental lexicon. More frequent (or probable) units should therefore require less effort to access and thus be processed more quickly. In other words, the more you practice the production and comprehension of a unit, the more entrenched this unit becomes and the better you master it until the point of automatization (Langacker 2008: 16). The simple underlying idea is that "[w]hat you do often, you do better and faster" (Divjak 2019: 1).

This metaphor of representation strength in the mental lexicon is able to explain several empirical findings of the last decades (see Divjak 2019 for an overview). To name just a few examples, more frequent words are faster recognized (Howes & Solomon 1951), more easily recalled (Hall 1954), retrieved with fewer errors (MacKay 1982), more resistant to analogical leveling in language change (Bybee 2007), and, importantly for this study, often pronounced with shorter durations (see, e.g., Lohmann 2018; Caselli et al. 2016; Gahl et al. 2012; Bell et al. 2009; Gahl 2008; Aylett & Turk 2006; Pluymaekers et al. 2005a, 2005b; Bell et al. 2003; Jurafsky 2003; Jurafsky et al. 2001; Bybee 2000; Losiewicz 1995). Contradicting the strict Chomskyan division between linguistic competence and performance, these findings paved further the road to a more usage-based perspective on language (Divjak 2019: 2). However, the nature of these frequency effects and the exact mechanisms behind them remain unclear to this day. The relation between frequency and mental representation strength might be considerably more complicated than assumed (Baayen et al. 2016). What is clear is that since frequency is closely interrelated with morphology, frequency effects are relevant to any morpho-phonetic investigation.

Measures of lexical frequency have played an important role in research on morphological storage and processing. They are assumed to be able to provide insight into which units are stored in the mental lexicon, and whether words are composed and decomposed in speech processing. This hinges on one crucial assumption that is commonly found in the literature, namely the rationale that when we observe frequency effects for a particular linguistic unit, that unit must be represented in the lexicon (Plag & Balling 2020; Arndt-Lappe & Ernestus 2020: 193). For example, let us assume the production or perception of a complex word like *happiness* is shown to be affected by the frequency of its base *happy*. Then, it is plausible that we must somehow have stored the frequency of *happy*, and thus potentially also the form *happy* itself. We must have made use of the form *happy* and its frequency in our processing of the complex word *happiness*. But what if our production or perception of *happiness* was not shown to be affected by the frequency of *happy*, but by the frequency of *happiness* itself? Then, it is plausible that we must have stored the frequency of *happiness*, and thus the form *happiness* as an undecomposed whole. Base frequency effects and word frequency effects are thus used to draw inferences about how complex words are stored in the mental lexicon. This is the rationale traditionally followed by many psycholinguistic studies (e.g., Lõo et al. 2018; Caselli et al. 2016; Bertram et al. 2000b; Bertram et al. 2000c; Zhou & Marslen-Wilson 1994; Cole et al. 1989; Burani & Caramazza 1987).

According to this rationale, the separate storage of morphemes is indicated by *base frequency* effects. These are thus consistent with the decompositional perspective. Base frequency effects have been found in a number of studies for speech comprehension as well as speech production (e.g., Caselli et al. 2016; Bien et al. 2011; New et al. 2004; Vannest et al. 2002; Baayen et al. 1997). In addition to frequency, decomposed storage is also supported by some evidence from speech errors and other experimental paradigms (see, e.g., the review in Cohen-Goldberg 2013). If properties of bases show effects on complex words, then bases may be stored, and multimorphemic words may be compositionally assembled during production and disassembled during comprehension. Morphemes (bases and potentially affixes)[4] might be the basic access units, while complex words do not need to be stored and can be computed by rules, avoiding redundancy in the lexicon (Fábregas & Penke 2020; Pirrelli et al. 2020). This also holds for separationist approaches to the morpheme, the difference being that the morphosyntactic and morphophonological properties are stored and computed separately on their respective levels, and then mapped onto each other (see again Section 2.1).

The decompositional view on storage, where monomorphemic words are stored but multimorphemic words are (or can be) computed, has been around since at least Taft & Forster (1975), and has been adopted in both traditional and more recent approaches since then (e.g., Solomyak & Marantz 2010; Marcus 2001; Clahsen 1999; Pinker 1999; Marslen-Wilson & Tyler 1997; Prasada & Pinker

---

[4] Note that studies in the tradition of the debate between composition and whole-word storage generally do not test for affix frequency effects. This might be because it is empirically not as straightforward to measure affix frequency as it is to measure base frequency. Since affixes never occur on their own, it is difficult to disentangle their frequency from the influence of the frequency of the complex word and the base.

1993). Stratal Phonology (Bermúdez-Otero 2018) and Levelt et al.'s (1999) speech production model (see Section 2.1), too, allow for the decomposed lexical representation of component morphemes. Note that some of the models above allow for whole-word storage in addition to decomposed storage at the same time (so-called *dual-route* models).

One important exception to decomposed storage, however, are irregular inflected words. Decompositional theories which view the morpheme as a sign assume that while regular words can be computed from and segmented into morphemes according to rules, irregular words will be stored as wholes (e.g., Halle 1973; or Minimalist Morphology, Wunderlich 1996). This is because irregulars cannot be generated from a rule that simply computes over morphemes. Reviewing evidence from some frequency and priming studies, Fábregas & Penke (2020) claim that generally, inflected irregulars seem to be stored and regulars to be computed. The debate about the storage of regulars versus irregulars in the literature has mainly focused on inflectional morphology. The present work is concerned with derivation.[5] However, a similar argument could be made for irregularity in derivation: similar to words which are inflected without any (overt) affixation, some cases of non-concatenatively derived words could qualify for whole-word storage. A dual-route mechanism (see, e.g., Vaan et al. 2011; Vaan et al. 2007; Baayen et al. 2007; Schreuder & Baayen 1997 for discussion)

---

[5] For inflection, however, two notes are in order. The first one concerns the separationist view of the morpheme. If we treat inflectional morphemes as spell-outs or placeholders rather than signs, the morphosyntactic level and the morphophonological level may differ with regard to computation (Fábregas & Penke 2020). Regular inflected words are computed at the morphosyntactic level (where abstract features like PLURAL are added) as well as at the morphophonological spell-out level (where exponents like /s/ are added). Irregulars, too, are computed at the morphosyntactic level, but not necessarily at the morphophonological spell-out level, depending on the theory. Irregular exponents may have a single lexical entry associated with multiple abstract features. To arrive from the decomposed abstract features on the morphosyntactic level at the single exponent on the morphophonological level, a special morphological component may fuse the components into one position of exponence (for a detailed explanation, see Fábregas & Penke 2020).
The second note concerns models which allow for both decomposed and whole-word storage. Some approaches can also be regarded as mixed when the contrast between stored and computed words does not map directly onto the contrast between irregular and regular words. In these cases, even though all words are computed, both regulars and irregulars can be stored as wholes as well as stored in a decomposed fashion. Decomposed irregulars would then be modified later through a readjustment rule, like in separationist accounts. Regulars could generally be accessed directly, but if needed be decomposed when the speaker hears an unfamiliar word or produces a new coinage (see Fábregas & Penke 2020 for such an interpretation of Halle 1973).

could then allow for both types of storage, depending on whether the word in question is actively derived by rule (e.g., for regular affixation) or not (e.g., for irregular cases). The irregular cases will not be the focus of analysis here, as the data in the present studies come from words derived by regular affixation. For such regular concatenative derivation, the decompositional perspective will generally predict complex words to be stored in a decomposed fashion, and to be computed from derivational rules.

Yet, the decompositional view on storage has been challenged by *word frequency* effects. According to the rationale outlined above, word frequency effects indicate that the word is stored as a whole, morphologically unanalyzed. Word frequency effects (of complex words) are thus not consistent with a decompositional perspective. To be more precise, they are not consistent with a decompositional perspective that in addition to computation does not also allow for the whole-word storage of complex words. Word frequency effects, more so than base frequency effects, have been found in countless studies (e.g., Lõo et al. 2018; Caselli et al. 2016; Bowden et al. 2010; Tabak et al. 2010; Balling & Baayen 2008; Lehtonen et al. 2006; Moscoso del Prado Martín et al. 2005; Bien et al. 2005; Moscoso del Prado Martín et al. 2004; Meunier & Segui 1999; Baayen et al. 1997). Indeed, the word frequency effect has been called "ubiquitous" (Milin et al. 2009: 216). Note that some of these studies (e.g., Tabak et al. 2010; Bien et al. 2005) found evidence for both decomposed and whole-word representations simultaneously, supporting dual-route models. However, some studies also found evidence for whole-word representations while failing to find any for decomposition (Janssen et al. 2008; Chen & Chen 2007, 2006; Ernestus et al. 2006). For example, for reaction time, Baayen et al. (2007) suspect that base frequency is not a robust predictor compared to word frequency. We thus need to explore more systematically how predictive base frequency (as against word frequency) is for different datasets with different morphological categories. The present investigation contributes to closing this gap.

The ubiquity of the word frequency effect caused some skepticism towards the decompositional perspective on storage. No longer a collection of the lawless, the mental lexicon came to be viewed by more and more approaches as a place of enormous storage capacities, where complex words can also be stored, even regular or frequent ones (Arndt-Lappe & Ernestus 2020: 191, 194). A model that does not acknowledge the lexicon's ability to store a large number of words is regarded by some as unconvincing (Plag & Balling 2020: 312). Being able to avoid redundancy in a formal description by capturing recurrent structures with rules does not mean that this simplicity must be reflected in the cognition of language users (Divjak 2019: 29). Knowing that human brains have "impressive neural capacity" (2019: 44) and therefore may not need to save memory space, there is no reason to assume that individual units and rules generalizing over them are not stored *both*. In addition to monomorphemic words and multimorphemic words, we could potentially even store units larger than the word, such as all kinds of collocations and multi-word sequences (Pirrelli et al. 2020).

This position against the decompositional perspective on storage has been adopted by different models, sometimes collectively referred to as *full-listing models* (e.g., Caramazza 1997; Butterworth 1983). Word and Paradigm Morphology (e.g., Matthews 1991), which I will discuss in the context of the non-decompositional perspective in Section 2.2, also assumes that we should be able to access complex words from the lexicon without morphemic decomposition. There are even models that allow individual words to be stored not as word types, but as clouds of tokens of words (exemplar models, e.g., Pierrehumbert 2001). Note, however, that while some models rejecting decomposed storage assume that all wordforms are stored, some of them again assume that only irregular wordforms are stored (e.g., A-Morphous Morphology, Anderson 1992; also Aronoff 1976). A regular wordform, in this case, will be derived from its lemma and, crucially, not from individual morphemes – a form of computation without decomposition (see, e.g., Fábregas & Penke 2020). I will discuss the non-decompositional perspective in more detail in Section 2.2.

I have outlined above how base frequency effects and word frequency effects have been found in both comprehension and production, in various experimental paradigms. Let us now turn specifically to frequency effects on acoustic duration. In accordance with the idea that "[w]hat you do often, you do better and faster" (Divjak 2019: 1), the general hypothesis is that more frequent linguistic units should be more quickly produced and thus more likely to be shortened. While this rationale is intuitive, it is at present unclear which exact combination of linguistic, cognitive, and social factors lead to the reduction of higher-frequency units (for discussions, see, e.g., Clopper & Turnbull 2018; Arnold & Watson 2015). Why should stronger representations lead to shorter pronunciations? One possibility is that the access time or processing time for frequent units is reduced, therefore speeding up articulation. This might be because frequent units have a higher baseline activation or higher weights on mental connections (see Divjak 2019 for discussion). However, it is not clear how exactly ease of access, activation, and processing should translate into speed of articulation. Another possibility is that frequent words hold a motor practice advantage that allows speakers to save articulatory effort. The more often you pronounce a unit, the more routinized (and therefore faster) the articulatory gestures required to produce this unit will become.

Several studies have indeed found that higher-frequency units are more likely to be phonetically reduced (e.g., Lõo et al. 2018; Lohmann 2018; Caselli et al. 2016; Gahl et al. 2012; Aylett & Turk 2006; Bell et al. 2009; Gahl 2008; Bell et al. 2003; Pluymaekers et al. 2005b). This seems to be the case for both base frequency as well as word frequency. For example, Caselli et al. (2016) found that both base frequency and word frequency independently predict the duration of English inflected words with *-ing*, *-ed* and *-s*. They conclude that this provides evidence for both morpheme-based representations and whole-word representations. However, word frequency effects are again more commonly found (and tested for) than base frequency effects.

One important question that arises at this point is which domain of durational measurement should be affected by which frequency measure. For example, if bases are stored, should we expect base frequency to just affect the duration of the base? Or should the frequential properties of one constituent affect other constituents, too? And, if words are stored as wholes, should we expect word frequency to affect the duration of the base or the affix individually?

An effect of base frequency should obviously be observable in the duration of the base itself, but can also be expected to influence word duration and has been found to do so (e.g., Caselli et al. 2016). However, the nature of such an effect remains unclear: Is the reduction of the word that we observe merely the reduction of the base, still being traceable at the word level? Or can a base frequency effect on duration perhaps carry over to constituents other than the base itself (i.e., the affix)? This might be because a higher base frequency indicates more practice in the computation of complex words with that base and might thus provide a general advantage in computational speed, affecting the output speed of the complex word throughout.

For word frequency, we can hypothesize based on previous studies that an effect on duration should manifest itself in all domains including the word and below. For example, whole-word frequency has not only been found to affect word duration, but also acoustic detail on levels smaller than the word, such as affix durations in Pluymaekers et al. (2006, 2005b) and even individual segment durations with word-initial /s/ in Umeda (1977), vowels in Coile (1987), or word-final /t, d/ in Jurafsky et al. (2001). This makes sense, given that the reduction of a word must somehow be traceable to at least some smaller domains which make up this word. It is, however, worthwhile to explore in which of these domains a reduction observed at the word level might manifest itself most prominently. At present, it is unclear at the theoretical level at which point a word frequency effect arises (e.g., before the onset of a word, or during its composition), as the timing and sequencing of the speech production process are still a mystery.

Because of these considerations, the present investigation tested for both word frequency effects and base frequency effects on the duration of the word, the affix, and the base. This makes it possible to specify more precisely where reduction effects can manifest themselves. We are now ready to formulate the hypotheses for the first two frequency measures investigated in the present book. Based on the rationale of the decompositional perspective on storage, where morphemes are accessed separately and then computed, we should expect the following:

H FREQ$_{BASE}$ Higher base frequency should be associated with acoustic reduction, i.e., shorter durations, of the word, its base, and its affix.

In contrast, based on the rationale of full-listing, non-decompositional approaches which assume words to be stored as wholes, we should expect the following:

H FREQ$_{WORD}$ Higher word frequency should be associated with acoustic reduction, i.e., shorter durations, of the word, its base, and its affix.

So far, I have addressed the two most important frequency measures, base frequency and word frequency. However, this distinction is complicated by a third frequency measure that has gained attention in recent years, namely *relative frequency*. Like base frequency, relative frequency is a measure whose rationale has traditionally been explained from the decompositional perspective, as it supposedly reflects *morphological segmentability*. It is to this measure that I will turn next.

2.1.2 Morphological segmentability

Morphological segmentability[6] refers to the degree to which speakers or listeners can decompose a complex word into its morphological constituents. This notion is thus firmly rooted in the decompositional perspective. However, in-

---

6 In the literature, morphological *segmentability* is also known as morphological *decomposability*. To prevent confusion of this individual measure with the decompositional perspective as a whole, I will use the term *segmentability* throughout the present studies.

stead of categorizing words as being either simplex (monomorphemic) or complex (multimorphemic), it assumes that there are different degrees of morphological complexity on a gradient scale: words can be more complex or less complex, morphological boundaries may be stronger or weaker. The strength of a morphological boundary in a given word can be gauged, for example, on the basis of semantic transparency, type of base, various frequential measures, and the degree of phonetic-phonological integration across that boundary.

Consider the verbs *dislike* and *discard*. From the decompositional perspective, both words are considered morphologically complex, as we can identify the bases *like* and *card*, which are prefixed with *dis-*. However, it seems that one of them is more complex than the other: *dislike* appears to be more easily decomposable than *discard*. One reason for this is because *dislike* is semantically more transparent than *discard*. Its meaning 'to not like' is more straightforwardly compositional, while *discard* 'to cast aside' is semantically more opaque and idiosyncratic.

One way of operationalizing morphological segmentability is through *relative frequency* (Hay 2003, 2001). Derivatives which occur frequently relative to their base are assumed to be less segmentable than derivatives whose base is more frequent than the derived form. This is illustrated in Equation 2.1. If we divide the frequency of the base by the frequency of the derived word, then a high value of the variable RELATIVE FREQUENCY means that the base occurs more often than the derivative, making the derivative highly segmentable.

$$relative\ frequency = \frac{base\ frequency}{word\ frequency} \qquad (2.1)$$

For example, the base *boring* has a frequency of 7483 in the *Corpus of Contemporary American English* (COCA, Davies 2008), while the derived word *unboring* has a frequency of only 4. This results in a relative frequency value of ≈ 1,871, which indicates a highly segmentable word. If the base is more frequent than the derivative, speakers are more likely to recognize the base as a constituent, and therefore more likely to perceive the derivative to be complex. Vice versa, the base *sinkable* has a frequency of 4 in COCA, but *unsinkable* has a frequency of 117. This results in a relative frequency value of ≈ 0.03, which indicates that the derived word is not very segmentable. If the derivative is more frequent than its base, it is more difficult for speakers to decompose the word into its constituents because they encounter the derivative more often than its individual parts. The derivative will be perceived as a more simplex word. The examples *dislike* and *discard* above have shown how morphological segmentability is closely related to the idea of semantic transparency. Hay (2001) demonstrated that unlike the absolute frequency of the derivative, the relative frequency of base and derived form is a good predictor for semantic transparency. Relative frequency has therefore been considered an important operationalization of segmentability.

However, semantic and frequential properties are not the only correlates of morphological segmentability. It has been proposed that semantic opacity, and hence morphological segmentability, correlates with phonological opacity. Hay (2003, 2001), in what is now known as the *segmentability hypothesis*, suggests that morphological segmentability plays a crucial role in phonetic reduction: more segmentable words are less easily reduced (also see Bell et al. 2020; Ben Hedia 2019; Bergmann 2018; Ben Hedia & Plag 2017). This hypothesis can be derived from two underlying ideas which both imply that multimorphemic words could be pronounced with longer durations than monomorphemic words.

The first idea, which has been adopted by many decompositional models of the lexicon (e.g., Marcus 2001; Clahsen 1999; Pinker 1999; Prasada & Pinker 1993), is that segments representing morphemes should be less reduced than nonmorphemic segments. In speech comprehension, the listener must recognize morphemes based on their phonological segments. Thus, it would be important that morphemic segments are reduced as least as possible compared to nonmorphemic segments. Support for this assumption comes from findings that nonmorphemic phonemes are more likely to be deleted than morphemic ones (e.g., MacKenzie & Tamminga 2021; Guy 1991; Labov 1989; Guy 1980, but see Hanique & Ernestus 2012). The second idea is that morphological boundaries between morphemes will, either directly or via prosodic structure, result in less phonological integration of these morphemes. This idea can be found, for example, in the heterogeneity of processing hypothesis (Cohen-Goldberg 2013). If morphemes have separate lexical representations and act as separate domains for postlexical processing, then postlexical processes should be weakened by a morphological boundary. For example, postlexical reduction should have no trouble applying to monomorphemic words, but may find it more difficult to act across the morphological boundary in multimorphemic words.

Crucially, if we now assume that complex words can be more segmentable or less segmentable – perceived as more complex or as more simplex – then only highly segmentable words should be less reduced. Arguing from the first idea that morphemic segments should be less reduced, phonetic segments must be more fully realized to facilitate morpheme recognition for lexical access only in derivatives which are infrequent compared to their base. This is because only in these cases, the derivative's meaning needs to be computed from its constituents. Only words with strong boundaries are parsed into morphemes, so here, it is important to fully produce individual segments to make it easier for the listener to recognize the constituents. In simplex words, in contrast, individual segments are less important for recognition. Thus, segments in words which are perceived as more simplex (and therefore likely accessed as wholes) should be more vulnerable to reduction than segments in words which are more complex or decomposable, and hence produced as multimorphemic. In short, the more meaningful a unit, the less easily can it be reduced. A similar argument can be made arguing from the second idea that postlexical reduction is inhibited by a morphological boundary. Only words which are perceived and accessed as multimorphemic in the first place can be protected against reduction by that boundary. Words with stronger boundaries, or more segmentable words, should thus be less subject to reduction or deletion.[7]

The segmentability hypothesis thus relies on assumptions that belong to two classes of explanations for reduction. The first of these classes is what Jaeger & Buz (2017) call a *communicative account*, i.e., a listener-oriented explanation for reduction. Here we can fit the idea that speakers want to make constituent recognition easy for the listener. This account evokes the classic notion of a balance between two forces in articulation: while speakers want to minimize articulatory effort, they also want to maximize intelligibility for the listener (e.g., Lindblom 1990). The second of these classes is the *production ease account*, which is speaker-oriented and relies on processing and memory demands (cf. Jaeger & Buz 2017). It is this account that fits best with the idea that words are accessed in different ways, or different stages of difficulty, and that this affects acoustic reduction. This second account is important because it shows how closely effects of segmentability are intertwined with the question of storage and computation in the mental lexicon. Segmentability effects are interpreted to provide evidence for both types of storage – of whole words and of morphemes. The degree of segmentability determines which route of access will win the race. This interpretation is consistent with models assuming that words can be stored both as wholes and in decomposed fashion (the dual-route idea, found in, e.g., Schreuder & Baayen 1997; Vaan et al. 2011; also in Stratal Phonology, Bermúdez-Otero 2018). Both assumptions of the segmentability hypothesis are, however, dependent on online reduction effects. This makes the segmentability hypothesis contrast with the third class of explanations, the

---

7 Note that the heterogeneity of processing hypothesis categorically distinguishes between simplex and complex words, which would not allow for different degrees of complexity. However, as acknowledged by Cohen-Goldberg (2013), it can be adapted to account for different degrees of boundary strength.

representational account, which argues that reduction is encoded offline in linguistic representations (Jaeger & Buz 2017). It is at present unclear which one of these classes of explanations comes closest to the truth, but several discussions suggest a complex interaction of the three dynamics (Clopper & Turnbull 2018; Jaeger & Buz 2017; Arnold & Watson 2015).

While many studies have investigated the effects of other segmentability-related measures on various response variables, only a handful of studies have focused on the effect of relative frequency on duration specifically. Compared to the research on base frequency and word frequency, which almost uniformly point towards frequency-induced reduction (see again Section 2.1.1), the studies on relative frequency and duration produce a very incongruent picture and warrant a more detailed review.

Let us start with the studies that find a positive effect of relative frequency on duration (Zuraw et al. 2020; Plag & Ben Hedia 2018; Hay 2007, 2003). The flagship study on durational effects of segmentability is Hay (2003). She finds relative frequency effects on the deletion of segments investigating the suffix -*ly* in English. In an experimental study, she had six undergraduate students read out -*ly*-affixed words containing a base-final /t/ (e.g., *swiftly*) embedded in carrier sentences. Relative frequencies were categorized into bins by arranging 20 words into four frequency-matched paradigms (consisting of five words each). She finds that base-final /t/ in highly segmentable words (like *abstractly*) is more likely to be fully realized than in low-segmentability words (like *exactly*). In a follow-up study, Hay (2007) finds a relative frequency effect on affix duration for the prefix *un-* in English. She conducted a corpus study on the ONZE corpus, analyzing 359 affixed and 310 monomorphemic forms containing the string *un-*. She finds that the *un-*string is more likely to be reduced in monomorphemic words than in more complex words. She also finds that *un-* is more reduced in words containing a "legal" phonotactic transition from the affix-final nasal to the base-initial onset (i.e., a transition that also occurs in monomorphemic words), as opposed to those containing an "illegal" transition (i.e., a transition that never occurs in monomorphemic words). Phonotactic transition probabilities can be seen as another correlate of morphological segmentability and will be controlled for in the present studies.

More recently, Plag & Ben Hedia (2018) find relative frequency effects for two of their four investigated affixes. In a study of the Switchboard corpus, relative frequency affects the affix duration of *un-* and *dis-* in the expected direction. The more segmentable a word derived with these prefixes, the longer the prefix becomes. And finally, Zuraw et al. (2020) find in a production experiment with 16 speakers of American English varieties that increasing word frequency and base frequency variables do reduce and promote aspiration, respectively. While they fail to find some effects for different ways of calculating relative frequency, they also observe that voice onset time becomes longer for infrequent words when their base frequency increases. In general, they interpret the results as overall providing support for the segmentability hypothesis.

Let us now move to studies that find the opposite of what the segmentability hypothesis predicts, i.e., a negative effect of relative frequency on duration (Schuppler et al. 2012; Pluymaekers et al. 2005b). Pluymaekers et al. (2005b) investigated frequency effects for four Dutch affixes in the Corpus of Spoken Dutch, also including relative frequency in their models. For *ge-*, they observe an effect counter to what Hay (2003, 2001) predicts. In their data, less segmentable words are associated with longer durations for *ge-*. The authors hypothesize that this could be because speakers are more likely to place stress on the first syllable in words they perceive as monomorphemic, given that Dutch monomorphemic words are usually stressed on the first syllable.

Similarly, Schuppler et al. (2012) find a relative frequency effect in the opposite direction (i.e., opposite to the expectations in Hay 2003, 2001) on the presence or absence of the suffix *-t* in Dutch. In a study on the ECSD corpus, they analyze 2110 tokens ending in the Dutch suffix *-t* and find relative frequency to be significantly correlated with the likelihood of /t/ presence. However, contrary to the segmentability hypothesis, /t/ is more likely to be deleted in words which are more segmentable. They hypothesize that this may have been due to differences in both setup and language. First, they measured reduction on the affix instead of on the base-final segment, like Hay did. Second, the uncertainty in choosing from the morphological paradigm was greater in their study, because speakers had to decide between different suffixes. This supposedly gives the /t/ a greater information load and therefore a strengthened realization.

Finally, let us briefly review the studies that found null effects of relative frequency on duration (Zuraw et al. 2020; Plag & Ben Hedia 2018; Ben Hedia & Plag 2017; Zimmerer et al. 2014; Pluymaekers et al. 2005b). Apart from the one unexpected effect mentioned above, Pluymaekers et al. (2005b) largely fail to find relative frequency effects on duration. The affixes *ont-*, *ver-*, and *-lijk* all do not yield any significant effect of relative frequency. Likewise, Zimmerer et al. (2014) do not find a relative frequency effect on /t/-deletion in German. They constructed a new corpus from recordings of ten German native speakers who were instructed to produce paradigms for specific verbs given a set of pronouns. In this dataset, relative frequency does not reach significance as a predictor for the deletion of morphemic /t/ in second- and third-person singular verbs. Further, Ben Hedia & Plag (2017) fail to find a relative frequency effect for the English prefixes *un-* and *in-*. In a study of the Switchboard corpus, they do find that double and singleton nasal durations at affix boundaries in words with *un-* are longer than in words with negative *in-*, which in turn are longer than in words with locative *in-*. This mirrors a descending hierarchy of segmentability. However, relative frequency as a gradient segmentability measure of individual words does not reach significance in any of their regression models. Similarly, Plag & Ben Hedia (2018) fail to observe relative frequency effects on affix duration for *in-* and *-ly*.

Finally, Zuraw et al. (2020) fail to find a categorical relative frequency effect on the aspiration of base-initial /t/ after the English prefixes *dis-* and *mis-*. They categorically coded for each word whether the word or its stem has a higher frequency. This variable did not yield a significant effect on /t/-aspiration. This may be related to their operationalization of relative frequency, as they binned the relative frequency distinction into two distinct categories instead of four as in Hay (2003), or instead of including it as a continuous variable. Moreover, an interaction of frequency (operationalized as the number of movies a word appears in) and the word's base frequency, which is another possible way to measure relative frequency, does not reach significance when predicting the likelihood of /t/ aspiration.

What do we make of these findings? At this point, it seems that the evidence is inconclusive (see also Hanique & Ernestus 2012 for a critical review of the findings of earlier studies). It is apparent that relative frequency does not always affect acoustic duration. In addition, there are also two further problems of previous research which need to be addressed. One problem is that earlier studies often only looked at few morphological categories individually. This makes it difficult to compare studies (with often different methodologies) across affixes. The second problem is that different studies investigated different domains of durational variation. For example, some studies investigated the duration of the affix, while others looked at the deletion of individual segments. This renders a comparison of studies even more difficult. It is clear that we need to explore more systematically whether we can find relative frequency effects or not, and in how far it is a reliable measure as a morphological predictor of acoustic duration.

Let us formulate the hypothesis for the present investigation. Based on the rationale outlined above, the higher the morphological segmentability (i.e., the higher the relative frequency as calculated by dividing base frequency by derivative frequency), the less reduction is to be expected, i.e., the longer will be the duration of the word. Crucially, such a protection against reduction is expected to occur in all domains, i.e., both in the affix and in the base. This is expected from both underlying ideas outlined above. First, both constituents need to be recognized in more complex words, and second, both constituents are subject to potential postlexical reduction against which a morphological boundary can protect. Both the affix and the base (and consequently the whole word) are thus expected to vary in duration due to relative frequency. The following hypothesis follows from these considerations:

H FREQ$_{RELATIVE}$ The higher the relative frequency of a derivative (i.e., the more segmentable a derivative is), the longer will be its word duration, affix duration, and base duration.

Aside from the question *whether* relative frequency effects can be found with a large number of morphological categories, the question remains *why* relative frequency has previously produced such an incoherent picture. This gap has been noted before, and there have been calls for research investigating when the phonetics of a derivative are influenced by its relative frequency and when they are not (Arndt-Lappe & Ernestus 2020: 199). One idea is that the difference in the emergence of relative frequency effects between affixes might arise because the affixes differ in their prosodic structure. It has been speculated (Plag & Ben Hedia 2018) that prosodic word integration might inhibit segmentability effects. I will discuss this in the following section.

2.1.3 Prosodic word integration

As they found relative frequency effects for *un-* and *dis-*, but not for *in-* and *-ly*, Plag & Ben Hedia (2018: 112) hypothesize that these mixed results may arise because of prosodic integration. The affixes *un-* and *dis-* are considered to form prosodic words and thus to not integrate into the prosodic word of their hosts, while prosodic word status is less clear for *in-* and *-ly*. The question arises if their different prosodic word status might provide an explanation for why the morphological categories differ with regard to where segmentability effects can emerge. It might be more difficult for such an effect to emerge in affixes that are phonologically integrated into the prosodic word of the derivative, compared to those that form independent prosodic words (Raffelsiefen 2007, 1999). To foreshadow this idea, this is because pre-boundary lengthening caused by a stronger word-internal prosodic boundary might counteract potential reduction effects. Let us examine this rationale in more detail.

Prosodic approaches, such as Nespor & Vogel (2007), map morphological structure onto prosodic structure. Thus, following a prosodic approach, morphological effects on phonetic detail might be caused or at least mediated by the prosodic structure of words. A central notion in prosodic phonology is the *prosodic word* (sometimes also referred to as *phonological word* or *pword*). A prosodic word may sometimes correspond to the morphological word and to the orthographic word, but it may also describe sound sequences that do not map onto these latter notions of word. The construct of the prosodic word has been proposed because it provides the researcher with a convenient domain over which to formulate phonological generalizations regarding word stress, phonotactics, and other phonological processes (Hall 1999). There are several diagnostics that can be used to justify postulating such a construct, such as violations of syllabic constraints (onset or coda conditions, violation of the law of initials, ambisyllabicity), stress, vowel changes, or semantic criteria (Hildebrandt 2015; Raffelsiefen 2007, 1999).

In the prosodic hierarchy (Figure 2.2), the prosodic word (represented by lowercase omega ω) is considered to be a constituent above the foot level and below the phonological phrase level (Hildebrandt 2015; Nespor & Vogel 2007; Hall 1999).

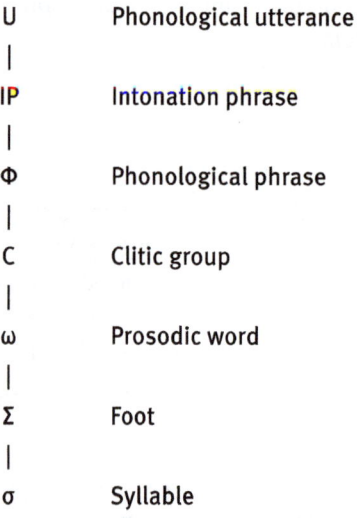

U	Phonological utterance
IP	Intonation phrase
Φ	Phonological phrase
C	Clitic group
ω	Prosodic word
Σ	Foot
σ	Syllable

Fig. 2.2: The prosodic hierarchy, adapted from Nespor & Vogel (2007: 11) and Hall (1999: 9).

The prosodic word is assumed to be the lowest constituent in the hierarchy that reflects morphological information, making it a key player in the transfer of morphological structure to phonetic output.

While some previous evidence suggests that "morphological effects on fine phonetic detail cannot always be accounted for by prosodic structure" (Pluymaekers et al. 2010: 523; also see Plag et al. 2017: 210), there is some evidence in favor of an effect of prosodic word boundaries in complex words on duration. For example, Sproat & Fujimura (1993) show that English /l/ is longer and more likely to be realized as [ɫ] before compound-internal boundaries, which are comparatively strong, than before affix boundaries, which are comparatively weak, or than within simplex words. Auer (2002) shows that final devoicing of /b/ in German suffixed words is characterized by a plosive release which is longer in derivatives with a word-internal prosodic word boundary than in derivatives with no such boundary. Sugahara & Turk (2009) find that segments in base-final rhymes of English affixed words preceding a stronger prosodic boundary are lengthened. Bergmann (2018) demonstrates that segments straddling a boundary in infrequent German derivatives are lengthened when these derivatives feature prosodic word-forming suffixes, compared to when they feature integrating suffixes. These findings suggest that the prosodic word structure of complex words impacts on their durational patterning and needs to be considered when investigating segmentability effects.

Within the prosodic hierarchy, researchers assume a number of constraints, one of which is especially important for the relationship between affix structure and prosodic word structure. Raffelsiefen (2007) suggests that the boundaries of grammatical categories must align with prosodic word boundaries, a constraint referred to as GP-ALIGNMENT. Crucially for the purposes of this present investigation, it follows from this constraint that whenever there are prosodic boundaries, they must coincide with morphological boundaries at the exact same place. This constraint, however, can be dominated by other constraints (such as, e.g., a constraint requiring syllables to have onsets). Because of this, if there are no prosodic boundaries, this does not necessarily mean that there are no morphological boundaries (Raffelsiefen 2007: 212). In other words, a morpheme cannot include multiple prosodic words, but a prosodic word can include multiple morphemes. This means that in the present investigation, there might be cases where an affix is a prosodic word on its own, as well as cases where the affix does not form a prosodic word on its own (for example, because it may just be a part of another prosodic word).

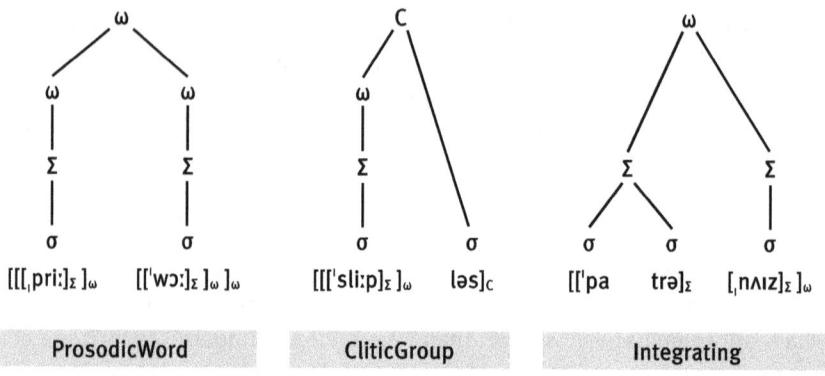

Fig. 2.3: Three types of prosodic word integration for affixes (following Raffelsiefen 1999), given as trees as well as in bracket notation. ProsodicWord: In this category, affixes form prosodic words on their own. CliticGroup: Here, affixes form a clitic group with their base. Integrating: In this case, affixes integrate into the prosodic word of their host base. Note that I use C to refer to the phonological domain of the clitic group, following the standard notation from the literature, whereas I use CliticGroup to refer to the category of derivatives in which such clitic group structure can be found.

From these constraints, Raffelsiefen (1999) deduces three possible scenarios that describe how an affix can integrate into prosodic word structure. The three structure trees with example words are given in Figure 2.3. First, an affix can form a prosodic word on its own (the ProsodicWord case). This is, for example, the case with the affix *pre-*. In the word *pre-war*, both syllables are stressed and heavy, hence both form a foot as well as a prosodic word each. Second, an affix might form a clitic group with the prosodic word of the stem (the CliticGroup case). An example of a clitic group affix is *-less*. In the word *sleepless*, the suffix is unstressed, hence it cannot form a prosodic word. Yet, the suffix does not fully integrate into the host prosodic word either, as the base-final plosive is not resyllabified into the affix syllable, despite /pl/ being a possible onset in English. Third, there are affixes that fully integrate into the prosodic word of their host (the Integrating case). This is the case with *-ize*. In a word like *patronize*, the base-final coda nasal resyllabifies into the onset of the derivative-final syllable. The whole derivative is therefore considered to be one prosodic word. In sum, we can see that from left to right, there is an increasing degree of prosodic word integration. Standalone prosodic word affixes are least integrated, while integrating affixes are most integrated. The question remains which potential consequences these structural differences have for acoustic duration.

One of the most important and well-known effects of (prosodic) constituent structure on acoustic duration is *pre-boundary lengthening*. Before a structural boundary, such as a phrase boundary or word boundary, phonetic material is lengthened, i.e., increases in duration. This phenomenon has long since been described in many different studies (e.g., Wightman et al. 1992; Campbell 1990; Beckman & Pierrehumbert 1986; Edwards & Beckman 1988; Vaissière 1983; Klatt 1975; also see Turk & Shattuck-Hufnagel 2020 for an overview) and is now considered to be a robust and reliable predictor of duration. Specifically, it has also been demonstrated to occur in complex words with different prosodic structure (Bergmann 2018; Sugahara & Turk 2009; Auer 2002; Sproat & Fujimura 1993). In the literature, the amount of lengthening is said to be dependent on two factors: the boundary strength and the position of the boundary type in the prosodic hierarchy.

First, how much a string of segments is lengthened depends on the amount, or strength, of the boundaries. The more constituents begin or end between two segments, the stronger the boundary, and the stronger the pre-boundary lengthening. This means that boundaries add up to form stronger boundaries. For example, the internal foot boundary in pre-war is stronger than the internal foot boundary in *sleepless* (Figure 2.3), because *pre-war* $[[[\ˌpriː]_\Sigma]_\omega[[\ˈwɔː]_\Sigma]_\omega]_\omega$ features a double foot boundary (one foot ends after the affix and provides a closing boundary, a second foot begins and provides an opening boundary), whereas *sleepless* $[[[\ˈsliːp]_\Sigma]_\omega ləs]_C$ just features a closing foot boundary after the base and no second foot. How strong a given boundary is, and consequently how much lengthening occurs before it, thus depends on the number of boundaries that co-occur together.

Second, the amount of lengthening depends on the position of the constituent providing the boundary in the prosodic hierarchy. Higher-level boundaries should be associated with stronger lengthening effects than lower-level boundaries. For example, segments before a prosodic word boundary are expected to be more lengthened than segments before a foot boundary, but less lengthened than segments before, e.g., a clitic group boundary. If the two boundaries in question belong to the same level in the prosodic hierarchy (like a prosodic word contained in another prosodic word), we would still expect the higher-level boundary in the tree to have the stronger lengthening effect than the lower-level boundary contained in the higher-level constituent. Based on these two factors governing prosodically induced lengthening, we can formulate predictions about how duration should vary between affixes affiliated with different prosodic word categories, as well as predictions about how prosodic word structure could interact with segmentability.

Coming back to the question of how the prosodic structure outlined above might interfere with morphological segmentability, we can hypothesize that morphological segmentability effects on duration might be counteracted by a strong prosodic boundary: according to the segmentability hypothesis, barely segmentable words should be more reduced than highly segmentable words, but if a barely segmentable word has a stronger internal prosodic word boundary, the preceding domain might be protected against reduction. In other words, pre-boundary lengthening effects introduced by prosody might cancel out reduction effects which low segmentability would have allowed for. We can complement the segmentability hypothesis **H** FREQ$_{RELATIVE}$ (see Section 2.1.2, repeated here for convenience) with this idea as follows:

H FREQ$_{RELATIVE}$ The higher the relative frequency of a derivative (i.e., the more segmentable a derivative is), the longer will be its word duration, affix duration, and base duration.

H PROS$_{FREQREL}$ The more prosodically integrated an affix is (the weaker the prosodic boundary), the less likely can higher relative frequency protect the derivative against reduction.

Second, prosodic word structure should have an effect on duration in general, independent of segmentability. It is important to think carefully about which domains should be more lengthened or less lengthened in specific prosodic categories, since these are nested with prefix or suffix status. For example, many English prefixes are considered to form prosodic words, whereas English suffixes supposedly never form prosodic words of their own (Raffelsiefen 1999).[8] Since the phenomenon of pre-boundary lengthening assumes lengthening only for the domain *preceding* the boundary in question, which prosodic category we look at will determine which domain (base or affix) we expect to be affected, depending on whether the affix is a prefix or a suffix.[9] We can formulate the following predictions for the contrasts between the categories, depending on whether we compare the domains affix and base within a prosodic category, or

---

[8] There are counterexamples to this claim, such as *-wise*.

[9] Since affix position is such an important criterion in formulating the predictions for duration, one could also hypothesize about and test effects due to affix position directly (i.e., simply test for a durational influence of an affix's status as prefix or suffix). However, as explained above, the following hypotheses are not just built on affix position, but on a variety of criteria relating to prosodic category (syllable and foot structure, stress, resyllabification). So, for example, *-ness* vs. *-ation*, or *-ment* vs. *-able* are predicted to behave differently, even though they are all suffixes. In English, affix position and prosodic category are not separable. The results (see Chapter 5) show that one would lose information by just testing for affix position, as there are effects of prosodic category that cannot be explained by position alone.

the prosodic categories within a domain. The hypothesis abbreviations use PW for the ProsodicWord case, INT for the Integrating case, and CG for the CliticGroup case.

Comparing bases and affixes

H PROS$_{PW}$ — ProsodicWord bases should be more lengthened than ProsodicWord affixes. This is because ProsodicWord affixes are prefixes and therefore the base will be subject to word-final lengthening, with the second base-final pword boundary in a word like [[[ˌpriː]$_Σ$]$_ω$[[ˈwɔː]$_Σ$]$_ω$]$_ω$ ranking higher than the two internal pword boundaries.

H PROS$_{INT}$ — Integrating affixes should be more lengthened than Integrating bases. The Integrating affixes in the present book are suffixes,[10] so the suffix will be subject most strongly to word-final lengthening, with the final pword boundary outranking the internal foot boundaries, as illustrated in [[ˈpatrə]$_Σ$[ˌnʌɪz]$_Σ$]$_ω$.

H PROS$_{CG}$ — CliticGroup affixes should be more lengthened than CliticGroup bases. The CliticGroup affixes are suffixes and lack a foot boundary and prosodic word boundary compared to the bases, as seen in [[[ˈsliːp]$_Σ$]$_ω$ləs]$_C$. However, the word-final C boundary ranks higher than the internal pword and foot boundaries, so word-final lengthening should be dominant.

Comparing prosodic categories

H PROS
BASE: PW-INT
— ProsodicWord bases should be more lengthened than Integrating bases. This is because ProsodicWord bases end with one foot boundary and two pword boundaries, and occur word-finally ([[[ˌpriː]$_Σ$]$_ω$[[ˈwɔː]$_Σ$]$_ω$]$_ω$), whereas Integrating bases end with just two foot boundaries and mostly occur word-internally ([[ˈpatrə]$_Σ$[ˌnʌɪz]$_Σ$]$_ω$).

---

[10] Note that according to Raffelsiefen (1999), English suffixes always either integrate or form a clitic group, i.e., they can never form a pword on their own. Prefixes, in contrast, generally form pwords on their own. There are some candidates for suffixes that form their own pword (e.g., *-wise*) and for prefixes that do not form their own pword (e.g., *be-*, *en-*); however, these are not included in the present investigation (see Section 3.1). In the present data, all prefixes form their own prosodic words, but no suffix does.

H PROS	Integrating affixes (all suffixes) should be more lengthened than ProsodicWord affixes (prefixes) due to word-final lengthening. The ProsodicWord prefix has two more boundaries provided by the derivative alone (compare [[[ˌpriː]$_\Sigma$]$_\omega$[[ˈwɔː]$_\Sigma$]$_\omega$]$_\omega$ and [[ˈpatrə]$_\Sigma$[ˌnʌɪz]$_\Sigma$]$_\omega$), but since the Integrating affix occurs word-finally, it will be followed by at least the same amount of potentially stronger boundaries belonging to whatever word or phrase comes next.
AFFIX: INT-PW	
H PROS	CliticGroup affixes should be more lengthened than Integrating affixes. This is because the word-final C boundary of CliticGroup affixes, as seen in [[[ˈsliːp]$_\Sigma$]$_\omega$ləs]$_C$, outranks the pword and foot boundaries of Integrating affixes, as seen in [[ˈpatrə]$_\Sigma$[ˌnʌɪz]$_\Sigma$]$_\omega$.
AFFIX: CG-INT	
H PROS	CliticGroup bases should be more lengthened than Integrating bases. The CliticGroup internal morphological boundary coincides with just one single foot boundary in words like [[[ˈsliːp]$_\Sigma$]$_\omega$ləs]$_C$ instead of a double foot boundary like for the Integrating bases in words like [[ˈpatrə]$_\Sigma$[ˌnʌɪz]$_\Sigma$]$_\omega$; however, the CliticGroup bases feature a higher-ranking internal pword boundary, which the Integrating bases do not.
BASE: CG-INT	
H PROS	CliticGroup affixes (all suffixes) should be more lengthened than ProsodicWord affixes (prefixes). CliticGroup affixes lack foot boundaries and pword boundaries compared to the ProsodicWord affixes (compare [[[ˈsliːp]$_\Sigma$]$_\omega$ləs]$_C$ and [[[ˌpriː]$_\Sigma$]$_\omega$[[ˈwɔː]$_\Sigma$]$_\omega$]$_\omega$), but CliticGroup affixes are suffixes in the present data and are therefore subject to the higher-ranking word-final C boundary lengthening compared to the ProsodicWord prefixes.
AFFIX: CG-PW	
H PROS	ProsodicWord bases should be more lengthened than CliticGroup bases due to word-final lengthening and because they feature an additional pword boundary compared to the CliticGroup bases (compare [[[ˌpriː]$_\Sigma$]$_\omega$[[ˈwɔː]$_\Sigma$]$_\omega$]$_\omega$ and [[[ˈsliːp]$_\Sigma$]$_\omega$ləs]$_C$).
BASE: PW-CG	

It is possible to summarize these predictions as follows (Table 2.1). I use the ▶ sign to mean 'should be more lengthened than':

Tab. 2.1: Summary of predictions for prosodic category effects on duration H PROS. The right arrow sign ▶ between categories means that the left-hand element is expected to be more lengthened than the right-hand element.

Comparing bases and affixes		
Integrating:	CliticGroup:	ProsodicWord:
affix ▶ base	affix ▶ base	affix ▶ base
Comparing prosodic categories		
bases:	affixes:	
ProsodicWord ▶ CliticGroup ▶ Integrating	ProsodicWord ▶ CliticGroup ▶ Integrating	

It has become clear that an empirical investigation is called for that investigates segmentability and prosodic word effects on duration simultaneously. It is further necessary to conduct a study which examines more affixes at the same time, so we can better compare when effects do and do not emerge in the same conditions. We need to assess whether relative frequency is a useful predictor for duration, and under which prosodic circumstances it is not. One aim of the present investigation is to account for this gap by testing the hypotheses outlined above, as well as by aiming for a larger-scale investigation than previous studies.

I have discussed three variables that have played an important role in modeling acoustic duration from a decompositional perspective on morphology – base frequency (as against word frequency), morphological segmentability, and prosodic word integration. I will now turn to the fourth and last decompositional measure investigated in this book, which is *affix informativeness*.

2.1.4 Affix informativeness

I have described in Section 2.1.2 the notion that in speech production, two forces are assumed to work against each other (Lindblom 1990). On the one hand, speakers want to minimize the effort required for articulation. On the other, the communicative account (Jaeger & Buz 2017) tells us that they want to cater to the listener by ensuring that they are being understood. Put simply, speakers are lazy, but not as lazy as to inhibit successful communication. We have seen in Section 2.1.2 that based on this, it is possible to hypothesize that morphemic segments, i.e., segments which on their own are more meaningful than segments which are just part of a larger morpheme, are more resistant to reduction.

More content demands more form. But this rationale may not only be applicable to segments. It may also apply to morphemes themselves.

Ben Hedia's (2019) research suggests that in addition to morphological segmentability, one vital morphological predictor for acoustic duration may be the morphological *informativeness* of an affix. In this view, how meaningful an affix is, and consequently how prone it is to being reduced, may be conceptualized as how semantically informative an affix is or how predictable it is in its context (e.g., Ben Hedia 2019; Hanique & Ernestus 2012). We should observe more resistance to reduction the more informative, and the less predictable an affix is. In Ben Hedia's work, the information load of different affixes emerged as one of the key explanations for morphological gemination and degemination in English derivatives (Ben Hedia 2019; Plag & Ben Hedia 2018; Ben Hedia & Plag 2017). It is, however, not trivial to decide how to conceptualize informativeness, and how to measure the information load of individual linguistic units.

Informativeness, also known as informativity, information density, or surprisal, can be operationalized in many ways. For example, it can be operationalized as paradigmatic probability, syntagmatic probability, prior probability, preceding or following joint probability, as unigram, bigram, or trigram conditional probability (each preceding, following, or surrounding), as preceding or following mutual information, affix- or word-specific information load, segmentability hierarchies, or as redundancy (see, e.g., Ben Hedia 2019; Hanique et al. 2013; Hanique & Ernestus 2012; Schuppler et al. 2012; Pluymaekers et al. 2010; Bell et al. 2009; Pluymaekers et al. 2005a; Jurafsky et al. 2001; Kuperman et al. 2007; also see Milin et al. 2009). These measures can be roughly divided into three groups: predictability measures, semantic information load measures, and redundancy measures. Many of them can either be affix-specific or word-specific. In addition, informativeness may not only be a property of morphemes, but it can also be a property of words or combinations of words.

Predictability measures all relate to some form of probability or frequency of occurrence. *Paradigmatic probability* is an affix-specific measure which represents how many competitors a suffix has in its morphological paradigm (Ben Hedia 2019: 74; Schuppler et al. 2012; Pluymaekers et al. 2010). The more competitors, the less probable, hence the more informative the suffix is. For example, in English, -*ly* is the only possible form for adverbs. There are no competitors for -*ly* and thus no paradigm, meaning that -*ly* has a maximum probability to realize adverbs (i.e., it is not informative in a paradigm). But a suffix like -*t* in Dutch, for instance, is paradigmatically more informative: -*t* is just one of three possible forms in its inflectional paradigm of Dutch present-tense verb conjugation. The suffix *-t* is therefore less probable in the paradigm and more informative than *-ly*.

Affix-specific *syntagmatic probability* measures how frequently an affix occurs due to its semantic and derivational function (Ben Hedia 2019: 74; Hanique et al. 2013; Hanique & Ernestus 2012). For example, because *-ly* creates almost all adverbs in English, it occurs very frequently in discourse. This means it has a high syntagmatic (adjacency-based) probability of following a base as part of a derived word. It is thus not very informative. An affix like *-wise*, on the other hand, generates semantically more specific derivatives and might therefore be more informative. The specific semantic function of *-wise* makes this suffix less probable to occur in a derived word than *-ly*. Thus, while for *paradigmatic probability*, we have seen that an affix is less informative when it is grammatically maximally predictable, for *syntagmatic probability*, an affix is less informative when it occurs more often in discourse (due to its semantic and derivational properties). Paradigmatic probability and syntagmatic probability, however, may also interact, for instance due to morphological complexity. For example, one segment (like Dutch /-t/) might be less informative in complex words than in simplex words. This is because all words with the past participle function are always realized with this segment in Dutch, the suffix is thus predictable in the context of adjacency to the verbal base. In this account, prefixes are generally less predictable, and thus more informative, than suffixes, as the base cannot serve as an early clue for the prefix to come. In addition, prefixes generally do not have a specific syntactic function.

Prior probability is a word-specific measure and refers to the frequency of a word in a corpus, adjusted for (divided by) the total number of tokens in the entire corpus (Bell et al. 2009: 97; Jurafsky et al. 2001). This is also called "relative frequency" sometimes, which is not to be confused with the notion of the same name in Hay (2007, 2003, 2001). Essentially, prior probability is a kind of normalized frequency. Similar to this, *joint probability* is also word-specific and measures the frequency of two words occurring together in a corpus, adjusted for (divided by) the total number of tokens in the corpus (Bell et al. 2009: 97; Jurafsky et al. 2001). This is also referred to as "string frequency" sometimes. Joint probability can be thought of as a prior probability of bigrams. It can be calculated for both preceding and following words.

Another predictability-related measure is *conditional probability*, which is word-specific. It usually refers to the conditional probability of a word given the previous (or following) word and is also called "transitional probability". Mathematically, it is the bigram frequency divided by the frequency of the preceding (or following) word (Bell et al. 2009: 97, 99; Jurafsky et al. 2001). Compared to joint probability, which is also bigram-based, conditional probability thereby controls for the frequency of the conditioning word. This measure is also possible with trigrams (e.g., including the two preceding words, the two following words, or the two surrounding words).

The final measure in this group, *mutual information*, is word-specific and measures the bigram frequency divided by the frequency of the first word, multiplied with the frequency of the second word. In other words, it is the ratio of the frequency of a word occurring together with the previous word to the product of the individual frequencies of the word and of the previous word (Bell et al. 2009: 97; Pluymaekers et al. 2005a; Jurafsky et al. 2001). The intuition behind this measure is that there is informational value in how likely two words occur together beyond what could be expected from the frequencies of the individual words (Bell et al. 2009: 99).

Second, there is a group of measures related to semantic information load. Semantic information load comes in an affix-specific version and a word-specific version. *Affix-specific semantic information load* measures how much an affix contributes to the meaning of a derivative (Ben Hedia 2019: 75, 36–37). The more lexical meaning the affix contributes, the more informative it is. This must be estimated by a careful qualitative semantic analysis of the affixes. For example, in Ben Hedia's (2019) data, the affix *-ly* is least informative, as it does not have lexical meaning; *un-* is most informative, as it always has a stable, negative meaning; and *in-* and *dis-* pattern in between. Other factors relevant to the classification can be, for example, productivity, semantic transparency, and the type of base the affix takes (free or bound). Additionally, Ben Hedia (2019) distinguishes between different hierarchies ranking affixes according to their information load depending on how the criteria are weighted (for example, depending on whether the researcher considers lexical meaning to be a more important criterion than productivity).

Word-specific semantic information load, on the other hand, describes how semantically transparent or opaque individual words are. In transparent words, an affix is more informative than in opaque words. Ben Hedia (2019), for example, used this measure to make a partly categorical classification, with *un-*derivatives always being very informative, *-ly*-derivatives always being uninformative, and *dis-* and *in-*derivatives being informative when they are transparent, and not being informative when they are opaque.

The third and last group of measures relate to the repetition of linguistic items in discourse. Sometimes called *redundancy*, these measures are word-specific and are usually calculated based on the occurrence of an item in the previous context, where "context" can be defined in different ways. In other words, it is the number of times that the same lexeme had been spoken previously in the conversation, either by the speaker or by the listener (Bell et al. 2009: 97).

As we can see, there are many ways to measure informativeness, and many effects of such measures in both speech comprehension and speech production have been reported in the literature (e.g., Ben Hedia 2019; Hanique et al. 2013; Hanique & Ernestus 2012; Schuppler et al. 2012; Pluymaekers et al. 2010; Bell et al. 2009; Pluymaekers et al. 2005a; Jurafsky et al. 2001; Kuperman et al. 2007; Aylett & Turk 2004). Interestingly, Sóskuthy & Hay (2017: 300) note that some studies have also found that word frequency effects (see Section 2.1.1) are not as robust when measures of informativeness are included in the same statistical model (Seyfarth 2014; Piantadosi et al. 2011). This is not surprising, since we can notice from the outline of operationalizations above that informativeness is conceptually closely related to frequency. Highly frequent words are more probable, therefore carry less information, so high frequency goes together with low informativeness. In fact, frequency and informativeness can both make sense of the production ease account (Jaeger & Buz 2017). High-frequency words are assumed to be accessed faster, and so are low-informativeness words. This is supposedly because units with high information load are more difficult or costly to access and process (Milin et al. 2009). However, this threefold relationship between processing difficulty, frequency, and informativeness (and the potentially manifold relationship with other variables) makes it notoriously difficult to disentangle such effects both empirically and conceptually. This is a central point of discussion for the present book and will be explored further throughout Chapters 4–8.

The alert reader will also have noticed that informativeness measures do not inherently have to be decompositional measures. Some of the operationalizations of informativeness outlined above, particularly some of the word-based ones, are fully compatible with a non-decompositional perspective. In principle, it is possible with many of these measures to mathematically quantify the informativeness of any unit – morphemes, words, phrases, and even larger structures. However, the present chapter is interested in finding decompositional measures of informativeness, namely measures that assume morphemic constituents. As this book investigates derivational affixes, the question arises which of the measures outlined above can qualify as measures of affix informativeness.

The measures *paradigmatic probability* and *syntagmatic probability* are not suited for this task. This is because it is unclear how to measure the differences in paradigmatic probability and in syntagmatic probability for different derivational prefixes (a problem noted before by Ben Hedia 2019). Several word-based measures are non-decompositional and are therefore of no further interest if one wants to explore the decompositional perspective. These are *prior probability*, *joint probability*, *mutual information*, and most versions of *redundancy*. In addition, *prior probability* is a normalized frequency measure and was thus considered conceptually too close to the measures used in the frequency studies (Section 2.1.1 and Chapter 4). A similar decision was made for *joint probability*, as bigram frequency (target plus following word) in the present studies was already controlled for (see Section 3.3.2). A *redundancy* measure was not feasible to use in the present investigation due to the structure of some of the extracted corpus data. This leaves two candidates, *conditional probability* and *semantic information load*.

Operationalizing informativeness as *conditional probability* has the major advantage that this measure does not include in its definition the frequency of the target word, which is of separate interest in the present book (see again Section 2.1.1). However, in the definitions found in the literature (Bell et al. 2009: 97, 99; Jurafsky et al. 2001), *conditional probability* is a non-decompositional measure. As explained above, *conditional probability* usually refers to the conditional probability of a word given the previous or following word. It was therefore decided to create a version of this measure that specifically encodes the conditional probability of an affix, *conditional affix probability*. This novel measure does not measure the probability of the whole derivative, treating it essentially the same as a monomorphemic word, but the probability of the affix itself. One major advantage of this measure is that it addresses the problem noted by Ben Hedia (2019) that it is challenging to qualitatively estimate the syntagmatic probability of derivational prefixes. While this measure does not estimate probability by qualitatively categorizing affixes based on concerns about semantics and derivational functions, it does provide a quantitative, usage-based alternative.

Conditional affix probability, then, measures the probability of the affix given the probability of the preceding linguistic item. In the case of prefixes, the preceding item will be the word preceding the derived target word in discourse. In the case of suffixes, the preceding word will be the base of the target derivative. This is schematically illustrated in Equation 2.2 and Table 2.2, where C_{aff} stands for conditional affix probability, p for probability, and A, B, and C for the respective positions illustrated in the table.

$$C_{aff} = \frac{p(AB)}{p(A)} \qquad (2.2)$$

Tab. 2.2: Example cases for the measurement of conditional affix probability. For suffixes, the derived word constitutes a base-affix bigram, whereas for prefixes, the bigram consists of the prefix and the preceding word in the utterance.

example of measurement for suffixes		example of measurement for prefixes		
A	B	A	B	C
random	-ize	her	pre-	determination

In both cases, *conditional affix probability* C_{aff} measures the probability of the affix given whatever linguistic unit precedes it. For suffixes, this is the probability of the suffix B given the probability of the base A, for prefixes, this is the probability of the prefix B given the probability of the preceding word A. Note that in the case of suffixes, the measure is equivalent to an inversed relative frequency measure (see Section 2.1.2). This will be discussed further in Section 6.3.

The second candidate for a decompositional informativeness measure is *semantic information load*. As explained above, this measure generally estimates how much an affix contributes to the meaning of a derivative. We have seen that there are two versions of this measure, *affix-specific semantic information load* and *word-specific semantic information load*. Even though the latter is word-based, both fit into the decompositional perspective. This is because both versions rely on semantic transparency versus semantic opaqueness, notions in which it is inherent that the meaning of a complex word can unveil or obscure the meanings of its individual constituents (base and affix). Two major advantages of these variables are that they are not confounded with frequency or other probability-based measures, and that they place special emphasis on semantics.

For the affix informativeness study, it was decided to investigate *affix-specific semantic information load*. This is because in order to explore the decompositional perspective, it was deemed particularly relevant to investigate the affix as such, rather than gradient, word-based properties. The affix-specific measure is particularly interesting because it treats affixes categorically and does not explicitly assume intra-affix variation in informativeness. Within the decompositional perspective, it thus provides an interesting contrast to word-based measures such as frequency and morphological segmentability (see Sections 2.1.1 and 2.1.2). The more an affix contributes to the meaning of a derived word, the more informative it is assumed to be (Ben Hedia 2019). Note that in Ben Hedia's (2019) study, criteria based on syntagmatic probability and on semantic information load are jointly evaluated to form an informativeness ranking of affixes. In the interest of distinctness of the two measures used in the present investigation, I estimated the categorical informativeness of the affix only based on criteria of semantic information load (namely, clearness of semantic meaning, type of base, semantic transparency, and productivity). I will describe the characteristics of each affix according to these criteria in Section 3.1, while the coding will be explained in Section 6.1.

We have arrived at two informativeness measures to use in the present study of affix informativeness, one predictability-based measure (*conditional affix probability*) and one semantic information load measure (*affix-specific semantic information load*). We are now ready to summarize the predictions for the two informativeness measures. As explained above, the more informative an affix is, the less reduction we should observe. This holds for both measures. Which domains should be affected by this? One could argue that from a communicative account, only the informative affix itself would need to be less reduced. However, because the argument for informativeness-induced differences in duration again partly relies on processing costs, we might expect speakers to be generally slowed down in production (for example, also before and after uttering the affix string). Note that most of the literature is not very specific about how far informativeness effects should be able to spill over into other domains. To explore this, I again investigated all three domains of potential reduction (the derived word, the affix, and the base), and I followed the assumption that informativeness could in principle affect all domains of potential reduction.

For the predictability-based measure, we can formulate the hypothesis that acoustic durations should become shorter the more probable (i.e., the less informative) an affix is given the probability of the preceding item.

H INF_{PROB} The higher the conditional affix probability (i.e., the less informative an affix is), the shorter will be the duration of the word, of the affix, and of the base.

For the measure based on semantic information load, we can formulate the hypothesis that acoustic durations should become longer the more the affix contributes to the meaning of the derivative (i.e., the more informative it is).

H INF_{SEM} The higher the semantic information load of the affix (i.e., the more informative an affix is), the longer will be the duration of the word, of the affix, and of the base.

I have discussed all four measures that the present book investigates from the decompositional perspective. It is now time to change perspectives.

2.2 The non-decompositional perspective

Like the decompositional perspective, approaches taking a non-decompositional perspective can be found among theories primarily concerned with the description of morphological structure as well as among models of speech processing (e.g., Baayen et al. 2019b; Matthews 1991; Rumelhart & McClelland 1986). However, approaches taking a non-decompositional perspective are fewer in number. As Blevins et al. (2016: 285) observe, for example, practically all approaches to morphology decompose complex words into bases and exponents except Word and Paradigm Morphology (e.g., Matthews 1991). Historically, the non-decompositional perspective emerged in parallel to decompositional ideas in structuralism and generativism (Blevins et al. 2016). The unifying idea behind non-decompositional approaches, and the idea that places them in opposition to decompositional approaches, is that words are not decomposed into smaller morphological units. Complex words are not analyzed into or computed from atomic morphemes, but words themselves are the atomic units of analysis, and potentially of lexical access. As a result, speech processing models or computational implementations taking the non-decompositional perspective are often characterized by a direct connection between phonology and phonetic realization on the one hand and the semantics of words on the other, rather than by a feed-forward structure in which specific mechanisms combine smaller units in-between.

Non-decompositional approaches are generally oriented more along the paradigmatic than along the syntagmatic axis (Milin et al. 2009). That is, rather than in the sequential organization of units in morphosyntactic arrangements, they are interested in the connection and choice between related units in a language. Paradigmatic relations govern the analysis and allegedly also the processing of (complex) words. Analyzing morphology as a syntax of words, where the organization of concatenated units like bases and affixes is conceptualized with tree structures, is not of interest to such an approach (Blevins et al. 2016). What is central to a non-decompositional approach to morphology is not the composition of complex words, but the relation of words to each other.

Consequently, the morpheme as a central morphological unit has no place in the non-decompositional perspective. The mapping of form and meaning does not require any intermediate constituents; morphemes do not mediate between semantics and phonology. In fact, morphemes as a theoretical construct are not required at all. Bases, affixes, exponents – they have no theoretical relevance or independent existence. Recurrent chunks of sublexical form are conceptualized not as fixed units, but merely as expressions of morphological categories: shared phonological and semantic similarities which have no ontological status. The basic building blocks of morphology are whole words, therefore such recurrent parts are merely abstractions over full forms which can be analyzed simply as analogies or similarities between words (see, e.g., Pirrelli et al. 2020; Plag & Balling 2020; Blevins 2006). Hence, approaches taking the non-decompositional perspective are also called *abstractive approaches* or *word-based approaches* (Blevins 2006). Importantly, if full words are the minimal units of morphological analysis, this means that contrary to the decompositional perspective, words do not have internal boundaries (see again Sections 2.1, 2.1.2, and 2.1.3). Measures concerned with the strength of word-internal boundaries, like morphological segmentability and prosodic word integration, are thus irrelevant or would have to be interpreted in a different way.

Just like for the decompositional perspective, analyzing morphological structure in a certain way also has implications for the storage of linguistic information in the mental lexicon. If words are the minimal building blocks, then words (not morphemes) might be the units we store and access in our memory to produce and comprehend speech. We have already seen in the discussion of frequency (Section 2.1.1) that the prevalence of word frequency effects was taken by many approaches to indicate whole-word storage in the lexicon. The metaphor of a collection of the lawless was replaced by the idea that all kinds of constructions could be stored with massive redundancy: regular words, highly frequent words, collocations, idioms, and more (Arndt-Lappe & Ernestus 2020; Pirrelli et al. 2020; Plag & Balling 2020; Divjak 2019). Non-decompositional approaches like Word and Paradigm Morphology (Matthews 1991) indeed share the idea of full-listing models (e.g., Caramazza 1997; Butterworth 1983) that we can access complex words as wholes from the lexicon. The computation of sublexical building blocks is no longer required. Morphological structure can emerge simply due to the mutual relation of redundantly memorized full complex words (Pirrelli et al. 2020).

There are (at least) three important variations on the idea of a non-decompositional conceptualization of the mental lexicon: computation without decomposition, storage of token information, and no traditional storage at all. The first variation, computation without decomposition, concerns the debate about the relevance of rules. As mentioned in Section 2.1.1, there are some models which, despite assuming a non-decompositional perspective, claim that for inflectional morphology, only irregular words are stored (e.g., A-Morphous

Morphology, Anderson 1992; also Aronoff 1976). In this case, a regular wordform is not stored but its lemma will have a general lexical entry to which rules can be applied to produce the required wordform. The computation of regulars in these non-decompositional models is different from the computation of regulars in decompositional models. From the non-decompositional perspective, words – not morphemes – are used as input to produce other words as output. This is also a form of computation, but crucially not of decomposition (see, e.g., Fábregas & Penke 2020). In this case, complex words are stored morphemically unanalyzed, but there are still rules that may derive them from related words in the morphological paradigm.

However, some researchers go further and question whether we even need any rules at all. Considering that there seems to be massive redundancy in the lexicon anyway, rules as input-output mechanisms may be irrelevant. Arndt-Lappe & Ernestus (2020), reviewing evidence for the storage of complex words in the mental lexicon, argue for the storage of all complex words with optional morpho-phonological rules, but emphasize that models which rely only on storage have the advantage that they do not require storage to be economical. Plag & Balling (2020) observe that rules are also often challenged by (sometimes widespread) exceptions, and by the fact that certain patterns often seem to be better accounted for by output-output rather than input-output relations. In fact, there are plenty of possibilities for morphology, other than rules, to handle whole words in order to be productive. For example, some approaches assume that we form words by analogy to existing words or that we generalize from words by forming schemata (e.g., in Construction Morphology, Booij 2018, 2010b). Using analogy, we derive words based on their similarity to a single other word or sets of words in the lexicon which are pertinent, or informative, for the target word. Using schemata, we abstract away from analogies and generalize over a set of related words, remembering generalizations with different degrees of abstractness that can serve as the basis for new words.[11] Thus, if we discard the idea of composition, we may as well discard the idea of rule-based computation.

A second variation of the non-decompositional view of the mental lexicon is that we do not only store all words as word types, but, in fact, information about individual word tokens. This is advocated most prominently by so-called exemplar-based models (e.g., Johnson 2004; Pierrehumbert 2002, 2001; Bybee 2001;

---

[11] Even though analogy versus schemata are often discussed separately (see, e.g., Arndt-Lappe & Ernestus 2020; Plag & Balling 2020), they are not necessarily in conflict but can be seen as extremes on a scale of schematicity (Booij 2010a).

Goldinger 1998, also see Pisoni & Levi 2007; Gahl & Yu 2006 for discussion). According to these models, humans store clouds of acoustically fully specified tokens (exemplars) for each word. Every time they encounter a new instance of a category (such as a word) in their environment, they subconsciously update this category with new information about that instance. This means that the mental lexicon does not just store words in abstracted form, but all forms with their concrete phonetic detail. Subtle subphonemic differences can be picked up and memorized based on experience. From a pocket calculator perspective on the mental lexicon which assumes storage capacities to be limited (see again Section 2.1.1, Baayen 2007), this is counterintuitive: nobody pronounces a word the same way twice. How could you possibly store all those possible variants? However, if we are willing to assume that the human brain has immense storage capabilities, exemplar models offer an elegant solution to many problems regarding subphonemic variation. For example, compared to feed-forward models (see Section 2.1), exemplar models have no difficulty explaining morphophonetic effects. Subphonemic differences, for example between morphological functions, are just memorized all directly from experience. Of course, one major unsolved question that remains in this type of approach is how these differences would arise in the first place.

A third variation on the non-decompositional view of the mental lexicon is to assume that there is no traditional "storage" at all. That is, human brains do not "contain" a list-like dictionary from which linguistic items can be retrieved (see, e.g., Baayen et al. 2019b). This is a radically different approach to linguistic memory – one that rejects the current metaphor of a mental lexicon as a collection of lexical entries altogether. All approaches discussed so far in this book make use of this metaphor in one way or another, whether they claim humans to store morphemes or whole words, rules or schemata, abstract word types or exemplars. But just as the metaphor of the pocket calculator, the storage metaphor is exactly that – a metaphor. The idea of traditional storage may as well be highly implausible and not transferable to cognition. Static representations in a lexicon, no matter what size or form, may not exist in the first place (Pirrelli et al. 2020: 28). But what could be the alternative to a mental dictionary of the commonly assumed type? This is where ideas of connectionism and discrimination come in. Let us now examine these ideas more closely.

One radically different way to conceptualize human memory and the morphological mechanisms operating in it is an associative network. This idea can be found, for instance, in connectionist approaches (e.g., the Distributed Connectionist approach by Rumelhart & McClelland 1986). In this case, the lexicon is not a dictionary where we "store" information as a list of items and possible operations. The word "storage" evokes images of fixed, permanent objects to collect and stow away – this is not the case here. Instead, the lexicon is a dynamic system, a neural network characterized by an ever-changing distribution of connections between its transient elements. Instead of statically memorizing information and placing it on a shelf in a cognitive library to later retrieve it by means of looking for the right entry, here we make use of a web of interactions whose strengths of association, states of activation and inhibition, and distributions are in constant flux. From a paradigmatic point of view, the higher weighted a connection between related words, the stronger associated these words are to each other.

Crucially, however, the idea of distributed connections can be applied not just to relations between words, but also to form-meaning relations. Thus, from a speech processing point of view, the higher weighted a connection between a word's form and a word's meaning, the stronger associated the form is to that meaning. For each encountered word or acoustically realized token of that word, we do not create a new "entry" (e.g., a stored word or exemplar), but instead strengthen or weaken the associations of its properties to all elements in the rest of the network. This perspective has been taken by so called *discriminative approaches* (for example, the Discriminative Lexicon, Baayen et al. 2019b). Discriminative approaches offer a new way of exploring and computationally implementing the idea of linguistic memory as a network, and the idea of non-decompositionality more generally, and have recently been successful in modeling several phenomena in speech comprehension and production. The present book focuses on discriminative learning to further explore the non-decompositional perspective. I will illustrate the idea of discrimination in detail in the following section.

2.2.1 Discriminative learning

Discriminative approaches (see, e.g., Chuang et al. 2020; Baayen et al. 2019b; Baayen et al. 2011; Ramscar et al. 2010; Ramscar & Yarlett 2007) are generally non-decompositional because, as the name suggests, they see form-meaning relations as *discriminatory* instead of compositional. That is, form-meaning relations are created in a system of difference, which distinguishes between features based on their similarity and dissimilarity and connects them to each other in a learning process. In discriminative approaches, "signs" in the semiotic sense of relations of form and meaning (Saussure 1916, see Section 2.1) are not fixed units. Like other non-decompositional models, discriminative models refrain from sublexical static representations such as morphemes, bases, affixes, or exponents in the lexicon. The brain does not contain stable lists of stored items. Instead, speech comprehension and production are the result of a dynamic learning process where relations between form and meaning are constantly recalibrated based on the speaker's experience. Linguistic memory is not a dictionary, but a network (Tomaschek et al. 2021).

This is best illustrated by reconsidering the simple example from Section 2.1. For convenience, the decompositional, sign-based view is repeated in Figure 2.4 next to the discriminative view. A complex wordform like *happiness* /hæpinəs/ 'the quality or state of being happy' is no longer analyzed as being composed of two form-meaning pairings, the base morpheme /hæpi/ 'happy' and the derivational suffix morpheme /nəs/ 'quality, state'. Instead, parts of the acoustic signal /hæpinəs/, here represented by overlapping triphone chunks (the hash # marks a word boundary) are mapped onto different meanings. It is important to note that these chunks do not constitute constituents in their own right; they are merely proxies for the acoustic signal and could in principle be of any size. Moreover, and crucially, these chunks do not "have" a meaning – they are connected to every possible meaning in the network, it is merely the differences in association strength that determine which connections will be activated.

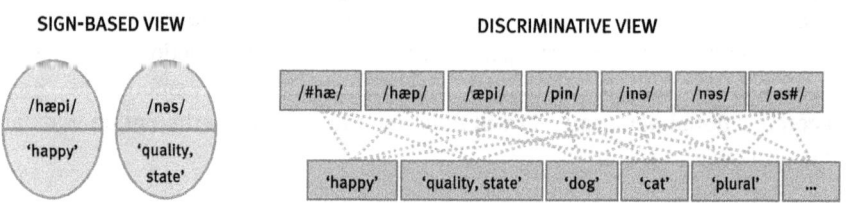

Fig. 2.4: Schematic illustration of a discriminative view of associations between form and meaning (right) versus a sign-based view of morphemes (left) for the complex word *happiness*.

How strong associations between given forms and meanings are in the system depends on how often specific forms occur together with specific meanings, and on how often they fail to occur together with others. Each time a speaker makes a new experience, i.e., encounters a form together with a specific meaning, all associations of forms and meanings in the system are updated to reflect this new state of learning. An association strength increases when a *cue* (such as a specific form) occurs together with an *outcome* (such as a specific meaning), and an association strength decreases when a cue does not occur with the outcome. Association strengths between forms and meanings, then, are dynamically calibrated in a discriminative system (for a textbook introduction, see Plag 2018).

As a consequence, morphology, in this approach, is rather implicit. Recurrent sublexical patterns that in other approaches would be described as morphemes or even phonaesthemes are at best treated as epiphenomenal, emerging from the same underlying associative structure. What we traditionally understand as units, e.g., morphemes, would in this view perhaps correspond to particularly strong associations between form and meaning (Plag & Balling 2020). Importantly, however, such linguistic structure emerges "through self-organization of unstructured input" (Pirrelli et al. 2020: 25). Linguistic contrast does not result from a priori meaningful signs or realizations, but from the pressure of discrimination to reduce uncertainty in a semiotic system (Blevins et al. 2016). Due to this pressure, cues are continuously competing against each other for how well they can predict an outcome. Pirrelli et al. (2020: 38) note that the metaphor of such constantly updating, adaptive activation flows chimes well with current approaches to quantum physics as well as approaches to biological systems. The metaphor of a discriminative network would thus certainly be an alternative more in keeping with contemporary zeitgeist than the metaphor of lexical storage.

The major advantage of a discriminative perspective for the present investigation is that compared to decompositional feed-forward models, it is theoretically far better equipped to explain morpho-phonetic effects. In Section 2.1, I have described how the observation that phonetic detail varies systematically with morphological properties is unaccounted for by decompositional models of the morphology-phonology interaction and of speech production (Roelofs & Ferreira 2019; Levelt et al. 1999; Dell 1986; Kiparsky 1982; Chomsky & Halle 1968). Established psycholinguistic models of speech production (e.g., Levelt et al. 1999) assume that morphological units select general phoneme templates without morphological information which are then passed on to an articulator module to be realized phonetically. Feed-forward models of the morphology-phonology interface (e.g., Kiparsky 1982) assume that morphological brackets around constituents are "erased" in the process of passing on a word through morphological and phonological levels of processing. Hence, these models do not allow for postlexical access of morphological information, and no trace of morphological structure should be left at the level of phonetic realization. In these approaches, morphological effects on the phonetic output are unexpected, and the mechanisms behind them are unclear.

However, from a discriminative perspective, observing morpho-phonetic patterns does not present a problem. A discriminative model lacks a feed-forward architecture which divides speech processing into separate levels. It is an end-to-end model that goes directly from form to meaning and from meaning to form. This means that the loss of morphological information between levels, e.g., through phoneme template selection or bracket erasure, is no longer an issue. Moreover, discriminative approaches refrain from postulating morphemes or even phonemes as psychologically relevant units in the first place. This opens the way for interpreting acoustic differences from a new perspective. In a discriminative approach, differences between morphological categories are expected to emerge naturally from sublexical and contextual cues. If we can model systematic acoustic variation between morphological categories with measures derived from a discriminative network, it is possible to explain potential effects by its theoretical principles of learning and experience. Morphophonetic patterns would simply serve to enhance discriminability, reduce the uncertainty in navigating the semiotic space, and thus facilitate processing and communication (also see Blevins et al. 2016). Discriminative approaches, then, are a promising alternative way for the present investigation to understand the patterning of durations in complex words, and, more generally, an alternative to better explain the morphology-phonetics interaction at the theoretical level.

To explore the discriminative perspective empirically, it is helpful to find a way of implementing this perspective as a computational model. This endeavor has increasingly gained attention in recent years – for good reason. Pirrelli et al. (2020) make a case for how a combination of psycholinguistics and computational linguistics is uniquely positioned to tackle questions of the mental lexicon and morphological processing. Embodying the shift from rules to learning from experience, the two linguistic subdisciplines are characterized by a methodological complementarity: psycholinguistics tries to explain the processing "black box" (the explanandum) by looking at behavioral data (the explanans), while computer simulations try to explain the behavioral data (the explanandum) by looking at the processing apparatus (the explanans) (Pirrelli et al. 2020). There are several possibilities to computationally implement the discriminative idea, however, two of the most prominent ones are *naïve discriminative learning* (NDL) and *linear discriminative learning* (LDL). Discriminative learning models (e.g., Chuang et al. 2020; Baayen et al. 2019b; Baayen et al. 2011; Ramscar et al. 2010; Ramscar & Yarlett 2007) implement the complex mappings of form and meaning outlined above in a mathematical fashion.

To explore the discriminative view, and the non-decompositional perspective more generally, the present study used *linear discriminative learning* (LDL, Chuang et al. 2021; Heitmeier et al. 2021; Chuang et al. 2020; Baayen et al. 2019b; Baayen et al. 2018). LDL is a methodological toolkit that implements Word and

Paradigm Morphology, and it has been proposed as part of a general model of the lexicon dubbed the *Discriminative Lexicon* (Baayen et al. 2019b). LDL is a new variant of naïve discriminative learning (NDL, Tomaschek et al. 2019; Baayen 2011; Baayen et al. 2011; Baayen et al. 2013). Like NDL, LDL is *discriminative* because its system of form-meaning relations is generated by discriminating between different forms and meanings instead of building them from compositional units. Like NDL, it is a system of *learning* because the association strengths between forms and meanings are continuously recalibrated in a process of experience. This learning is simple and interpretable because, in contrast to deep learning, it features just two layers, an input layer and an output layer, both of which are linguistically transparent. Unlike NDL, however, LDL is *linear* and no longer "naïve". Its networks are linear mappings between form matrices and meaning matrices (which serve as either the input layer or the output layer, respectively). In this approach, forms are represented by vectors, and meanings are also represented by vectors. I will explain this in more mathematical detail in Section 7.1. The general idea is that if we can express both forms and meanings numerically, we can mathematically connect form and meaning. In LDL, the network is no longer naïve because where NDL represents word meanings with binary vectors and thereby naïvely assumes meaning outcomes to be independent, LDL uses real-valued vectors, taking into account that words cannot only be similar in form, but also in meaning.

The idea of representing word meanings with real-valued vectors might be familiar to the reader, as it comes from distributional semantics (see, e.g., Lapesa et al. 2018; Landauer & Dumais 1997). In semantics, the distributional hypothesis states that words with similar distributions should be similar in meaning (Acquaviva et al. 2020: 378). This hypothesis goes back to older ideas that "the meaning of a word is its use in the language" (Wittgenstein 2009 [1953]) and "you shall know a word by the company it keeps" (Firth 1957, also see Harris 1954). In such an approach, the frequency of co-occurrence of a word with other words is used to determine how close the meaning of the word is to the meanings of other words. Simplifying the approach, for each word, the values of its co-occurrence frequency with other words make up a vector, which represents that word's meaning. The distance between word vectors gauges these words' semantic similarity. The strong version of the distributional hypothesis claims that semantic distributions have cognitive reality, because experiencing co-occurrence gradually forms corresponding representations in the lexicon (Acquaviva et al. 2020). While Acquaviva et al. (2020) observe that a distributional view on semantics can be contrasted with relational (structuralist), symbolic (generativist), and conceptual (cognitive linguistics) views on semantics, they also note that the distributional view is in fact heavily indebted to structuralism. This is because distributional semantics assumes the meaning of a linguistic item to be determined by that item's relation to other items. It is therefore also important to emphasize that distributional semantics itself does not have to be semantically non-decompositional: for example, it would also be possible to model the distribution and relation of morpheme semantics to each other.

This has interesting implications for discriminative learning. While NDL is a hybrid model which uses subsymbolic forms but symbolic meanings, LDL can use real-valued vectors in the spirit of distributional semantics to represent the semantics of words subsymbolically (Heitmeier et al. 2021). However, which "chunks" of meaning are represented subsymbolically is a matter of operationalization. This opens up researcher degrees of freedom to explore different morphological scenarios. The present study is interested in exploring different approaches to morphological structure. It is therefore important to investigate how potential morpho-phonetic effects might differ depending on how much information an LDL network has about the semantics of morphological categories. To address this, the present LDL study trained three different networks which differ in what kind of explicit information they have about the semantics of a word's morphological category (i.e., about the semantics of DIS, NESS, LESS, ATION, and IZE). Further below in Section 7.1.3, I will explain how this is implemented, and in the discussions in Section 7.3 and Chapter 8 I will discuss in detail the implications.

From the LDL networks, the researcher can then derive measures that can be used as predictors in statistical models. Of course, there are many measures that one could investigate from a non-decompositional perspective more generally. I have already hinted at some of these measures with word frequency (Section 2.1.1) and word-based informativeness measures (Section 2.1.4). However, as the present study uses LDL to explore the non-decompositional perspective, I will focus on measures from discriminative models specifically.

Recent research has shown that measures from discriminative models seem to be able to model behavioral data successfully. For example, discriminative approaches have already been used to successfully model reaction time (e.g., Chuang et al. 2020; Baayen et al. 2011) and to simulate speech production of individuals with aphasia (Heitmeier & Baayen 2020). However, there is still a general lack of studies testing measures derived from discriminative networks. Furthermore, the question arises whether a discriminative approach is also able to predict acoustic duration. Recently, Tomaschek et al. (2019) and Schmitz et al. (2021b) modeled the duration of English word-final [s] and [z] of different morphological status. The former study used NDL, while the latter study used LDL. In addition, Tucker et al. (2019a) used NDL to model the duration of stem vowels in English verbs. In all three studies, the measures derived from the networks were predictive and indicated, for example, that higher semantic activation diversity is associated with shorter durations. Chuang et al. (2020), too, found several LDL measures to be predictive for duration when combined in a principal components analysis. However, there were also some differences between the studies. For example, certainty in producing a morphological function was associated with lengthening in one study (Tomaschek et al. 2019), and with shortening in the other (Schmitz et al. 2021b). In addition, while most of these studies focused on inflection, it is necessary to also test how well discriminative approaches can deal with derivational morphology. The present work aims to fill this gap.

It is possible, then, to summarize the aims of the present LDL study as follows. Given the highly explorative nature of this study, I will formulate as guidelines only research questions instead of hypotheses. The first aim is to investigate how well LDL can account for the durational variation in the data. Given that LDL is claimed to provide a powerful alternative to the decompositional perspective, one could expect the LDL-derived measures to perform at least as well as the measures assuming decomposition (see again Sections 2.1.1 to 2.1.4). Note that in the study taking the non-decompositional perspective, only word durations were modeled.

Q $LDL_{PREDICT}$ Are measures derived from linear discriminative learning networks comparable to traditional measures in their predictiveness for the acoustic duration of derived words?

The second aim is to explore which measures will affect acoustic duration in what way. Again, given that the present study is highly exploratory in nature, and given that we do not have much literature yet on the effect of LDL-derived measures on acoustic duration, it is dispreferred to formulate specific hypotheses about individual measures at this stage. Potential expectations will be discussed in Section 7.1.5, where I will explain the LDL measures in detail. It is possible at this stage to ask more generally if LDL-derived measures can successfully (i.e., significantly) predict derivative durations. If they do, the effects of LDL-derived measures should be interpretable with regard to speech production. For example, they should mirror the finding by Schmitz et al. (2021b), Tomaschek et al. (2019), and Tucker et al. (2019a) that higher activation diversity is associated with shorter durations. It will be of major interest to explore how we can interpret potential effects conceptually, and what they tell us about the mechanisms of speech processing.

Q LDL$_{\text{INTERPRET}}$ What do effects of measures derived from linear discriminative learning networks on acoustic duration tell us about speech processing?

The third aim is to explore in how far the operationalization of the semantics of complex words, and hence the amount of morphological information (as foreshadowed above), leads to different network structures and different effects on duration. Will we observe differences between the networks, depending on whether or how we specify the semantics of the morphological category a derivative belongs to?

Q LDL$_{\text{NETWORKS}}$ How will LDL networks differ in their structure and in the effects of their measures on acoustic duration when we build them with different operationalizations of semantic and morphological information?

I have outlined the general theoretical principles of discriminative learning as one way of conceptualizing and computationally implementing a non-decompositional perspective on morphology and the lexicon. How exactly LDL is implemented mathematically and statistically will be explained in detail in Section 7.1. Before we turn to the four studies testing measures from the decompositional perspective and the non-decompositional perspective, let me briefly summarize the predictions I have derived in the sections of the present chapter.

2.3 Summary of hypotheses and questions

In a nutshell, approaches taking a decompositional perspective assume words to be decomposed into smaller morphological units, while approaches taking a non-decompositional perspective do not. We have seen that the decompositional perspective and the non-decompositional perspective can be explored from various angles and with various measures. Many findings of previous studies seem to be consistent with the decompositional perspective, such as base frequency effects, the degree of segmentability, and affix informativeness.

However, we have seen that there are empirical as well as theoretical problems, including problems of reliability and validity. The empirical problem is one of reliability: some effects have been inconsistent or have failed to emerge in several cases. Larger-scale studies like the present one can help to shed light onto how reliable these effects really are. The theoretical problem is that it is unclear how to account for such effects. First, speech production models and theories of the morphology-phonology interface in the decompositional perspective generally do not allow for morphological structure to be reflected in phonetic detail. Second, in many cases, effects of specific measures have been interpreted to provide evidence for one perspective or the other, but it is not always clear if these effects could also in fact be explained from the opposite perspective. This is a problem of validity: it might be the case that such measures are predictive not because they capture decomposition, but due to some other underlying mechanism or structure. One way of addressing this is to also explore the non-decompositional perspective and see if whatever underlies morpho-phonetic effects can be captured by non-decompositional measures, such as measures derived from linear discriminative learning networks. Can morpho-phonetic effects also emerge from nonmorphemic morphological structure without any fixed one-to-one mapping of form and meaning, and without fixed representations in the lexicon?

As outlined in Chapter 1, the present book investigates the decompositional measures with durational data from the morphological categories NESS, LESS, PRE, IZE, ATION, DIS, UN, and IN in British English varieties and the categories NESS, ATION, DIS, UN, ABLE, ITY, MENT, and RE in New Zealand English varieties. The measures derived from the linear discriminative learning networks are tested with the morphological categories DIS, NESS, LESS, ATION, and IZE in British English varieties. I will describe the selection and characteristics of these categories in Section 3.1. In the present chapter, I have formulated several predictions and questions that help explore the decompositional and non-decompositional perspective with these morphological categories in four empirical studies. I will report these studies in Chapters 4 to 7. The first of these four studies (Chapter 4) investigated the frequency measures, i.e., base frequency, word frequency, and relative frequency (supposedly reflecting morphological segmentability). For this study, the following hypotheses are relevant:

H $\text{FREQ}_{\text{BASE}}$ Higher base frequency should be associated with acoustic reduction, i.e., shorter durations, of the word, its base, and its affix.

H $\text{FREQ}_{\text{WORD}}$ Higher word frequency should be associated with acoustic reduction, i.e., shorter durations, of the word, its base, and its affix.

H FREQ_{RELATIVE} The higher the relative frequency of a derivative (i.e., the more segmentable a derivative is), the longer will be its word duration, affix duration, and base duration.

The second study (Chapter 5) investigated prosodic word integration and its interaction with morphological segmentability. For this study, I have derived the following hypotheses:

H PROS_{FREQREL} The more prosodically integrated an affix is (the weaker the prosodic boundary), the less likely can higher relative frequency protect the derivative against reduction.

H PROS Affix durations and base durations should pattern according to the following hierarchy, where the right arrow sign ▶ between prosodic categories or domains means that the left-hand element is expected to be more lengthened than the right-hand element:

Integrating affix ▶ base	bases ProsodicWord ▶ CliticGroup ▶ Integrating
CliticGroup affix ▶ base	affixes CliticGroup ▶ Integrating ▶ ProsodicWord
ProsodicWord base ▶ affix	

The third study (Chapter 6) investigated affix informativeness, as gauged by the conditional probability of an affix and by its semantic information load. We can expect:

H INF_{PROB} The higher the conditional affix probability (i.e., the less informative an affix is), the shorter will be the duration of the word, of the affix, and of the base.

H INF_{SEM} The higher the semantic information load of the affix (i.e., the more informative an affix is), the longer will be the duration of the word, of the affix, and of the base.

Finally, the fourth study (Chapter 7) investigated how we can model morphophonetic effects in English derivational morphology with linear discriminative learning. I have proposed the following explorative questions:

Q LDL_{PREDICT} Are measures derived from linear discriminative learning networks comparable to traditional measures in their predictiveness for the acoustic duration of derived words?

Q LDL_{INTERPRET} What do effects of measures derived from linear discriminative learning networks on acoustic duration tell us about speech processing?

Q LDL_{NETWORKS} How will LDL networks differ in their structure and in the effects of their measures on acoustic duration when we build them with different operationalizations of semantic and morphological information?

The four studies reported in this book have their individual methodology. However, they also share many methods, procedures, and variables. The following chapter will therefore first describe those parts of the methodology that are applicable to all four studies.

3 General method

The four studies of the present book are, to varying degrees, exploratory in nature. Exploratory studies are often characterized by an adjustment of parts of their methodology during the research process with the aim of identifying patterns. This is especially the case for the study on linear discriminative learning (Chapter 7) since no concrete hypotheses regarding specific measures were formulated in advance. The aim, rather, was to explore if – and if so, which – measures are predictive in the first place (see again Section 2.2.1). However, while the other three studies (frequency measures, prosodic word integration, and affix informativeness, Chapters 4–6) do test specific predictions about effects of predefined measures, they too are exploratory rather than confirmatory. This is because these studies explored many variations of different statistical models for a single dataset. Roettger et al. (2019: 2) importantly note that confirmatory studies

> [allow] for only a single theoretically motivated model to be fitted to the data. Subsequently, model criticism is carried out to clarify whether the resulting model is actually appropriate for the data. In a genuinely confirmatory analysis, there is no place for repeated modeling during data collection, no place for adding or removing interactions, and no place for including or removing control variables. As soon as a second model is fitted to a given dataset, the analysis is no longer confirmatory, but exploratory [...].

The present studies explored several researcher degrees of freedom during the research process, whose exploitation could potentially be harmful when interpreted as if in a confirmatory setting. Following Wicherts et al.'s (2016) list, these include measuring additional variables to select as covariates and choosing them for statistical modeling (see Section 3.3), correcting, coding, and discarding acoustic data in a non-blinded manner (Section 3.2.2), deciding how to deal with violations of statistical assumptions and with outliers in an ad hoc manner, and choosing between different statistical models (Section 3.4). It is thus vital to report the present studies as exploratory, especially given that confirmatory and exploratory methods often intermingle in practice (Roettger et al. 2019). One way of mitigating against spurious results in exploratory studies that set out to test null hypotheses is to set more conservative alpha levels (Roettger et al. 2019), which I implemented in several places throughout the studies (see chapters below).

While the methodological procedures specific to each analysis will be described in Chapters 4–7 respectively, the present chapter will outline the general strategies pertinent to all analyses. Section 3.1 will describe the selection and characteristics of the morphological categories investigated in the present book. Section 3.2 will describe how the datasets were extracted, cleaned, and prepared for analysis. The coding and computation of the response variable and the predictor variables will be explained in Section 3.3, followed by a description of the general modeling strategy in Section 3.4.

3.1 Selection of morphological categories

The morphological categories chosen for analysis are NESS, LESS, PRE, IZE, ATION, DIS, UN, IN, ABLE, ITY, MENT, and RE. The term *morphological category*, in this book, is used to refer to groups of words that share a particular morphologically expressed meaning. In the decompositional perspective, the morphological categories NESS, LESS, PRE, IZE, ATION, DIS, UN, IN, ABLE, ITY, MENT, and RE correspond to the affixes *-ness, -less, pre-, -ize, -ation, dis-, un-, in-, -able, -ity, -ment,* and *re-*. Referring to the decompositional perspective (as well as to acoustic segmentation and durational measurement), I use these italicized written representations of these affixes, together with the term *morpheme* or *affix*. However, from a general perspective (as well as from a non-decompositional perspective) I use the written representations of morphological categories in small caps and refrain from referring to the corresponding affixes. This is because the present work debates the very nature of morphological categories and hence the existence of minimal signs combining a form and a meaning (e.g., *-ness* / nəs/ 'quality, state'). In addition to *morphological category*, I use the terms *morphological function* or *derivational function* to refer to the semantic or grammatical contribution of a particular category (e.g., NESS). The terms *category* and *function* better reflect the fact that in the non-decompositional perspective, derived words might be grouped into categories sharing similar semantics or features but are not composed of form-meaning building blocks.

The morphological categories above were chosen based on two criteria. The first criterion was that the categories should feature enough observations in the corpora. This is important to ensure sufficient power for statistical analysis. The second criterion was that the categories should be diverse in terms of their semantic properties and, importantly, in terms of the prosodic classification of the affixes associated with the morphological categories. All three types of prosodic word integration should be represented by at least two affixes each. The prosodic classification is based on Raffelsiefen (2007, 1999) and, whenever she does not explicitly mention the affix in question, on the application of her criteria for determining prosodic word status, like syllable and foot structure, stress, and resyllabification (see again Section 2.1.3). Table 3.1 gives an overview of the classification, together with the corpus study affiliation of the affixes.

Tab. 3.1: Investigated affixes in the three corpora, sorted by prosodic word category.

	ProsodicWord	CliticGroup	Integrating
Audio BNC	*dis-, in-, pre-, un-*	*-ness, -less*	*-ation, -ize*
QuakeBox corpus	*dis-, un-, re-*	*-ness, -ment*	*-ation, -able, -ity*
ONZE corpus	*dis-, un-, re-*	*-ness, -ment*	*-ation, -able, -ity*

Note that the selected affixes are the same across the QuakeBox and ONZE corpora, but partly different for the Audio BNC. This is because after initial sampling from the Audio BNC, some of the morphological categories did not yield enough tokens in the New Zealand corpora and were therefore replaced by others (see Section 3.2.2). Morphological categories not represented by an affix in Table 3.1 that would have fulfilled the criteria were judged to feature too few word types or tokens to provide adequate statistical power. The morphological categories that were considered for analysis but not included for this reason in either corpus study are WISE, DE, MEGA, POST, SUPER, ATE, EE, EN, HOOD, and ORY. In addition, the category LY was considered but discarded because its token counts are larger than those of the other categories by several orders of magnitude, making it impracticable to manually check the automatic forced alignment (see Section 3.2.2 below).

Let us briefly have a look at some of the characteristics of the affixes in Table 3.1 from the decompositional perspective (following Plag 2018; Bauer et al. 2013). The ProsodicWord affixes are *dis-, in-, pre-, un-,* and *re-*. These affixes have in common that they are all prefixes and are characterized by relatively clear semantics: *dis-, in-,* and *un-* have a clear negative meaning, while *re-* is clearly iterative and *pre-* can carry spatial or temporal meaning. The ProsodicWord affixes mostly take free morphemes as bases and their derivatives tend to be rather transparent. They vary in their productivity, with *pre-* and *un-* being considered very productive, and *dis-, in-,* and *re-* somewhat productive. They are generally assumed to be secondarily stressed, although there is some variability, with unstressed or main-stressed attestations. Most of the prefixes are not obligatorily subject to phonological alternation except *in-*, which assimilates to the following base-initial onset (e.g., *irregular, illegal, impossible*). None of the affixes cause resyllabification. It must be noted that the prefixes *dis-* and *in-* are considered to be prosodic words only most of the time, i.e., in semantically transparent derivatives with words as bases. In opaque derivatives with bound roots, they are expected to integrate into the host prosodic word. However, this is irrelevant for the present purposes, as I excluded all derivatives whose base is not a word in order to be able to properly calculate the base frequency, which is needed for relative frequency (see dataset description in Section 3.2.2). All the *dis-* and *in-*affixed words in the present studies are therefore associated with the ProsodicWord structure.

The CliticGroup affixes are the suffixes *-ness*, *-less*, and *-ment*. Their semantics are generally a little less straightforward than those of the ProsodicWord affixes. While *-less* has a clear privative meaning, the meanings of *-ness*, which can denote abstract states, traits, or properties, and *-ment*, which can denote processes, actions, or results, are not always predictable. Like the ProsodicWord affixes, however, the CliticGroup affixes mostly take free bases and produce mostly transparent derivatives. Both *-ness* and *-less* are considered to be highly productive, whereas *-ment* used to be productive but has lost some of that capability in contemporary English varieties (but see Kawaletz 2021). The CliticGroup affixes are never stressed, not subject to phonological alternations (with exceptions for *-ness* in specific configurations), and not involved in resyllabification processes.

Finally, the Integrating affixes are the suffixes *-ation*, *-ize*, *-able* and *-ity*. Compared to the other affixes, their semantics are rather multifaceted, covering a wide range of meanings each. For example, *-ize* can have locative, ornative, causative, resultative, inchoative, performative or similative meaning, *-ation* denotes events, states, locations, products or means, *-able* is used to express capability, liability or quality, and *-ity* denotes properties, states, qualities, sometimes with a "nuance of pomposity" compared to *-ness* (Bauer et al. 2013: 248), and has various idiosyncratic derivatives, too. Their bases are mostly free morphemes, but all of them can attach to bound roots as well. They are mostly transparent, but overall less so compared to the affixes in the other two prosodic categories. The most productive of them by far is *-able*, whereas *-ity* is more restricted in its application. Integrating affixes can cause differences in the stress patterns of the derivatives, either being mostly secondarily (*-ize*) or primarily (*-ation*) stressed themselves, or capable of causing stress shifts and other phonological alternations within their bases (*-able*, *-ation* and *-ity*). Resyllabification is commonplace among all of them, making them clear cases of the Integrating category.

Having categorized the affixes associated with the morphological categories used in the present studies, let us now turn to the data I used to represent these categories.

3.2 Building the datasets

The present studies use three different corpora from two varieties of English, each corpus study including eight morphological categories each. There are at least three advantages to such a wide corpus approach. The first advantage is the amount of data. While in experimental data, the researcher can generate balanced sets of observations also for rare phenomena, such as less frequent morphological categories, it is often difficult to elicit a lot of observations due to constraints of time and resources. In corpus studies, however, it is possible to analyze a lot of data, without having to carry out large-scale experiments in different places. With corpus data, it is possible to analyze more morphological categories overall than with experimental data.

The second advantage is that the type of data is conversational speech produced outside of a lab context. It has been suggested that experimental research may fail to replicate some kinds of effect, particularly frequency effects (Gahl et al. 2012). This is because when speakers read words in similarly structured carrier phrases or in word lists, they tend to adjust their speech rate in such a way that it may override potential frequency effects. Note that "conversational speech" does not necessarily exclude lab speech – conversational speech can also be elicited, and many alleged drawbacks of experimental speech, like the list reading effect, can be alleviated with careful design of experimental setup and stimuli (Xu 2010). However, there is hardly a way to come closer to a reflection of everyday use of language than by using spontaneous speech outside of the experimental context, without any input by the researcher. While it is true that in experiments, it is possible to construct stimuli in a way that controls for many potentially intervening variables, it has been argued (e.g., Tucker & Ernestus 2016) that research on speech production in particular needs to shift its focus to spontaneous speech to be able to draw valid conclusions about language processing. It is assumed that corpora with conversational speech enable the researcher to investigate a more authentic process of language production.

Third, and finally, much psycholinguistic research has been conducted on experimental data that have often not been elicited to guarantee spontaneousness or casualness. However, it is generally important to use a diversity of methods in linguistic research: as we have seen, spontaneous and non-spontaneous speech both come with their advantages and disadvantages and might yield different results in the investigation of linguistic phenomena. This work contributes to the diversification of psycholinguistic research by using non-elicited conversations.

One priority in selecting the corpora is to ensure that it is possible to find enough tokens for as many different morphological categories as possible. The corpora need to be large enough to yield a sufficient number of observations per category. Three corpora in particular were judged to fulfill this criterion: the Audio BNC (Coleman et al. 2012), the QuakeBox corpus (Walsh et al. 2013), and the ONZE corpus (Gordon et al. 2007).

3.2.1 Description of the corpora

The Audio BNC (Coleman et al. 2012) is the largest of the three corpora. It consists of both monologues and dialogues from different speech genres of a number of British English varieties, and contains about 7.5 million words. The data can be extracted via its web interface (Hoffmann & Arndt-Lappe 2021; Hoffmann & Evert 2018), which is available at bncweb.lancs.ac.uk. Just as the other two corpora, the Audio BNC comes phonetically aligned by an automatic forced aligner. While the size of this corpus is very large, it was found that many of the recordings are not optimal in quality, and therefore that the alignment was in many cases wrong or imprecise. This resulted in some additional data loss during the cleaning procedure, which I will describe below in Section 3.2.2.

The QuakeBox corpus (Walsh et al. 2013) consists of mainly monologues spoken by inhabitants of Christchurch, New Zealand, who tell the interviewer about their experiences surrounding the 2010–2011 Canterbury earthquakes. For this corpus, a shipping container was transformed into a mobile recording studio, aptly named the "QuakeBox". This container was placed in various parts of the city that had been affected by the earthquake. One advantage of this corpus compared to the other two corpora is that the conversational context and the conversation topics are much more consistent across speakers. This is because all speakers were asked to tell the interviewers their personal experience of a single event, the earthquake. Since these stories were recorded in a soundproof space, the audio is also of very high quality compared to the Audio BNC. I extracted the data on-site in Christchurch via the LaBB-CAT interface (Fromont & Hay 2012; Fromont 2003–2020). At the time of extraction, the corpus contained about 800,000 tokens, or 86 hours of speech spoken by 758 participants.

Finally, the ONZE corpus (Gordon et al. 2007) consists of three collections of recordings from different New Zealand English varieties, the historical Mobile Unit (with speakers born between 1851–1910), the later Intermediate Archive (with speakers born between 1890–1930), and the contemporary Canterbury Corpus (with speakers born between 1930–1984), as well as some additional recordings from various projects. The ONZE corpus is thus a collection of subcorpora rather than one uniform corpus. For this reason, the ONZE corpus studies will include one additional covariate compared to the studies on the other two corpora. This covariate controls for the respective subcorpus of the ONZE in which each observation appears (see Section 3.3.2). The ONZE corpus, too, is available at the University of Canterbury, Christchurch. As with the QuakeBox corpus, I used LaBB-CAT to extract the data. At the time of extraction, all subcorpora together contained about 3.3 million tokens, or 392 hours of speech spoken by 1,589 participants.

3.2.2 Data extraction and cleaning

Wordlists, recordings, and textgrids were obtained by entering query strings into the corpora interfaces. These query strings searched for all word tokens that begin (for prefixes) or end (for suffixes) in the phonological and orthographic affix representation of each of the investigated morphological categories. The exact string and the wildcards used depended on the type of interface used to access the corpus. For the Audio BNC, it is possible to use CQP syntax. For example, I used the string [phon=".*NAH0S" & word= ".*ness"] to find all instances of words phonologically ending in /nəs/ and orthographically ending in <ness>. For the QuakeBox and ONZE corpora, I used the LaBB-CAT interface (Fromont & Hay 2012; Fromont 2003–2020). In the LaBB-CAT syntax, for example, tokens with -*ness* could be extracted with the string _^(.*n.s)$_^(.*ness)$_^(n)$, which searches for all words with a syllable starting with /n/ and ending with /s/, with the word-final orthography <ness>, and including the segment /n/. Specifying syllable and segment criteria in addition to orthographic criteria is necessary to access the different layers (syllable layer, segment layer) into which the New Zealand corpora are organized. For all three corpora, it is then possible to extract the list of results in the form of wordlists in spreadsheets, as well as to extract the corresponding recordings and textgrids. The spreadsheets include corresponding meta-information and variables which have already been coded in the corpora.

The wordlists were cleaned manually, excluding words which were monomorphemic (e.g., *bless, pregnant, station*), whose semantics or base were unclear (e.g., *harness, predator, dissertation*), or which were proper names or titles (e.g., *Guinness, Stenness, Stromness*). It was decided to only include derivatives with words as bases, not bound roots, meaning that the bases had to be attested as independent words with a related sense to the derivative. This is important because the frequency of the base word outside of the derivative is needed in order to calculate relative frequency.[1] The existence of such bases was determined by consulting pertinent dictionaries such as the Oxford English Dictionary Online 2020, as well as web attestations.

If the researcher needs to identify derived words and their bases, they face two challenges. The first one is posed by derivatives that belong to more than one morphological category, i.e., by derivatives that (from the decompositional perspective) are multi-affixed words. First, the target affixes could potentially appear inside a derivative instead of word-initially or word-finally, making it difficult to compare durations. This problem was solved by the way the query strings were formulated, only considering words in which the target affixes appear at the beginning or end of the derivative. Second, it can be difficult or sometimes impossible to define the base word of a derivative because the order of affixation is unclear. In these cases, it was decided not to speculate on the order of affixation, but to always consider non-target affixes to be part of a base to which the target affix is then attached. For example, in the *-ation* dataset, the word *recreation* was considered to have the structure of *recreate + ion*, while in the *re-* dataset, it was *re + creation*. Following previous research (e.g., Sóskuthy & Hay 2017; Seyfarth 2014; Bell et al. 2009; Gahl 2008; Pluymaekers et al. 2005b), I also included all wordforms of a given type (e.g., *discover, discovered, discovering* etc.). This is important because frequencies might differ substantially between wordforms of the same lemma (Sóskuthy & Hay 2017).

The second challenge pertains to etymology. Sometimes, bases may have been borrowed from a different language, such as Latin, and only later may have undergone derivational processes in the English language. But at other times, borrowed words had already been derived when adopted into English. In these latter cases, it is more difficult to decide if English native speakers without etymological knowledge would even consider a word morphologically complex. This issue was addressed by ignoring etymological criteria altogether and only considering words whose base was attested in current English as a separate word. It did not matter whether the base existed first or was formed by backformation processes.

Once the wordlists had been cleaned in this way, I removed all audio files and textgrids corresponding to the excluded words. However, the remaining

---

[1] Including bound roots is also possible using workarounds such as categorically assigning a low frequency (of, e.g., 1) to them (e.g., Baayen et al. 2006), or counting their occurrence in other derivatives (e.g., Gahl & Plag 2019). The empirical and theoretical consequences of such workarounds are not clear.

audio files also needed to be cleaned themselves. Because the alignments had been produced by the automatic forced aligners of the three corpora, they were not optimal. Before starting the acoustic analysis, manual inspection of all items was therefore necessary to exclude items that were not suitable for further analysis.

The alignment of the items was checked by visually and acoustically inspecting the items in the speech analysis software Praat (Boersma & Weenik 2001). This was done by seven trained student assistants and the author. Items were excluded that fulfilled one or more of the following criteria: the textgrid was a duplicate or corrupted for technical reasons, the target word was not spoken or inaudible due to background noise, the target word was interrupted by other acoustic material, laughing, or pauses, the target word was sung instead of spoken, the target word was not properly segmented or incorrectly aligned to the recording. In cases where the alignment did not seem satisfactory, we specifically examined three boundaries to decide whether to exclude the item: the word-initial boundary, the word-final boundary, and the boundary between base and affix. We considered an observation to be correctly aligned if none of these boundaries would have to be shifted to the left or right under application of the segmentation criteria in the pertinent phonetic literature (cf. Ladefoged & Johnson 2011; Machač & Skarnitzl 2009). Following Machač & Skarnitzl (2009: 25–26), we considered the shape of the sound wave to be the most important cue, followed by the spectrogram, followed by listening. A segmentation example that was considered adequate is given in Figure 3.1.

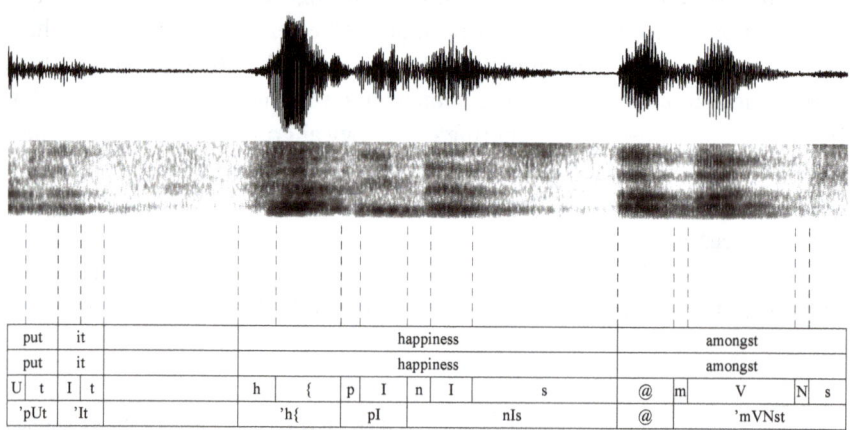

Fig. 3.1: Example of a token of *happiness* from the ONZE corpus considered to be correctly aligned.

For comparison, an example of a token considered to be aligned incorrectly is given in Figure 3.2. The incorrect alignment of *sadness* in Figure 3.2 is evident when comparing the boundary placement to the spectrogram and soundwave. The end boundary of the word-final segment /s/ in *sadness* is placed in the middle of the suffix-internal schwa, and the boundaries of the following word *and* are incorrectly placed during this schwa up until the beginning of the suffix-final fricative. It is only later in the sound file that the word *and* is spoken.

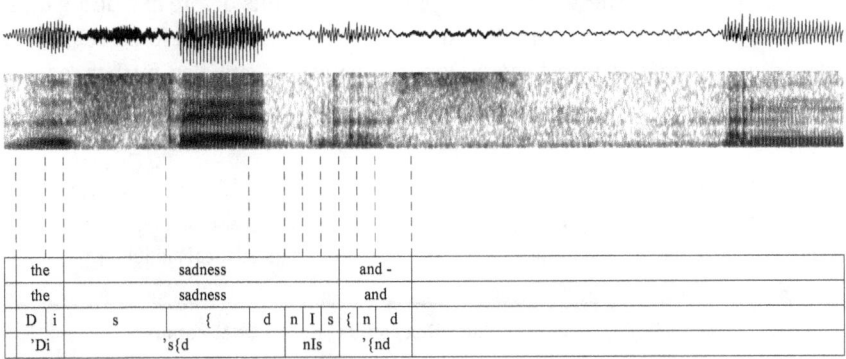

Fig. 3.2: Example of a token of *sadness* from the QuakeBox corpus considered to be incorrectly aligned.

I also excluded derivatives with geminates (e.g., *openness*, *unnecessary*), since in these cases it is usually impossible to determine the acoustic boundary between base and affix (also see Ben Hedia 2019). Finally, derivatives were removed in cases where within a dataset of an individual morphological category, only one or two tokens represented one level of the NUMBER OF SYLLABLES variable (see Section 3.3.2) in order to avoid statistical problems.

After reducing the datasets in this manner, I checked whether each morphological category still contained enough observations to be suitable for statistical analysis. It was decided that a token count of fewer than 100 per morphological category would result in too problematic a lack of statistical power. Further, I made sure that the type count was satisfactory as well. For example, the category WISE (associated with the suffix *-wise*) was excluded because almost all tokens belonged to the high-frequent word type *otherwise*. As mentioned above, the discarded categories were WISE, DE, MEGA, POST, SUPER, ATE, EE, EN, HOOD, and ORY (as well as LY, see Section 3.1). Eight categories per corpus remained. As explained in Section 3.1, because of this restriction, the selected categories are partly different for the Audio BNC from those in the QuakeBox and ONZE studies.

The remaining morphological categories were NESS, LESS, PRE, IZE, ATION, DIS, UN, and IN for the Audio BNC, and NESS, ATION, DIS, UN, ABLE, ITY, MENT, and RE for the QuakeBox and ONZE corpora. As mentioned before, it was made sure that all three types of prosodic word integration were sufficiently represented, which is relevant for the analysis of prosodic word boundary effects on duration in Chapter 5. Table 3.2 gives an overview of the token counts and type counts in the remaining data. These numbers represent the counts before excluding outliers during statistical modeling. For analyses that used mixed-effects regression instead of standard multiple regression, the datasets were also further reduced to only those types (or types and speakers) for which there are more than a fixed number of observations. This will be described later in Section 5.1.

Tab. 3.2: Overview of initial types and tokens sorted by corpus and morphological category, before excluding outliers and further dataset reductions during statistical modeling.

	Audio BNC		QuakeBox corpus		ONZE corpus	
	Tokens	Types	Tokens	Types	Tokens	Types
NESS	468	125	156	39	125	43
LESS	216	59				
PRE	123	68				
IZE	474	66				
ATION	3979	373	492	94	1082	186
DIS	689	159	179	58	262	67
UN	958	277	295	67	348	80
IN	339	69				
ABLE			199	50	285	61
ITY			594	46	447	79
MENT			345	46	705	73
RE			379	72	403	95

Note that some datasets are smaller than others due to the nature of corpus data. Thus, there might be variations in statistical power between the datasets. In a null hypothesis significance testing (NHST) framework, the larger the dataset, the more likely one is to observe "significant" effects. This will be important to consider in the discussion of cases where we observe effects in a dataset of one morphological category but not of another.

3.3 Variables

Acoustic duration may be affected by several variables other than the variables of interest, and it is vital to control for as much variation as possible. The following sections describe in detail those variables that will be relevant to all the analyses. Variables specific to certain analyses, such as informativeness variables and variables derived from the LDL networks, will be described later in the pertinent sections.

3.3.1 Response variable

DURATION DIFFERENCE
The way many studies use duration as a response variable is by simply measuring the absolute acoustic duration in milliseconds, as read from the pertinent intervals in the annotated textgrids. The present studies, too, started out by measuring this absolute acoustic duration in milliseconds of the derived word, its affix, and its base, respectively. This was done by reading out the textgrid files with scripts written in Python, using the TextGridTools module (Buschmeier & Włodarczak 2013). The resulting variables are correspondingly called OBSERVED WORD DURATION, OBSERVED AFFIX DURATION, and OBSERVED BASE DURATION. Using this absolute acoustic duration poses no problem in studies that compare the durations of one individual segment or one segment cluster across words. However, the present studies need to compare the durations of entire derived words, affixes, and base words, which vary in length, i.e., in their number of segments. In addition, when analyzing spontaneous speech from a corpus, one cannot control which words exactly are spoken. This means that words are uncontrolled for phonological and segmental makeup.

One way to control for the length of a linguistic unit is to incorporate a covariate with word length information in the statistical modeling, such as the number of syllables or the number of segments (e.g., Bell et al. 2009). In theory, this should factor out the variation introduced by the varying length of different word types. However, this method does not factor out the variation introduced by *which* segments the pertinent units contain. Some types of segments, such as most vowels, are by nature longer in duration than other types of segments, such as plosive consonants. A more optimal solution would therefore be to not only control for the number of segments, but also for the kinds of segments.

This can be done by first calculating the mean duration of each segment in a large corpus (for the present studies, I used the QuakeBox corpus, Walsh et al. 2013).[2] Then, it is possible to compute for each target unit (a derived word, an affix, or a base word) the sum of the mean durations of its segments. This sum of the mean segment durations is also known as BASELINE DURATION, a measure that has been successfully used as a covariate in other corpus-based studies (e.g., Engemann & Plag 2021; Sóskuthy & Hay 2017; Caselli et al. 2016; Seyfarth 2014; Gahl et al. 2012). Conceptually, the variable BASELINE DURATION represents the duration that would be expected purely based on a unit's segmental makeup. Depending on the durational domain of investigation, I will refer to the variables as WORD BASELINE DURATION, AFFIX BASELINE DURATION, and BASE BASELINE DURATION, respectively.

However, there is one major problem with using BASELINE DURATION as a covariate. If one needs to have other covariates in the models, such as the number of syllables (which can control not only for word length, but also for compensatory shortening, see Section 3.3.2), BASELINE DURATION will be highly collinear with these measures. The problem of multicollinearity will be explained in more detail in Section 3.4. In short, collinearity may cause coefficients in regression models to become unstable, and therefore unreliable.

One way to solve this problem is to not use BASELINE DURATION as a covariate, but to factor it into the response variable itself. This can be done by subtracting the baseline duration from the observed duration. I will refer to this variable as SUBTRACTED BASELINE DURATION. This creates a new response variable that represents only the difference in duration to what is expected based on segmental makeup.

However, SUBTRACTED BASELINE DURATION is also a rather crude way of merging these two variables. Simple subtraction is not very precise specifically when the relation between OBSERVED DURATION and BASELINE DURATION is not constant across words with different word lengths. Because this relation was indeed not constant in the data of the present studies, this variable also seemed to behave strangely in some datasets. During the analysis, it was found that a more accurate way of representing the relationship between OBSERVED DURATION and BASELINE DURATION is to fit a simple linear regression model predicting OBSERVED DURATION as a function of BASELINE DURATION. The residuals of this model can then be

---

[2] I used the QuakeBox corpus for all studies because the other corpora, particularly the Audio BNC, do not provide this information in an accessible and reliable form.

used as a response variable. I will refer to this final response variable as DURATION DIFFERENCE, with WORD DURATION DIFFERENCE, AFFIX DURATION DIFFERENCE, and BASE DURATION DIFFERENCE, respectively. The complex relationship between the different durational variables is best illustrated with an example.

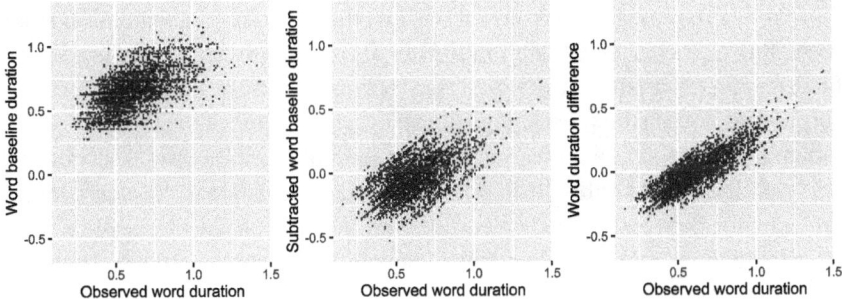

Fig. 3.3: Comparison of duration variables. Word baseline duration, subtracted word baseline duration, and word duration difference (in seconds) are plotted against the observed duration (in seconds) of derived words in the ONZE corpus.

Figure 3.3 shows, as an example case, the three durational variables BASELINE DURATION, SUBTRACTED BASELINE DURATION, and DURATION DIFFERENCE plotted against the observed duration of derived words from the ONZE corpus. The first panel compares BASELINE DURATION against OBSERVED DURATION. The positive trend of the datapoints in this panel confirms that BASELINE DURATION essentially measures what it is supposed to measure: longer words are expected to be longer, based on their segmental makeup. The second panel compares the SUBTRACTED BASELINE DURATION against OBSERVED DURATION. Here, we can see that the difference in duration to what is expected based on segmental makeup is not constant across longer and shorter words. Instead, we observe a clear positive trend: the longer the observed duration of the word is, the higher the value of SUBTRACTED BASELINE DURATION. This means that for longer words, the underlying variable BASELINE DURATION, i.e., the duration expected based on segmental makeup, systematically underestimates the actual duration. Similarly, for shorter words, it systematically overestimates the actual duration.

Finally, the third panel compares DURATION DIFFERENCE, i.e., the residuals of a linear model regressing OBSERVED DURATION against BASELINE DURATION. We can see that the tendency of overestimating the duration of long words and underestimating the duration of short words is still present for DURATION DIFFERENCE. However, the datapoints cluster much more closely together and are overall closer to the line $y = 0$, which means that DURATION DIFFERENCE is a little bit less prone to over- and underestimating the durations than SUBTRACTED BASELINE DURATION. In other words, using the residuals of a linear model, regressing OBSERVED DURATION on BASELINE DURATION, as a response variable is more precise in controlling for variation based on segmental makeup than using the results of a subtraction of BASELINE DURATION from OBSERVED DURATION.

For this reason, DURATION DIFFERENCE, i.e., the residuals of a regression model predicting OBSERVED DURATION as a function of BASELINE DURATION, was used as the final response variable in the analyses. For each dataset (i.e., for subsets by corpus and subsets by morphological category), I built these regression models individually to obtain a more precise estimation of DURATION DIFFERENCE for each study. Using this variable, it is possible to mitigate against the non-constant relationship between the expected duration and the observed duration. I will refer to the domain-specific variants of DURATION DIFFERENCE with WORD DURATION DIFFERENCE, AFFIX DURATION DIFFERENCE, and BASE DURATION DIFFERENCE, respectively.

3.3.2 Predictor variables

WORD FREQUENCY

There are many ways to operationalize frequency. One way is to count the occurrence of words in a corpus of natural speech. Another way is to ask speakers for a familiarity rating ("How often do you think this word occurs in the language?"). Since the former method is considered more reliable than speakers' subjective ratings (but see the discussion in Section 4.3), for the present studies it was decided to use corpus-based word counts. One problem with this approach, however, is that derived words are often rare words (see, e.g., Plag et al. 1999). For this reason, very large corpora are necessary to obtain frequency values for derived words. It was therefore decided to use the *Corpus of Contemporary American English* (COCA, Davies 2008).

COCA is much larger than the BNC or the New Zealand corpora themselves, and therefore had a much higher chance of the words (and their bases) being sufficiently attested. It was considered important to prioritize covering a bigger frequency range with more tokens. Moreover, it is important to use the same frequencies consistently across the three studies. As corpora in different varieties have different sizes, it is difficult to compare effects of frequency for sets of words of which many have very low frequencies, or do not occur at all in one or two of the three corpora. Note that while COCA covers a different group of English varieties than the three audio corpora, these three corpora already differ in the varieties they cover. It is therefore not possible to avoid using frequency values from varieties that are not covered in at least one of the three investigated corpora.

I extracted the WORD FREQUENCY, i.e., the frequency of the derivative, from the 2014 DVD version of COCA with the help of the corpus tool Coquery (Kunter 2016). Following Sóskuthy & Hay (2017) and Gahl (2008), frequency counts were estimated based on orthographic wordforms, i.e., it was not differentiated between homographs or homophones belonging to different parts of speech. It is currently unclear whether homophones share a lemma and/or their wordform, and thus might influence each other in their properties such as frequency (see, e.g., Sternke 2021; Ferreira & Griffin 2003; Jescheniak & Levelt 1994; Dell 1990), or whether they are represented by different lemmas whose wordforms do not inherit any frequency information of their respective counterpart homophone (see, e.g., Lohmann & Conwell 2020; Lohmann 2018; Gahl 2008; Caramazza et al. 2001). As explained in Section 2.1.1, on a more general level, it is unclear whether frequency-induced reduction is a motor practice effect at the wordform level, or an effect originating from lexical properties that govern retrieval speed at the lemma level (or something else entirely, like the artifact of a listener-oriented speed adjustment to ensure the intelligibility of unpredictable items, or a combination of these and/or other factors). It is important to keep in mind that using wordform-based frequency counts is potentially more accurate in representing motor practice information, but potentially less accurate in representing lexical frequency information of individual lemmas. However, analyses by Sóskuthy & Hay (2017) for their data suggest that these inaccuracies are not likely to cause a substantial difference in either direction, as the proportion of English homographs is small.

Finally, all sections of COCA were used when retrieving the frequency counts (instead of just the spoken section). This is because, first, both spoken and written frequencies can be expected to influence speech processing across modalities (note, however, that this biases against capturing a motor practice effect). Second, spoken and written frequencies are usually highly correlated. And third, it has been found that for some data (such as auditory lexical decision reaction time), using frequency information from the entire COCA is more accurate, i.e., provides a better fit, than restricting the frequency information to its spoken component (Tucker et al. 2019b).

Psycholinguistic research has found that the relation between frequency and behavioral measures is often logarithmic, so that effects are larger in low-frequency ranges than in high-frequency ranges (Gahl 2008; Hay 2002; Howes &

Solomon 1951). Following standard procedures, I therefore log-transformed WORD FREQUENCY before it entered the models instead of using raw frequency. Before transformation, I added a constant of +1 to the variable in order to be able to take the log of the zero frequency of non-attested derivatives (cf. Baayen 2008; Howes & Solomon 1951).

BASE FREQUENCY

I extracted the BASE FREQUENCY, i.e., the frequency of the target derivative's base occurring outside of the derivative, from the *Corpus of Contemporary American English* (COCA, Davies 2008) with the help of the corpus tool Coquery (Kunter 2016), in the same way as described above for WORD FREQUENCY. I added a constant of +1 and log-transformed the variable.

RELATIVE FREQUENCY

The RELATIVE FREQUENCY of a base word, compared to the derived word in which it appears, was calculated by dividing BASE FREQUENCY by WORD FREQUENCY. Calculated this way, the higher the relative frequency, the more segmentable the item is assumed to be (see Section 2.1.2). I log-transformed the variable before it entered the models.

SPEECH RATE

How fast we speak influences the duration any produced linguistic unit will have. SPEECH RATE can be operationalized as the number of syllables a speaker produces in a given time interval (see, e.g., Plag et al. 2017; Pluymaekers et al. 2005b). In the utterance in which the target word appeared, I divided the number of syllables in the utterance by the duration of the utterance. *Utterance* was defined as the window containing the target word plus one second before and one second after it. For this purpose, I extracted textgrids and audio files with this time window from the corpora, in addition to the textgrids containing the target word only.

The window of ±1 second was considered to be a good compromise between a maximally local speech rate, which just includes the adjacent segments but allows the target item to have much influence, and a maximally global speech rate, which includes larger stretches of speech but is vulnerable to changing speech rates during this larger window. I extracted the utterance duration and the number of syllables in the utterance window from the textgrids with a Python script. Pauses (i.e., periods of silence where no syllables were annotated) were not factored into the total duration of the utterance, nor into the total syllable count. It is expected that the higher the speech rate (i.e., the more syllables are produced within the utterance window), the shorter the durations of word, base, and affix should become.

NUMBER OF SYLLABLES

Researchers have observed a compression effect where segments are reduced if they are followed by more syllables or phonemes (Frazier 2006; Munhall et al. 1992; Lehiste 1972; Nooteboom 1972; Lindblom 1963). This effect has been found for both monomorphemic and multimorphemic words. It is sometimes referred to as *compensatory shortening*, or *polysyllabic/polysegmental shortening* (also see Turk & Shattuck-Hufnagel 2020 for an overview).

If the present studies modeled absolute observed durations, a higher number of syllables would be expected to lead to longer durations, because more syllables mean more phonetic material. However, the number of segments, and thereby indirectly the number of syllables, is already controlled for in the response variable DURATION DIFFERENCE. It is therefore possible to expect NUMBER OF SYLLABLES to be negatively correlated with duration due to compensatory shortening. I extracted the NUMBER OF SYLLABLES in a given unit with Python scripts from the textgrids and converted it into a categorical variable.

BIGRAM FREQUENCY

BIGRAM FREQUENCY refers to the frequency of the target derivative occurring together with the word following it in COCA. It has been found that the degree of acoustic reduction can be influenced by the predictability conditioned on the following context (see, e.g., Torreira & Ernestus 2009; Bell et al. 2009; Pluymaekers et al. 2005a). It is thus expected that the higher the bigram frequency, the shorter the duration. Following standard procedures, BIGRAM FREQUENCY was log-transformed before it entered the models. Similarly to the other frequency measures, I added a constant of +1 to the variables in order to be able to take the log of non-attested bigrams (cf. Baayen 2008).

BIPHONE PROBABILITY

The variable BIPHONE PROBABILITY refers to the sum of all biphone probabilities (the likelihood of two phonemes occurring together in English) in a given target derivative divided by the number of segments. It has been found that segments are more likely to be reduced or deleted when they are highly probable given their context (see, e.g., Turnbull 2018; Edwards et al. 2004; Munson 2001; also see Hay 2007 on transition legality effects on reduction). There are two possible lines of reasoning behind this. First, from the viewpoint of storage in the mental lexicon, the more probable a biphone is, the easier it should be to access it. This is because with higher probability speakers have a stronger representation of phoneme templates occurring in succession. Note that, as mentioned in Section 2.1.1, this idea of reduction based on lexical access speed is debated in the literature (see, e.g., Clopper & Turnbull 2018; Arnold & Watson 2015). Second, the more probable a biphone is, the better our phonotactic motor skills of pronouncing the biphone will be, as our articulator muscles are trained better in pronouncing segment sequences that we pronounce often. Thus, biphone probability can be expected to negatively correlate with duration: the more probable the biphones, the shorter the durations.

It is also possible to have a competing hypothesis about the direction of such probability effects. In an alternative account, we can read high probability as high *certainty*: biphone probabilities could be interpreted to reflect how certain a speaker is in the production of specific words. In this account, the more probable a phonological string is, the more certain the speaker becomes, and the longer the durations should be. This is because a speaker may want to invest more energy in maintaining the acoustic signal when they are certain, and less energy when they are uncertain, in order to not prolong a state of uncertainty (Tucker et al. 2019a). This should lead to shorter durations of low-probable strings (not of high-probable ones). Higher certainty has been found to be associated with longer duration when operationalized in various ways (Tucker et al. 2019a; Tomaschek et al. 2019; Cohen 2015, 2014; Kuperman et al. 2007). I will discuss this in more detail in the context of linear discriminative learning in Section 7.3 and Chapter 8. Whatever the expectation for the direction of the effect may be, it seems clear that biphone probability is an important control variable that needs to be included in the models.

Biphone probabilities were calculated by the Phonotactic Probability Calculator (Vitevitch & Luce 2004). For this, I first manually translated the target derivatives' ASCII transcriptions of the Audio BNC, as well as the QuakeBox and ONZE transcription systems, into the coding referred to as Klattese, as this is the computer-readable transcription convention required by this calculator. I then summed the biphone probabilities for each word and divided the result by the number of this word's segments to obtain the average biphone probability for each word.

SUBCORPUS

As described in Section 3.2.1, the ONZE corpus consists of multiple subcorpora. Some of these are older than others. For example, the historical Mobile Unit features speakers born between 1851–1910, the later Intermediate Archive features speakers born between 1890–1930, and the contemporary Canterbury Corpus features speakers born between 1930–1984. Sóskuthy & Hay (2017) found that across these subcorpora of the ONZE corpus, word duration decreases over time. The authors attribute this to the fact that speakers from the Mobile Unit and the Intermediate Archive were older at the time of recording, as well as to the higher level of formality in these older subcorpora. I therefore added the variable SUBCORPUS to control for these effects. This variable was only included in analyses of the ONZE corpora.

AFFIX

AFFIX is a categorical variable used in the decompositional perspective studies, coding which affix is included in the derivative. This is to account for any potential idiosyncrasies in durations of morphological category.

OTHER VARIABLES

All other variables will be explained in the pertinent sections (Chapters 4–7).

3.4 General modeling procedure

Data in the present studies were modeled by multiple linear regression models and mixed-effects regression models, using R (R Core Team 2022), the lme4 package (Bates et al. 2015) and lmerTest (Kuznetsova et al. 2016). Both multiple linear regression and mixed-effects regression have the advantage that they can deal with unbalanced datasets, and that the researcher can investigate the predictor of interest while controlling for confounding variables at the same time (cf. Baayen 2008). That is, a linear regression model

$$Y = \beta_0 + \beta_1 X_1 + \beta_2 X_2 + \cdots + \beta_p X_p + \varepsilon, \tag{3.1}$$

where Y is the response variable, β_0, β_1, β_2, ... β_p are the coefficients to be estimated from the data, and ε is a random error in the approximation, includes X_1, X_2, ... X_p as the set of predictor variables to predict Y simultaneously (Chatterjee & Hadi 2006: 2).

However, linear regression and mixed-effects regression also both come with their unique advantages and disadvantages. Mixed-effects regression has the extra advantage that in addition to the predictors of interest and covariates outlined above (the so-called *fixed effects*), it can also include so-called *random effects*. These random effects control for unknown idiosyncrasies, in psycholinguistic research typically idiosyncrasies of word types and speakers. For each word type or speaker, mixed-effects regression allows the intercepts and/or the slopes of the regression line to be different. However, one disadvantage of this method is that it requires word types to be represented by multiple tokens, and to be spoken by multiple speakers. Because this is not always the case in corpus data, many observations need to be excluded. This can potentially result in a considerable loss of data. Moreover, it might be the case that random effects are nested with a fixed effect. For example, a random effect for word type might be nested with a fixed effect of word frequency, because word frequency is a property of word type. This might result in statistical problems. For many analyses in the present studies, it was therefore decided to use standard multiple linear regression.

One major decision that must be taken when modeling individual linguistic units, like derived words, is whether to model types or tokens. It is possible to take for each word type the mean durational values of its tokens, as well as the mean values of its tokens for all predictors and covariates (see, e.g., Gahl 2008). In the models, each observation will represent a word type for which individual token-based measurements have been aggregated. One advantage of this is that it makes the datasets more balanced. In corpus data, some types are naturally overrepresented, while other types are represented by very few tokens. However, multiple linear regression modeling already accounts for the imbalance of datasets. What is more, the duration of an individual token is influenced by many unique situational factors, which means that much information is lost when averaging over them (Lohmann 2018). It was therefore decided to conduct token-based analyses for the present studies.

Both multiple linear regression and mixed-effects regression models were generally built in the same fashion. The predictors of interest and covariates were first fitted to the response variable in a maximal model. Because linear regression assumes the residuals of the model to be normally distributed, I carefully examined if the residuals of each model fulfilled this assumption. This was done for the maximal model first. If the normality assumption was not met, I trimmed the datasets in order to improve the residual distribution. In these cases, datapoints with a standardized residual greater than either ±2.5 or ±2.0 (decided based on visual inspection of the distribution) were considered outliers. That is, observations whose residuals were more than 2.5 or 2.0 standard deviations away from the mean were removed, and then the model was refitted to the data (see, e.g., Bien et al. 2011; Baayen & Milin 2010). This procedure led to a satisfactory distribution of the residuals. After each step of model simplification (see below), it was checked again that the residuals were still distributed satisfactorily. As this distribution did not notably change as a function of model simplification, no further trimming was necessary in these cases. In general, for some very problematic distributions, the standard procedure of applying a standard deviation cutoff may not work and may require the researcher to manually exclude individual datapoints. However, this turned out not to be necessary for the models in the present studies.

One major problem that needs to be addressed in regression modeling with multiple variables is *multicollinearity* (see, e.g., Tomaschek et al. 2018; Baayen

2008). Multicollinearity occurs when two or more predictor variables correlate with each other. In this case, the model can no longer reliably estimate the contribution of each of the two correlated variables to the explained variance in the data. In the worst case, this can lead to unstable effects, and even to unstable effect signs, because effects enhance or suppress each other (Tomaschek et al. 2018). One way to prevent multicollinearity is to simply refrain from including predictor variables that are correlated with each other in the same model. I applied this strategy, for instance, in the analysis of the frequency measures. Since the frequencies of the derived word, of the base, and the relative frequency of the base compared to the word are usually strongly correlated, it was decided to make separate models for each of those three frequency predictors. This strategy was also applied in the analysis of the linear discriminative learning variables, where it was made sure that only weakly correlating and conceptually different predictors were included simultaneously.

To ensure that multicollinearity was not an issue even after applying this strategy, I checked for each model reported in this study the variance inflation factors (VIFs). Variance inflation factors can be used as a diagnostic for estimating how strongly affected a model is by multicollinearity. According to Chatterjee & Hadi (2006), a VIF value of 10 or more is critical and indicates that the data may have collinearity problems. The VIF values of the predictors in almost all final models reported in the present studies were smaller than 2, with a maximum value in one model of 3.84, which is still far below this critical value. VIF values were higher for models including interaction terms, but collinearity diagnostics are naturally inflated for models with interaction terms. In these cases, I created separate models with the respective variables but without their interactions. All VIFs in these cases were smaller than 2.

I first built maximal models, i.e., full models including all predictors of interest and relevant covariates. Unless otherwise specified, I then simplified the models according to the standard procedure of removing non-significant terms in a stepwise fashion. An interaction term or a covariate was eligible for elimination when it was non-significant at the .05 alpha level. Non-significant terms with the highest p-value were eliminated first, followed by terms with the next-highest p-value. This was repeated until only variables remained in the models of which at least one level reached significance at the .05 alpha level.[3]

---

[3] This alpha level for model simplification applied to all studies, including those in which it was decided to only interpret as meaningful (but not exclude) effects at the .001 alpha level (see Section 4.1).

We are now ready to move on to the four individual studies. The chapters associated with those studies (Chapters 4–7) will describe study-specific methods and present the results and pertinent discussion.

4 Frequency measures

How do frequency measures affect the acoustic duration of English derived words? As explained in Section 2.1.1, the decompositional perspective assumes the frequency of a derived word's base word (such as *happy*) to be associated with acoustic reduction (**H** FREQ$_{BASE}$). From a non-decompositional perspective, however, we would only expect the frequency of the derived word itself (such as *happiness*) to be associated with reduction (**H** FREQ$_{WORD}$). Finally, in a decompositional perspective we can assume relative frequency, which supposedly reflects how morphologically segmentable a complex word is at its boundary between base and affix (*happi | ness*), to be associated with longer durations (**H** FREQ$_{RELATIVE}$). This chapter will report which effects on duration were detected in a large-scale study investigating all three frequency measures.

4.1 Method

The predictors of interest for the present study are given below, together with a shortened explanation (for a detailed description of these variables, the reader is referred back to Section 3.3):

WORD FREQUENCY	The log-transformed wordform frequency of the target derivative from COCA.
BASE FREQUENCY	The log-transformed wordform frequency of the target derivative's base word from COCA.
RELATIVE FREQUENCY	The wordform frequency of the base word divided by the wordform frequency of the derivative from COCA, log-transformed. Higher values indicate more segmentability.

As mentioned in Section 3.4, one of the cautionary measures against potential multicollinearity was to create separate models, each with a different predictor of interest: the frequency of the derived word (WORD FREQUENCY), the derivative's base word (BASE FREQUENCY), and the relative frequency of the base word compared to the derived word (RELATIVE FREQUENCY). The collinearity in this case arises because, first, the frequencies of the derived word and its base are usually correlated, since more frequent derivatives often contain more frequent bases. Second, both WORD FREQUENCY and BASE FREQUENCY are usually very strongly correlated with RELATIVE FREQUENCY, given that the latter is calculated based on the former.

One problem with durational analyses in general is that the locus of reduction or lengthening is often not clear. Especially for segmentability effects, it has not been sufficiently investigated where in a word they manifest (see again Section 2.1.2). It was therefore decided to model three kinds of duration separately to obtain a more nuanced picture: the duration of the derived word (WORD DURATION DIFFERENCE), the duration of the affix (AFFIX DURATION DIFFERENCE), and the duration of the derivative's base word (BASE DURATION DIFFERENCE).

For each corpus, I modeled the data in two ways, in an across-category analysis and in separate category-internal analyses. The across-category analysis investigated the whole dataset including all morphological categories in each corpus study. The category-internal analyses, on the other hand, investigated one morphological category at a time. For example, in the Audio BNC study, I built models just for the NESS dataset, and different models for the LESS dataset, and so on. This means that for each corpus study, there were 3 x 3 x 8 category-internal models: three separately modeled frequency predictors (WORD FREQUENCY, BASE FREQUENCY, RELATIVE FREQUENCY), for each of these models three different durational response variables (WORD DURATION DIFFERENCE, AFFIX DURATION DIFFERENCE, BASE DURATION DIFFERENCE), and each of those models for eight different morphological categories (NESS, LESS, PRE, IZE, ATION, DIS, UN, and IN for the Audio BNC, and NESS, ATION, DIS, UN, ABLE, ITY, MENT, and RE for the QuakeBox and ONZE corpora). In total, this amounts to 72 category-internal regression models per corpus study.

One major problem in the null hypothesis significance testing (NHST) framework is that the higher the number of models, the higher the likelihood of obtaining false positives. For example, assuming the standard threshold for rejecting the null hypothesis of $p < .05$, the probability of obtaining at least one false positive in 72 models is

$$1 - (1 - 0.05)^{72} \approx 0.98. \qquad (4.1)$$

That is, it is almost a hundred percent certain that there will be one false positive across the models. It was therefore decided for the category-internal models to only interpret effects below a lowered conventional p-value threshold of

.001.[1] In this case, the chance of obtaining one false positive across the 72 models is reduced to

$$1 - (1 - 0.001)^{72} \approx 0.07. \qquad (4.2)$$

This conservative strategy serves to bias against the risk of incorrectly rejecting the null hypothesis, i.e., that the frequency measures will have no effect on duration.

As explained in Chapter 3, for small datasets – in this case, especially for the category-internal subsets – standard multiple linear regression is often better suited than mixed-effects regression due to the potential loss of data. The frequency measures were therefore investigated with multiple linear regression models. Model creation, criticism, and simplification followed the procedure described in Section 3.4. For the number of observations lost during trimming in each model, please refer to the materials at https://osf.io/4h5f3/. The initial models included the respective frequency measure (either WORD FREQUENCY, BASE FREQUENCY, or RELATIVE FREQUENCY) fitted to the respective durational response variable (either WORD DURATION DIFFERENCE, AFFIX DURATION DIFFERENCE, or BASE DURATION DIFFERENCE). In addition, each maximal model included the following covariates (for a detailed description of these variables, the reader is referred back to Section 3.3):

SPEECH RATE	The number of syllables in a window of ±1 second around the target derivative divided by the duration of that window.
NUMBER OF SYLLABLES	The number of syllables of the target derivative.
BIGRAM FREQUENCY	The log-transformed frequency of the target derivative occurring together with the word following it in COCA.
BIPHONE PROBABILITY	The sum of all biphone probabilities (the likelihood of two phonemes occurring together in English) in a target derivative divided by the number of segments.
SUBCORPUS	The subcorpus of the ONZE corpus (used only for the models with ONZE corpus datasets).

---

[1] Note that the threshold of .001 is only used to decide which effects to interpret as meaningful. Effects at the .05 alpha level still remained in the models during simplification (see Section 3.4).

4.2 Results

This section presents the results for the three frequency measures. I will first look at the category-internal analyses, followed by the across-category analysis.

4.2.1 Category-internal analyses

Overviews of the effects of interest in all category-internal models are given in Figure 4.1 for the Audio BNC, Figure 4.2 for the QuakeBox corpus, and Figure 4.3 for the ONZE corpus. Due to the high number of models, the full models will not be reported and discussed individually here. This is for practical reasons, but also for reasons of good statistical practice: in such large-scale analyses, it is important to carefully focus on the overall picture and to avoid over-interpretating individual effects that may merely be noise. However, the interested reader can access all full models in the HTML markdowns and R scripts at https://osf.io/4h5f3/.

The figures can be read as follows. The columns group models for the three different frequency predictors: the first column contains models for WORD FREQUENCY, the second column contains models for BASE FREQUENCY, and the third column contains models for RELATIVE FREQUENCY. The rows group models for the three different durational responses: WORD DURATION DIFFERENCE in the first row, AFFIX DURATION DIFFERENCE in the second row, and BASE DURATION DIFFERENCE in the third row. Each "cell" of this matrix contains an overview of eight models, one for each morphological category (here, affix). For each model, i.e., for each affix, the overview provides the estimated effect size (the β coefficient) of the respective frequency predictor, together with the significance level (with three asterisks indicating a p-value < .001). Since the non-significant predictors of interest were removed during model simplification, the values for these models were taken from the maximal models (before the simplification procedure) to be able to compare them to the significant ones.

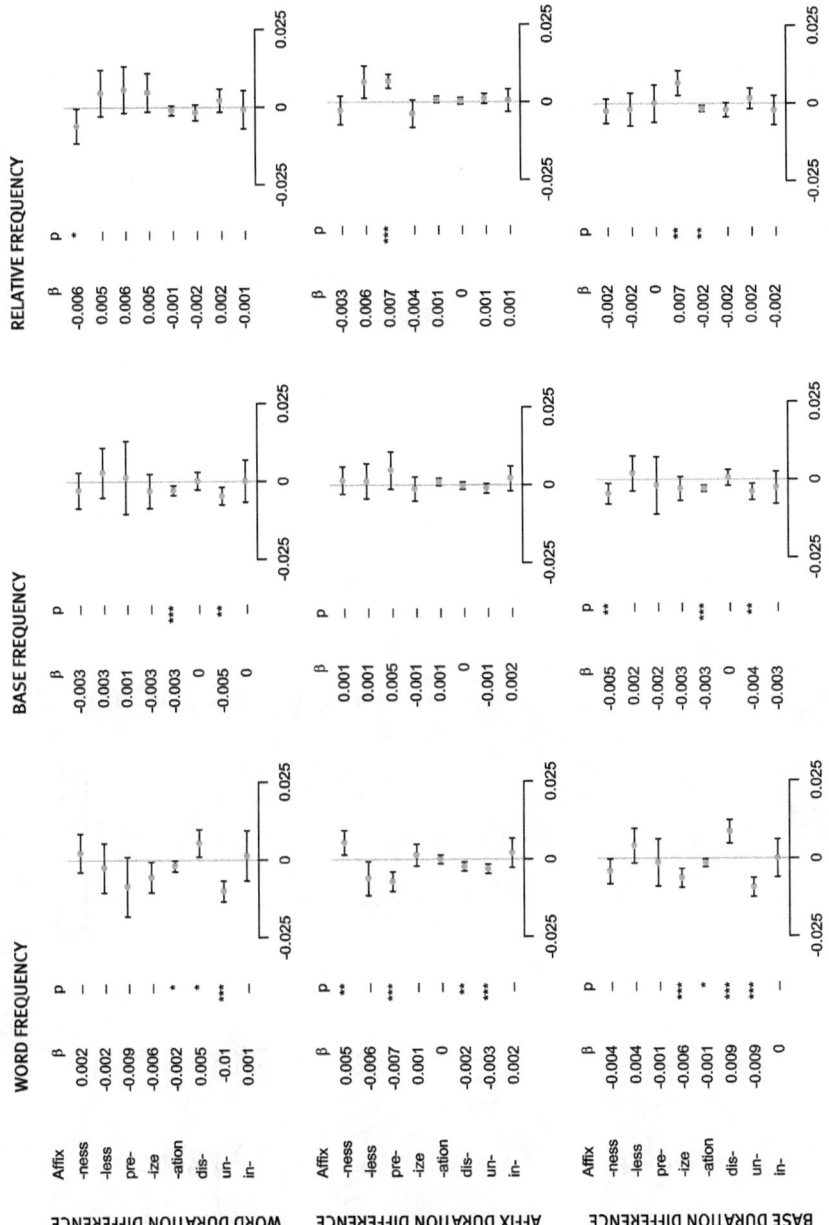

Fig. 4.1: Overview of frequency effects in the Audio BNC. Orange (light-shaded) dots represent the estimated coefficient β, bars represent its confidence intervals. In case a coefficient of the predictor of interest turned out non-significant during model simplification (p > .05), the coefficients for this predictor are taken from the maximal model.

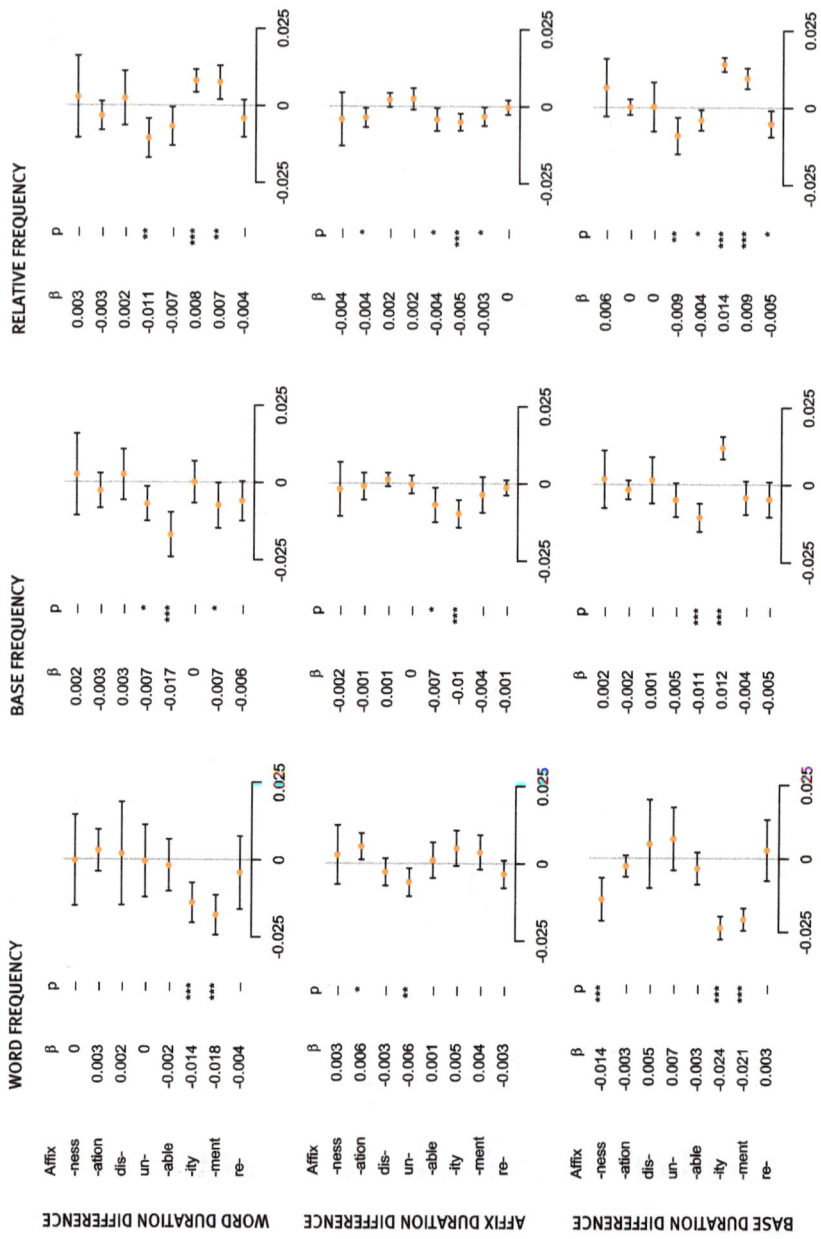

Fig. 4.2: Overview of frequency effects in the QuakeBox corpus. Orange (light-shaded) dots represent the estimated coefficient β, bars represent its confidence intervals. In case a coefficient of the predictor of interest turned out non-significant during model simplification (p > .05), the coefficients for this predictor are taken from the maximal model.

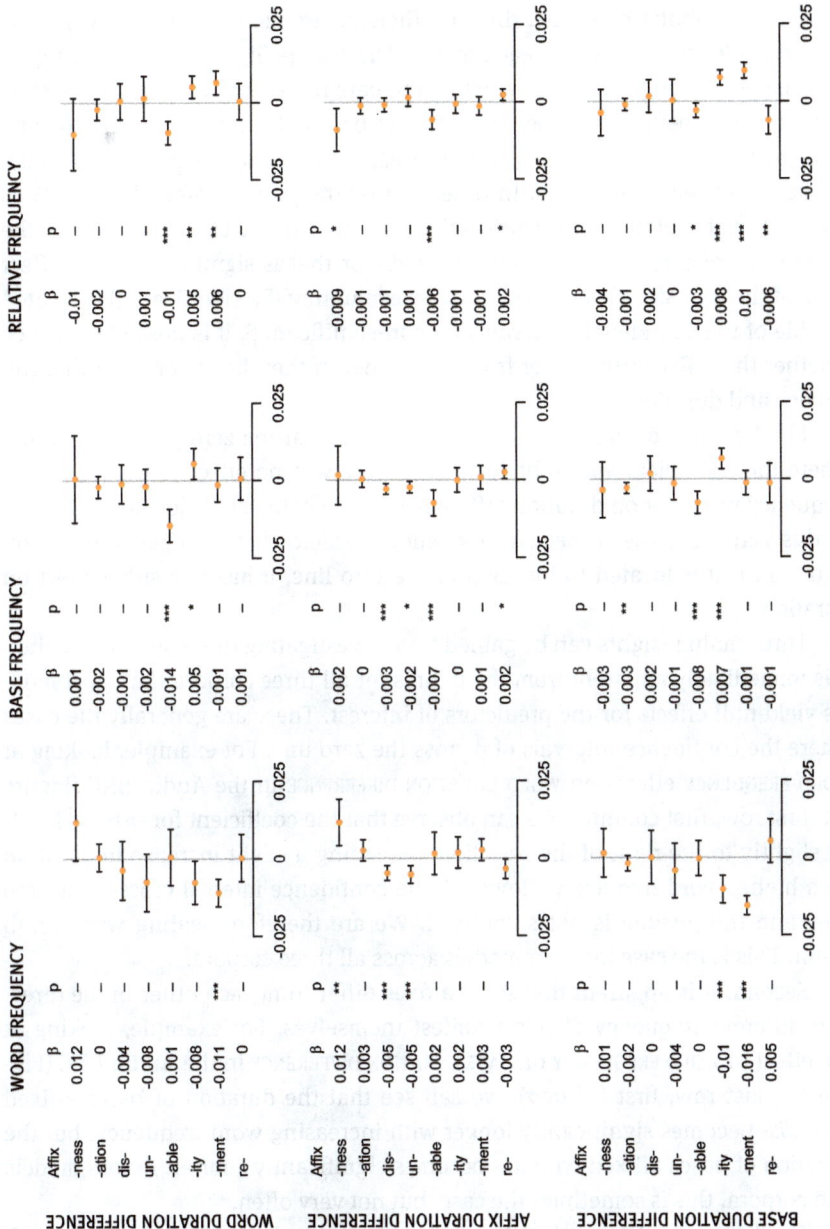

Fig. 4.3: Overview of frequency effects in the ONZE corpus. Orange (light-shaded) dots represent the estimated coefficient β, bars represent its confidence intervals. In case a coefficient of the predictor of interest turned out non-significant during model simplification (p > .05), the coefficients for this predictor are taken from the maximal model.

Next to this tabular overview, the β coefficients are plotted together with their 95 % confidence intervals for each model. The orange (light-shaded) dots represent the estimated β coefficients, while the bars represent the confidence intervals of these coefficients. The extent of the bars indicates that when drawing samples from the data, in 95 % of the cases, the true coefficient will fall somewhere in-between those bars. In other words, the plotted interval has a 95 % probability of containing the true coefficient value. This is useful to compare the effect sizes of a respective frequency predictor that is significant to the effect sizes of the non-significant predictors. By evaluating if a significant β is located outside of the confidence intervals of a non-significant β, it is possible to check whether the affixes truly differ from each other in their behavior regarding frequency and duration.

Finally, each of the plots contains a grey line at the zero point, indicating where the coefficient would be located if there was no effect of the respective frequency predictor on duration difference. If the coefficient is located to the left of this zero line, the respective frequency predictor has a negative effect on duration. If it is located to the right of the zero line, it has a positive effect on duration.

Three main insights can be gained from investigating these overviews. First, it is immediately apparent from the figures for all three corpora that most models yield null effects for the predictors of interest. These are generally the cases where the confidence intervals of β cross the zero line. For example, looking at WORD FREQUENCY effects on WORD DURATION DIFFERENCE in the Audio BNC (Figure 4.1, first row, first column), we can observe that the coefficient for *-ness* is located slightly to the right of the zero line, indicating a slight increase in duration with higher word frequency. However, the confidence interval crosses the zero line, and the p-value is not significant. We are therefore dealing with a null result. This is the case for most models across all three corpora.

Second, it is apparent that some affixes differ from each other in the direction different frequency effects manifest themselves. For example, looking at the effect of WORD FREQUENCY on BASE DURATION DIFFERENCE in the Audio BNC (Figure 4.1, last row, first column), we can see that the duration of bases affixed with *dis-* becomes significantly longer with increasing word frequency, but the duration of bases affixed with *un-* becomes significantly shorter. Across models and corpora, this is sometimes the case, but not very often.

Third, we can observe that there seems to be no clear pattern in the way effects manifest themselves and do not manifest themselves. There are differences between affixes, between the three corpora, between domains of durational measurement, and of course between frequency measures. In order to obtain a clearer picture, it is helpful to abstract further from the individual models.

Table 4.1 provides an overview in which models are grouped by affix. As described above, because of the high number of models, it was decided to only interpret as meaningful those effects with a significance level of p < .001. Consequently, Table 4.1 only marks effects with p < .001. Columns in this table refer to the response variable DURATION DIFFERENCE, where values for the WORD, the AFFIX, and the BASE repeat for each affix, in this order. Rows refer to the FREQUENCY predictors, divided into the frequency of the WORD, the BASE, and RELATIVE frequency. Each affix block thus represents a matrix with nine cells, one for each of the predictor-response combinations. Cells that are marked in purple (darker shade) indicate models where the respective frequency predictor was significant at p < .001 in the expected direction.

To recap, the expected direction for WORD FREQUENCY and BASE FREQUENCY was that with increasing frequency values, durations should become shorter. For increasing values of RELATIVE FREQUENCY, durations were expected to become longer. Models with effects in the opposite direction from what was expected are marked in blue (lighter shade). Models in which the predictor of interest did not reach significance at p < .001 are represented by empty cells. We can observe WORD FREQUENCY effects in 16 out of 72 possible cases, BASE FREQUENCY effects in 11 out of 72 possible cases (of which 2 effects unexpectedly indicate longer durations instead of shorter durations), and RELATIVE FREQUENCY effects in 9 out of 72 possible cases (of which 3 effects unexpectedly indicate shorter durations instead of longer durations).

Tab. 4.1: Overview of category-internal frequency effects with a conservative threshold of p < .001 in all three corpora, grouped by affix. Purple cells (darker shade) mark models with frequency effects in the expected direction (shorter durations for increasing WORD FREQUENCY and BASE FREQUENCY, and longer durations for increasing RELATIVE FREQUENCY). Blue cells (lighter shade) indicate frequency effects in the opposite direction from what was expected. Empty cells indicate that there was no significant effect at the p < .001 level.

Audio BNC

DURATION DIFFERENCE		WORD DUR	AFFIX DUR	BASE DUR	WORD DUR	AFFIX DUR	BASE DUR	WORD DUR	AFFIX DUR	BASE DUR	WORD DUR	AFFIX DUR	BASE DUR
affix		-ness			-ize			-ation			dis-		
FREQUENCY	WORD FREQ						purple						purple
	BASE FREQ								purple		purple			
	REL FREQ													
affix		-less			pre-			un-			in-		
FREQUENCY	WORD FREQ					purple			purple	purple				
	BASE FREQ													
	REL FREQ					purple								

QuakeBox

DURATION DIFFERENCE		WORD DUR	AFFIX DUR	BASE DUR	WORD DUR	AFFIX DUR	BASE DUR	WORD DUR	AFFIX DUR	BASE DUR	WORD DUR	AFFIX DUR	BASE DUR
affix		-ness			-ity			-ation			dis-		
FREQUENCY	WORD FREQ		purple				purple						
	BASE FREQ					purple	blue						
	REL FREQ				purple	blue	purple						
affix		-able			-ment			un-			re-		
FREQUENCY	WORD FREQ					purple							
	BASE FREQ	purple		purple									
	REL FREQ						purple						

ONZE

DURATION DIFFERENCE		WORD DUR	AFFIX DUR	BASE DUR	WORD DUR	AFFIX DUR	BASE DUR	WORD DUR	AFFIX DUR	BASE DUR	WORD DUR	AFFIX DUR	BASE DUR
affix		-ness			-ity			-ation			dis-		
FREQUENCY	WORD FREQ						purple					purple	
	BASE FREQ					blue					purple		
	REL FREQ					purple							
affix		-able			-ment			un-			re-		
FREQUENCY	WORD FREQ		purple					purple					
	BASE FREQ												
	REL FREQ	blue	purple			purple							

- purple: p < .001 expected direction
- blue: p < .001 unexpected direction

Together, even more strikingly than the previous overview, this overview tells us that mostly, reliable frequency effects of any of the three kinds fail to emerge in the vast majority of cases. Out of the 216 cells for all three corpora together, only 36 represent models with reliably significant effects, and only 31 of these models support the expectations of the present study. Moreover, not only do frequency effects mostly not emerge; if they emerge, they also do not emerge in any consistent pattern. This becomes especially apparent if we compare the same affixes across corpora. Table 4.1 reveals that while the effects in the QuakeBox and ONZE corpora are generally more similar to each other than the effects of the two New Zealand corpora are to the effects in the Audio BNC, many of the affixes do not behave consistently. This suggests that the differences cannot be attributed to some systematic variation between affixes but are rather random artifacts.

Moreover, the emergence of effects can also not be attributed to the different dataset sizes. For example, with the *-ation* datasets having by far the highest number of tokens, they should display the most or the strongest effects due to statistical power, if the effects were real. But the *-ation* matrices in Table 4.1 reveal that this is not the case. Datasets with very few tokens can show effects (for example *pre-* in the Audio BNC), and datasets with very many tokens can fail to yield effects (for example *-ation* in both New Zealand corpora). In addition, I checked whether the differences can be attributed to the different ranges of the frequency measures. Naturally, in some datasets, the most highly frequent word is more frequent than the most highly frequent word in other datasets. This gives the frequency measures a different range in different datasets, and therefore presumably a different potential of exhibiting effects. The differences cannot be attributed to the frequency ranges, as some effects appear with lower frequency ranges while others do not appear with higher ones.

It is interesting to note that whenever there is an expected (positive) effect of RELATIVE FREQUENCY, there is an expected (negative) effect of WORD FREQUENCY.[2] It seems that whether RELATIVE FREQUENCY affects duration is mainly dependent on whether WORD FREQUENCY affects duration. This makes sense, as RELATIVE FREQUENCY is calculated based on WORD FREQUENCY and the two measures are therefore correlated. This finding will be discussed in further detail in Section 4.3.

To foreshadow the discussion, the results for the frequency measures are not convincing enough to speak in favor of any of the three frequency hypothe-

---

[2] In the two cases where the effect of relative frequency is unexpected (negative), there is an expected (negative) effect of base frequency.

ses. Before discussing the implications of this, let us have a brief look at the across-category models.

4.2.2 Across-category analysis

Below, Table 4.2 provides an overview of the effects of the three frequency measures in the across-category models. To recap, these models include the observations of all morphological categories at the same time, amounting to 7252 tokens for the Audio BNC, 2647 tokens for the QuakeBox corpus, and 3674 tokens for the ONZE corpus. Again, the interested reader can examine the individual models at https://osf.io/4h5f3/.

Tab. 4.2: Overview of across-category frequency effects with a conservative threshold of p < .001, grouped by corpus. Purple cells (darker shade) mark models with frequency effects in the expected direction (shorter durations for increasing WORD FREQUENCY and BASE FREQUENCY, and longer durations for increasing RELATIVE FREQUENCY). Blue cells (lighter shade) indicate frequency effects in the opposite direction from what was expected. Empty cells indicate that there was no significant effect at the p < .001 level.

We can see that overall, the ratio of effects and null effects is not as imbalanced as in the category-internal models. Of 27 possible effects, 16 effects could be detected, 14 of these in the expected direction. This might be due to the fact that with a larger amount of data, it is extremely likely for any effect to turn out "significant," even with the cautionary measure of lowering the alpha level. Of the three frequency measures, we observe the fewest significant effects for RELATIVE FREQUENCY (4 out of 9 possible cases in the expected direction). For BASE FREQUENCY, 5 out of 9 effects emerge as significant, but one of them is unexpected (higher base frequency is associated with longer affix durations in the

ONZE corpus). Finally, for WORD FREQUENCY, 7 out of 9 effects are significant, with one effect being unexpected (higher word frequency is associated with longer affix durations in the QuakeBox corpus).

Taken together, we again find differences in effects between the three corpora, between domains of durational measurement, and between frequency measures, without a clear pattern that could be attributed to any of these three factors. Effects both emerge and do not emerge for different corpora, different domains of durational measurement, and different frequency variables. However, the observation that whenever there is an expected (positive) effect of RELATIVE FREQUENCY, there is an expected (negative) effect of WORD FREQUENCY, generally holds true for this dataset as well. In one case, a positive effect of RELATIVE FREQUENCY is accompanied by an unexpected (positive) effect of BASE FREQUENCY instead (Table 4.2, affix duration in the ONZE corpus).

I will now proceed to discuss these findings in detail with regard to the hypotheses of the present study, and with regard to the theoretical and methodological implications.

4.3 Discussion

The present chapter reported a large-scale study testing for word frequency, base frequency, and relative frequency effects on word duration, base duration, and affix duration in three different corpora with eight morphological categories each, using a streamlined and consistent modeling procedure, controlling for important covariates and collinearity, using non-elicited, conversational speech. The results clearly show that under these strict but realistic conditions in such a global approach, where we abstract away from individual effects and investigate the larger picture, frequency effects of all three kinds mostly fail to emerge. Frequency effects are by far not as ubiquitous or reliable as often claimed in the literature.

Let us first discuss in more detail the results for BASE FREQUENCY and WORD FREQUENCY. From the decompositional perspective, it was hypothesized with H FREQ$_{BASE}$ that a higher frequency of the base should be associated with the acoustic reduction of the derived word and its constituents (base and affix). This is generally not the case. It must be noted that in the very few cases where we do observe effects (11 out of 72 category-internally, 5 out of 9 across categories), BASE FREQUENCY predicts acoustic duration as expected. That is, the higher the frequency of the base, the shorter the durations become. However, in three cases, the higher the base frequency, the longer the durations become (longer durations of *-ity* bases in the QuakeBox and ONZE corpora, and overall longer affix durations in the ONZE corpus). Importantly, base frequency mostly does not affect acoustic duration at all. Based on the data in the present study, I therefore reject **H** FREQ$_{BASE}$. According to the rationale followed by much psycholinguistic literature outlined in Section 2.1.1, this does not provide support for the idea of decomposed storage and access in the mental lexicon. The processing and hence production of derived words is not facilitated by higher base frequency. The present study thus does not find convincing evidence for models that allow bases to be stored and then computed together with affixes to form complex words (e.g., Solomyak & Marantz 2010; Marcus 2001; Clahsen 1999; Pinker 1999; Levelt et al. 1999; Marslen-Wilson & Tyler 1997; Prasada & Pinker 1993; Taft & Forster 1975).

The fact that we fail to observe a negative base frequency effect or sometimes even observe a positive effect dovetails with some previous observations concerning reaction times in lexical decision and word naming, for instance by Milin et al. (2009) and Baayen et al. (2007). Like the present study, these authors find base frequency effects to be not very robust. For Baayen et al. (2007), word frequency emerged as a much more robust predictor of reaction times in lexical decision, while effects of base frequency were negligible. For Milin et al. (2009), an information-theoretical approach to base frequency (although base frequency was operationalized slightly differently than in the present study) reveals that higher base frequency may facilitate, but also inhibit processing. The authors suggest that if base frequency has both a facilitatory and an inhibitory component, this may explain why base frequency effects are not as reliably attested in the literature compared to word frequency effects. From a theoretical perspective, base frequency might not even be a good measure of decomposed storage. This is because when it occurs outside of the derived word, the base may not be very informative about the morphological and semantic role it plays in the context of its derivative (Baayen 2007).

However, the present study also casts doubt on the robustness of word frequency effects. From the non-decompositional perspective, it was hypothesized with **H** FREQ$_{WORD}$ that a higher frequency of the derived word should be associated with its acoustic reduction (wherever in the word it might manifest). This is mostly not the case. In cases where we do observe effects (16 out of 72 category-internally, 7 out of 9 across categories), WORD FREQUENCY predicts acoustic duration as expected. That is, the higher the frequency of the derived word, the shorter the durations become. In one case, the higher the word frequency, the longer the durations become (longer durations of affixes in the QuakeBox corpus). But like base frequency, word frequency mostly does not affect acoustic duration in the present datasets. **H** FREQ$_{WORD}$ can be rejected at this point. I do not find support for the idea that derived words are stored and accessed as wholes in the mental lexicon (see Section 2.1.1). The processing and hence production of derived words is not facilitated by their frequency, which speaks against full-listing models which assume this to be the case (e.g., Caramazza 1997; Butterworth 1983).

This seems to be at odds with the observation that word frequency effects are "ubiquitous" (Milin et al. 2009: 216). The literature claims that frequency effects are among the most robust psycholinguistic effects. However, it must be noted that "ubiquitous" does not mean that word frequency effects are necessarily found ubiquitously in the data, but rather, that they are ubiquitously reported in the literature. One obvious possible reason for the discrepancy between the ubiquity claim and the present findings – even though it is the least interesting reason from a theoretical perspective – could be that studies not finding word frequency effects are less likely to be published (Roettger 2019; Roettger et al. 2019; Nicenboim et al. 2018; Wicherts et al. 2016). The word frequency effect might seem consistently reliable because while many frequency effects are reported in the literature, null effects are not reported (with some exceptions, e.g., Bowden et al. 2010; Pluymaekers et al. 2005b).

Another reason might be that most of the studies reporting effects of word frequency (see Section 2.1.1) are concerned not with acoustic duration, but with other response variables, like the rate of speech errors in production or, most prominently, reaction time in comprehension. It might be the case that these other variables are more robustly influenced by frequency. Given that it is not clear how frequency of occurrence would translate into phonetic reduction in the first place (e.g., via an advantage in processing speed due to facilitated access, or via motor practice allowing to save articulatory effort), one might even say that we lack the theoretical motivation to assume that it does.

The question of how frequency information translates into articulation raises an interesting question for the interpretation of the present results. Recall the operationalization of frequency from Section 3.3.2. Frequency was estimated based on orthographic wordforms. This means that the present operationalization does not necessarily assume frequency information to be stored at the lexical level. Form frequency counts capture motor practice information more accurately than lexical frequency information of individual lemmas.[3] It could thus be argued that the fact that most models in the present study fail to yield frequency effects primarily speaks against a motor practice effect at the wordform level

---

[3] However, notice again that the present study did not only use spoken, but also written frequencies. This potentially biases against capturing motor practice information.

frequency (see again Sternke 2021; Ferreira & Griffin 2003; Jescheniak & Levelt 1994; Dell 1990), rather than against the notion of lexical retrieval speed at the lemma level (see again Lohmann & Conwell 2020; Lohmann 2018; Gahl 2008; Caramazza et al. 2001). However, wordform frequencies and lemma frequencies are usually highly correlated. Using either of them is unlikely to cause substantial inaccuracies for the other, given that the number of English homophones and homographs is small (cf. Sóskuthy & Hay 2017). It is therefore likely that if a frequency-induced effect of lexical retrieval speed on articulation were real, word frequency effects would have emerged more consistently in the present study.

The problem of how to operationalize word frequency – and of how to interpret its effects (or lack thereof) on articulation – leads to the more general problem of what it is that we measure when we measure word frequency. Similarly to base frequency effects, word frequency effects may not even indicate a specific type of storage and processing. This is because we could also interpret word frequency as morpheme n-gram frequency (Plag & Balling 2020). Word frequency effects may come about because of the frequencies of their respective bases (and perhaps affixes), which would indicate morphemic processing. Effects of word frequency, in this interpretation, do not indicate that the word is stored as an undecomposable unit, but rather that its morphemes are assembled more quickly (Divjak 2019: 143). If the word frequency effect does in fact depend on the base frequency effect, then the absence of base frequency effects in the present study could explain the absence of word frequency effects. The rationale behind both **H** FREQ$_{BASE}$ and **H** FREQ$_{WORD}$, then, brings along major problems of interpretation. It is not clear whether base frequency effects really indicate decomposed storage and morpheme-based processing, or whether word frequency effects really indicate whole-word storage and word-based processing.

What really are frequency effects, then, and what do they indicate? In recent years, some researchers have increasingly voiced criticism of frequency counts as a proxy for properties of human memory. Some have criticized the use of orthographic frequencies without disambiguating semantics and taking into account surrounding context (Baayen et al. 2016), while others have criticized the estimation of frequency counts by using linguistic corpora more generally (for an overview of this debate, see Divjak 2019: 134). In addition, individual speakers exhibit considerable differences in their linguistic exposure throughout life, and hence in the frequency information potentially encoded in their lexica (Dąbrowska 2015). From a cognitive perspective, it is not even clear how relevant repetition (as encoded by frequency) is as a measure of what speakers register in memory. We cannot equate "crude" frequency counts with experience: there is at least one other important factor, attention, which acts as a filter for exposure but has been neglected in linguistic research (Divjak 2019: 4–6, 130, 161–202, 274). Frequency measures used in linguistics, this study included, are merely simplistic approximations and can never really reflect actual encoding strength in individuals.

On top of this, frequency measures have been shown to be collinear with a variety of other measures, such as semantic diversity, word length, measures of valence, arousal, and dominance, neighborhood density, dispersion, and age of acquisition (Baayen et al. 2016). This correlation with other measures indicates that some "frequency effects" may in fact not be attributable to frequency as such. Instead, frequency might simply capture some underlying properties of linguistic knowledge and structure that we do not yet have a metaphor to describe. In Section 2.1.4, I have already outlined that frequency also has a negative relationship with informativeness. Frequency, informativeness, predictability, certainty – these might simply be words that describe the same underlying force operating on human memory. Measures derived from discriminative learning, too, have been found to correlate with frequency (Baayen et al. 2016; Baayen 2011). As we have seen, frequency effects do not necessarily imply that words must be stored. Frequency effects can also result from underlying association strengths between sublexical forms and meanings (see Section 2.2.1). It remains to be seen how informativeness and LDL-derived variables fare in predicting acoustic duration in Chapters 6 and 7.

Taken together, the discussion of the findings for H $FREQ_{BASE}$ and H $FREQ_{WORD}$ has shown that base frequency effects and word frequency effects do not only face empirical problems (a lack of robustness demonstrated in the present study, and in a few other studies), but also theoretical problems. Let us now turn to the discussion of the third frequency measure, relative frequency, and the hypothesis H $FREQ_{RELATIVE}$ associated with morphological segmentability.

From the decompositional perspective, it was hypothesized with H $FREQ_{RELATIVE}$ that higher segmentability, i.e., a higher frequency of the base relative to the frequency of its derivative, will be associated with longer acoustic durations. In the overwhelming majority of models, this is not the case. Relative frequency effects could be observed in only 9 out of 72 possible cases category-internally, and in 4 out of 9 possible cases across categories. These effects generally go in the expected direction (longer durations with higher relative frequency) except in 3 category-internal models (shorter durations of the affix -*ity* in the QuakeBox corpus, and shorter durations of -*able* derivatives and affixes in the ONZE corpus). Based on this data, the segmentability hypothesis must be rejected. There is no convincing evidence from relative frequency that complex words which are morphologically more segmentable are more resistant to reduction (Hay 2003, 2001).

In a way, expected effects, unexpected effects, as well as null effects are consistent with the existing literature on relative frequency effects on duration. This is because previous research (see the review in Section 2.1.2) has found positive, negative, and no effects. An association of higher relative frequency with increased duration has been found by Zuraw et al. (2020), Plag & Ben Hedia (2018), Hay (2007), Hay (2003), and in ten of the models of the present study. These findings seem to support the idea that words with a stronger morphological boundary are protected against reduction. On the other hand, an association of higher relative frequency with more reduction has been found by Schuppler et al. (2012), Pluymaekers et al. (2005b), and in three of the models of the present study. How could such an unexpected finding be explained? One way is to argue in terms of paradigmatic probability, like Schuppler et al. (2012) do in their study. They argue that the Paradigmatic Signal Enhancement Hypothesis (Kuperman et al. 2007) might work against Hay's idea of segmentability and predict exactly the opposite. According to this idea, the most probable choice in a morphological paradigm is acoustically enhanced. This is supposedly the case because speakers pronounce the most probable choice with more confidence or certainty than when selecting and pronouncing a less probable one. Words which are highly frequent compared to their bases (i.e., words that according to Hay should be less segmentable and therefore shorter) are the most likely candidate in the paradigm and should thus be pronounced with longer durations.

However, the present study does not provide convincing support for either of these alternatives due to the prevalence of null effects. No association of relative frequency and acoustic duration has been reported for models by Zuraw et al. (2020), Plag & Ben Hedia (2018), Ben Hedia & Plag (2017), Zimmerer et al. (2014), Pluymaekers et al. (2005b), and for 68 of the models of the present study. Similarly to base frequency and word frequency, relative frequency seems to lack robustness. This is also in line with Hanique & Ernestus (2012), one of the earlier attempts to consolidate work on the effects of morphological segmentability on acoustic duration. Reviewing several studies and re-analyzing data by Hay (2003) after identifying methodological issues, these authors conclude that the hypothesis that more easily decomposable words are longer in duration is not convincingly supported. And, similarly to base frequency and word frequency, relative frequency is not just empirically, but also conceptually problematic.

The first conceptual problem is a problem of mathematical operationalization. Relative frequency effects may be driven by word frequency effects. As illustrated in Equation 2.1 in Section 2.1.2, relative frequency is calculated by a simple division of base frequency by word frequency. It is thus highly collinear with these two frequency measures, which is why the present study opted for a separate modeling approach. The results have demonstrated that in all cases but one, when we observe an expected positive effect of relative frequency, there is an expected negative effect of word frequency in the same dataset. The few relative frequency effects that we do find may emerge simply because relative frequency is calculated based on word frequency. If the relative frequency effect is truly a word frequency effect, then it is no wonder that it often fails to emerge, given that word frequency effects also fail to emerge (Bowden et al. 2010; the present study). In addition, in statistical modeling, both underlying frequency measures (base frequency and word frequency) are in a sense included in the same regression model, due to the way relative frequency is calculated. However, both underlying frequencies are forced to have the same coefficient with the same algebraic sign. This may obscure individual effects of inhibition or enhancement that base frequency and word frequency might have. Conceptually, it may be better to include base frequency and word frequency in one model as separate variables (also see Plag & Baayen 2009: 134 f. concerning reaction times). However, this is usually not possible due to issues of multicollinearity.

The second conceptual problem is one of interpretation. For Hay (2003, 2001), a high base frequency relative to a low word frequency leads to higher segmentability, which should lead to longer durations. However, it is also possible to reconceptualize relative frequency as transitional probability from a learnability perspective (Harald Baayen, personal communication). This leads to opposite predictions for suffixes. If the base of a suffixed word is high-frequent, but the derived word is low-frequent, then the derived word features a low transition probability at the morphological boundary between base and suffix. That is, given that the base occurs more frequently on its own, it is less likely for a suffix to follow. From a perspective of learnability, a low probability of the transition cue at the boundary can be imagined as a highly salient predictor for the whole word. Speakers might better learn or discriminate these words because of their unusual transition, compared to words with highly probable transitions (i.e., compared to less segmentable words with a higher frequency of the word as a whole). Therefore, a high base frequency relative to a lower word frequency could be hypothesized to be facilitatory for articulation, leading to shorter durations. This could explain the unexpected effects of relative frequency found in the present study and other studies. The idea of transitional probability will be discussed further in Section 6.3.

In addition, research has questioned the very premise on which the segmentability hypothesis is built, namely the rationale that segments that are important for morpheme recognition are enhanced. For instance, Poplack (1980) shows that Puerto Rican Spanish /s/ is frequently deleted even when it is a morphemic plural marker. Bybee (2017, 2002) suggests that morphemic strings may be durationally enhanced simply because they occur in contexts that disfavor reduction, compared to contexts of nonmorphemic strings. Finally, Hanique & Ernestus (2012) review several studies investigating the hypothesis that the morphemic status of segments is associated with longer durations and conclude that there is no convincing evidence for such an effect. Segments which are more relevant for the identification of a morpheme (e.g., word-initial segments or morphemic segments, i.e., single-segment morphemes) are not longer than less relevant segments (e.g., word-final segments). Previous studies either have failed to demonstrate an effect of a segment's morphological status on reduction, suffer from methodological issues, or can be interpreted differently. Several studies, however, support the idea that segments that are more relevant for the identification of a complete *word* are enhanced. This indicates that rather than morphemic structure, it is word-based information load that affects duration.

It must be noted that the present results do not speak against the idea of morphological segmentability in general – different operationalizations of segmentability may be more successful than relative frequency. However, they indicate that frequency measures, including relative frequency, are less than ideal predictors of acoustic duration. As discussed in Section 2.1.3, one other possibility why relative frequency effects often fail to emerge might be that the integration of an affix into its prosodic host word might inhibit segmentability effects. This will be the focus of the next study.

5 Prosodic word integration

As explained in detail in Section 2.1.3, prosodic structure might interact with morphological segmentability. The present study investigates whether relative frequency is less likely to protect the derivative against reduction the more prosodically integrated an affix is (**H** PROS$_{\text{FREQREL}}$). This means that it also again examines **H** FREQ$_{\text{RELATIVE}}$ at the same time, testing for relative frequency effects on duration. Lastly, the study examines whether affix durations and base durations generally pattern according to the hierarchy of constituents and prosodic categories derived in Section 2.1.3 (**H** PROS).[1]

5.1 Method

Similarly to the previous study (Chapter 4), the present study investigated relative frequency, which was defined as follows:

RELATIVE FREQUENCY   The wordform frequency of the base word divided by the wordform frequency of the derivative from COCA, log-transformed. Higher values indicate more segmentability.

To investigate the effect of prosodic word integration, two additional variables were devised. The first variable is the predictor of interest, PROSODIC CATEGORY. The second one is a new variable called TYPE OF MORPHEME, which makes it possible to investigate affix durations and base durations at the same time, in a single statistical model. I will now explain these variables in detail.

PROSODIC CATEGORY
This predictor variable was categorically coded for each affix by assigning the value PW (prosodic-word-forming), CG (clitic-group-forming), or INT (integrating) to each observation containing the pertinent affix (see Section 3.1 and Raffelsiefen 2007, 1999 for the classification criteria). For convenience, Table 5.1 repeats the overview of the classification, together with the corpus study affiliation of the affixes.

---

[1] An earlier version of the study in the present chapter was published in Stein & Plag (2022). It was only minimally altered for this book.

Tab. 5.1: Review: Investigated affixes in the three corpora, sorted by prosodic word category.

	ProsodicWord	CliticGroup	Integrating
Audio BNC	dis-, in-, pre-, un-	-ness, -less	-ation, -ize
QuakeBox corpus	dis-, un-, re-	-ness, -ment	-ation, -able, -ity
ONZE corpus	dis-, un-, re-	-ness, -ment	-ation, -able, -ity

TYPE OF MORPHEME

In the investigation of the influence of prosodic boundaries on duration, it is especially important to compare different durational domains, in this case the affix and the base. Instead of building separate models for affix duration and base duration, it was thus decided for this study to investigate AFFIX DURATION DIFFERENCE and BASE DURATION DIFFERENCE simultaneously.

To do so, the present study included for each word token in the dataset two durational measurements, one for the affix and one for the base (see again Section 3.3.1), at the same time. This results in two observations per word token. Each measurement was paired with the value affix or base in an additional variable (labeled TYPE OF MORPHEME) that coded whether the measurement was for the affix or for the base. This coding had the advantage that one can look at base durations and affix durations in a single statistical model. The new response variable is simply labeled DURATION DIFFERENCE, as it encodes both information about the duration of the affix and of the base. The variable TYPE OF MORPHEME can thus take two values, base or affix.

The data were analyzed by fitting mixed-effects regression models. It was decided to include a random intercept for WORD, i.e., the target derivative type, for SPEAKER, and for AFFIX. In order to be able to include a random intercept for WORD and SPEAKER, only word types and speakers for which there are at least three observations were included. For WORD, this reduced the data by 953 tokens for the Audio BNC, 377 tokens for the QuakeBox corpus, and 563 tokens for the ONZE corpus (leaving 6299, 2270, and 3111 tokens, respectively). For SPEAKER, 735 tokens were lost for the Audio BNC, 226 tokens for the QuakeBox, and 573 tokens for the ONZE (leaving 5564, 2044, and 2538 tokens, respectively). For AFFIX random intercepts, the token counts remain unchanged. The final counts are presented in Table 5.2.

Tab. 5.2: Overview of types and tokens, at least three observations per type, sorted by corpus and morphological category, before outlier exclusion.

	Audio BNC		QuakeBox corpus		ONZE corpus	
	Tokens	Types	Tokens	Types	Tokens	Types
NESS	300	34	106	13	62	7
LESS	144	21				
PRE	40	10				
IZE	365	27				
ATION	3370	193	375	36	772	76
DIS	503	61	112	19	159	25
UN	594	73	203	26	224	23
IN	248	26				
ABLE			150	19	207	19
ITY			532	21	323	24
MENT			287	24	541	35
RE			279	24	250	36

Model creation, criticism, and simplification followed the procedure described in Section 3.4. The trimming resulted in a loss of 114 tokens (2 % of the data) for the Audio BNC, 85 observations (4.2 % of the data) for the QuakeBox corpus, and 112 observations (4.4 % of the data) for the ONZE corpus.

Models were fitted with interactions between the variables of interest. The models included interactions between RELATIVE FREQUENCY and PROSODIC CATEGORY, PROSODIC CATEGORY and TYPE OF MORPHEME, and RELATIVE FREQUENCY and TYPE OF MORPHEME. To investigate the differences between different interaction levels I relevelled the dataset for each contrast, i.e., for each reference level constellation of base and affix, and of prosodic categories. The initial models included the following covariates (for a detailed description of these variables, the reader is referred back to Section 3.3):

SPEECH RATE   The number of syllables in a window of ±1 second around the target derivative divided by the duration of that window.

NUMBER OF SYLLABLES   The number of syllables of the target derivative.

BIGRAM FREQUENCY	The log-transformed frequency of the target derivative occurring together with the word following it in COCA.
BIPHONE PROBABILITY	The sum of all biphone probabilities (the likelihood of two phonemes occurring together in English) in a target derivative divided by the number of segments.

5.2 Results

I report the p-values for the analysis of variance of the fixed effects in the three final models in Table 5.3. These p-values were calculated with the Anova() function (Type III) from the car package (Fox & Weisberg 2011). I document the full models for one respective reference level each in Table 5.5. The interested reader can access the models in the scripts at https://osf.io/4h5f3/.

Before I discuss the effects which turned out significant and remained in the models, let us first examine the null results. We can see from Table 5.3 that the interaction between RELATIVE FREQUENCY and PROSODIC CATEGORY was not significant in any of the corpora and was therefore removed from the models. The lack of interaction between RELATIVE FREQUENCY and PROSODIC CATEGORY means that we already must dismiss $H_{PROS_{FREQREL}}$ at this point. I do not find evidence that the effect of relative frequency depends on prosodic integration or vice versa.

One problem within the null hypothesis significance testing (NHST) framework is that it is strictly speaking not possible to interpret non-significance as the non-existence of an effect. While I do not find support for an interaction between RELATIVE FREQUENCY and PROSODIC CATEGORY and thus no support for $H_{PROS_{FREQREL}}$, we cannot claim that the opposite is true, i.e., we cannot "confirm" the null hypothesis. To more confidently claim that prosodic word integration does not affect whether relative frequency protects against reduction, it can be useful to quantify the evidence for the null. One way to do this is by using the BIC approximation to the Bayes Factor (Wagenmakers 2007). With this method, one can approximate the Bayes Factor by using the difference between BIC values of a full model for $H_{PROS_{FREQREL}}$ (including the interaction between RELATIVE FREQUENCY and PROSODIC CATEGORY) and a model for its null hypothesis (i.e., a model that does not include this interaction). If one assumes that it is a priori equally plausible that RELATIVE FREQUENCY and PROSODIC CATEGORY interact and that they do not interact, one can estimate the models' posterior probabilities with the help of the Raftery (1995) classification scheme. Table 5.4 compares the BIC and Bayes Factor estimates for the three corpora.

Tab. 5.3: ANOVA p-values for prosodic integration models. The table displays fixed effects fitted to DURATION DIFFERENCE (Type III Wald chi-square tests). For empty cells, the predictors were non-significant and thus removed from the model during the fitting procedure.

	Audio BNC				QuakeBox				ONZE			
	Chi²	DF	Pr		Chi²	DF	Pr		Chi²	DF	Pr	
Intercept	12.7	1	0.000	***	18.8	1	0.000	***	4.0	1	0.045	*
RELATIVE FREQUENCY	0.3	1	0.564									
TYPE OF MORPHEME	236.7	1	0.000	***	832.4	1	0.000	***	434.9	1	0.000	***
PROSODIC CATEGORY	11.0	2	0.004	**	51.4	2	0.000	***	12.9	2	0.002	**
SPEECH RATE	2467.2	1	0.000	***	742.4	1	0.000	***	929.3	1	0.000	***
BIGRAM FREQUENCY	6.1	1	0.014	*					4.7	1	0.031	*
BIPHONE PROBABILITY	23.2	1	0.000	***					9.2	1	0.002	**
NUMBER OF SYLLABLES	56.5	4	0.000	***	15.4	4	0.004	**	6.6	4	0.160	[2]
RELATIVE FREQUENCY: PROSODIC CATEGORY												
RELATIVE FREQUENCY: TYPE OF MORPHEME	19.4	1	0.000	***								
TYPE OF MORPHEME: PROSODIC CATEGORY	409.3	2	0.000	***	1495.1	2	0.000	***	862.6	2	0.000	***

Tab. 5.4: BIC approximation to the Bayes Factor (BF) comparing the models for H PROS$_{\text{FREQREL}}$ (a full model including the interaction between RELATIVE FREQUENCY and PROSODIC CATEGORY) and H$_0$ (the same model but without this interaction) for the three corpora.

	BIC H PROS$_{\text{FREQREL}}$ model	BIC H$_0$ model	BIC difference	BF H PROS$_{\text{FREQREL}}$	BF H$_0$
Audio BNC	-29,087.43	-29,123.82	36.39	1.25e-08	79,795,562
QuakeBox	-9,923.55	-9,954.07	30.52	2.36e-07	4,236,810
ONZE	-13,146.06	-13,179.25	33.19	6.20e-08	16,120,645

---

2 This covariate is non-significant in the ANOVA summary, but was not eliminated because one contrast between the levels of this covariate is significant in the full model (documented in Table 5.5).

We can see that in all three cases, the null hypothesis model (i.e., the one that assumes prosodic word integration to not have an influence on relative frequency effects) provides the better fit because of its lower BIC, and that it has the higher Bayes Factor value. The Bayes Factor, roughly speaking, tells us how many times "more" we should believe in the respective hypothesis. According to Raftery (1995), if we start with the belief that the hypothesis and the null hypothesis are equally likely, a Bayes Factor of > 150 constitutes "very strong" evidence for the respective hypothesis (i.e., a posterior probability of > .99). One can thus say that for all three corpora, the present study finds very strong evidence for the null. Prosodic word integration does not play any role in whether higher relative frequency can protect against reduction.

In addition, Table 5.3 shows that RELATIVE FREQUENCY was generally removed from all models both as interaction and as main effect due to non-significance, except from the Audio BNC. In the Audio BNC, there is one significant interaction between RELATIVE FREQUENCY and TYPE OF MORPHEME, where RELATIVE FREQUENCY is significant only if we look at the affix. In all three cases (despite the "significant" effect in the Audio BNC), though, the BIC approximation to the Bayes Factor for the models with versus without RELATIVE FREQUENCY again tells us that these models constitute very strong evidence for the null (BF > 8000, posterior probability > .99 for all three corpora). **H** FREQ$_{\text{RELATIVE}}$ is thus not well supported either: RELATIVE FREQUENCY generally does not affect duration in the present set-up.

Before turning to the significant variables of interest, let us briefly look at the covariates. As seen in Table 5.5, the covariates generally behave as expected in the three models: SPEECH RATE is always very highly significant and negatively correlated with duration. BIGRAM FREQUENCY is significant in the Audio BNC and ONZE and negatively correlated with duration. BIPHONE PROBABILITY is significant in the Audio BNC and ONZE models and is also negatively correlated with duration. Finally, NUMBER OF SYLLABLES is positively correlated with duration in the three models.

Let us now examine the variables of interest that remained in the models, starting with RELATIVE FREQUENCY. RELATIVE FREQUENCY only showed one significant interaction with TYPE OF MORPHEME, namely in the Audio BNC. The interaction is illustrated in Figure 5.1. The x-axis represents the log of RELATIVE FREQUENCY, the y-axis represents the response variable DURATION DIFFERENCE. I use a blue, solid line to represent the slope of RELATIVE FREQUENCY when looking at the base, and an orange, dotted line to represent the slope of RELATIVE FREQUENCY when looking at the affix. Significance is indicated next to a given slope with asterisks, which means that only the slope of the dotted line is significantly different from zero.

Tab. 5.5: Final prosodic integration models fitted to DURATION DIFFERENCE for all three corpora. Full models are documented at https://osf.io/4h5f3/. Empty cells indicate that the variable was removed during model simplification.

	Audio BNC			QuakeBox			ONZE		
	Estimate	SE		Estimate	SE		Estimate	SE	
INTERCEPT	-0.0398	0.0112	*	-0.0531	0.0122	***	-0.0247	0.0123	
RELATIVE FREQUENCY	-0.0010	0.0017							
TYPE OF MORPHEME affix	0.0223	0.0014	***	0.0804	0.0028	***	0.0477	0.0023	***
PROSODIC CATEGORY CG	0.0196	0.0153		0.0204	0.0160		0.0050	0.0172	
PROSODIC CATEGORY PW	0.0421	0.0129	*	0.0943	0.0138	***	0.0488	0.0148	*
SPEECH RATE	-0.0338	0.0007	***	-0.0336	0.0012	***	-0.0299	0.0010	***
BIGRAM FREQUENCY	-0.0017	0.0007	*				-0.0021	0.0010	*
BIPHONE PROBABILITY	-0.0063	0.0013	***				-0.0085	0.0028	**
NUMBER OF SYLLABLES 3	0.0183	0.0040	***	0.0057	0.0073		0.0022	0.0063	
NUMBER OF SYLLABLES 4	0.0223	0.0050	***	0.0167	0.0085		0.0090	0.0073	
NUMBER OF SYLLABLES 5	0.0362	0.0054	***	0.0398	0.0109	***	0.0200	0.0091	*
NUMBER OF SYLLABLES 6	0.0593	0.0112	***	0.0024	0.0216		0.0237	0.0181	
RELATIVE FREQUENCY: TYPE OF MORPHEME affix	0.0056	0.0013	***						
TYPE OF MORPHEME affix: PROSODIC CATEGORY CG	-0.0374	0.0047	***	-0.0929	0.0053	***	-0.0796	0.0040	***
TYPE OF MORPHEME affix: PROSODIC CATEGORY PW	-0.0571	0.0028	***	-0.1790	0.0047	***	-0.1092	0.0041	***
N two observations per token	10901			3918			4852		
N SPEAKER	595			264			312		
N WORD	441			178			242		
N AFFIX	8			8			8		
R^2 fixed	0.2274			0.3523			0.2932		
R^2 total	0.3870			0.4821			0.4836		

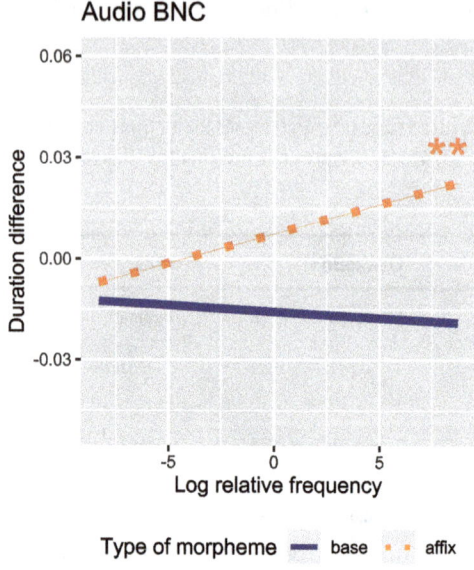

Fig. 5.1: Interaction of TYPE OF MORPHEME with RELATIVE FREQUENCY in the Audio BNC.

In general, and in accordance with hypothesis **H** FREQ_{RELATIVE}, higher relative frequency is expected to lead to increased durations of both base and affix. In the Audio BNC, this is indeed the case for affixes, but not for bases: affix durations in the Audio BNC increase with increasing relative frequency (i.e., increasing segmentability). In other words, in the one case where RELATIVE FREQUENCY interacts with TYPE OF MORPHEME, a relative frequency effect manifests itself only on the affix, not on the base. All the other cases yield a null result: base durations in the Audio BNC, and affix and base durations in the two New Zealand corpora, do not increase with higher relative frequency. As mentioned above, thus, the data do not convincingly support the segmentability hypothesis **H** FREQ_{RELATIVE}, even though we find one effect in the expected direction. This is in line with the results from the larger-scale study in Chapter 4. In addition, as discussed above, there were no interactions of RELATIVE FREQUENCY with PROSODIC CATEGORY.

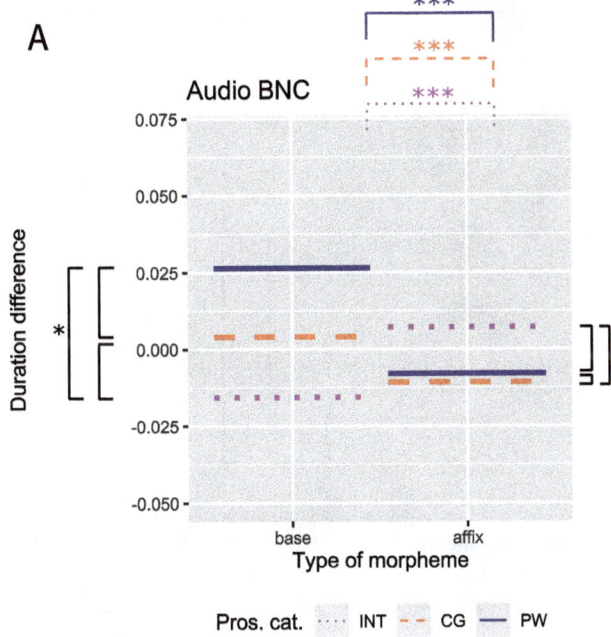

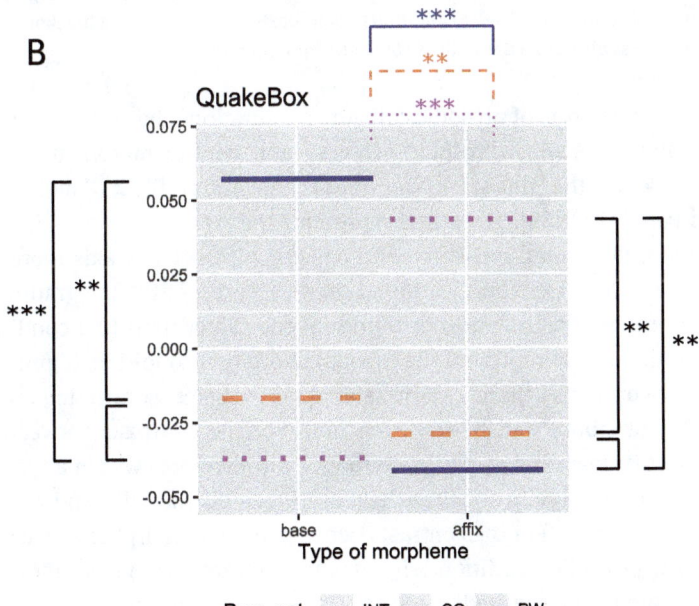

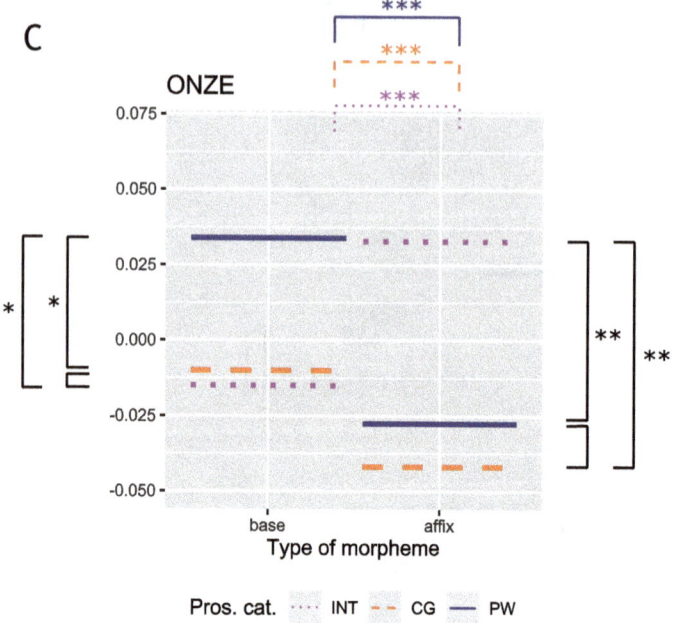

Fig. 5.2: Interaction effects between PROSODIC CATEGORY and TYPE OF MORPHEME in the three corpora. Significance levels of contrasts between conditions are indicated by asterisks on brackets. Abbreviations: PW for ProsodicWord, CG for CliticGroup, INT for Integrating.

Next, let us turn to the effects of prosodic category on duration. Figure 5.2 shows the interaction effects between prosodic category and type of morpheme on duration difference in the three corpora (Panel A: Audio BNC, Panel B: QuakeBox, and Panel C: ONZE). The x-axis represents the TYPE OF MORPHEME, i.e., the two domains of durational measurement, base or affix. The y-axis represents DURATION DIFFERENCE. I use purple, dotted lines to represent the Integrating (INT) condition; orange, dashed lines to represent the CliticGroup (CG) condition; and blue, solid lines to represent the ProsodicWord (PW) condition. Significance between the contrasts is indicated by asterisks on brackets connecting the respective conditions above and beside each plot. For the contrasts between prosodic categories (Integrating vs. CliticGroup vs. ProsodicWord) within a type of morpheme condition, significance brackets are given on the left-hand and right-hand side of each plot. For the contrasts between types of morpheme (base vs. affix) within a prosodic condition, significance brackets are given above each plot with colored solid, dashed, or dotted lines, corresponding to the prosodic category within which base and affix durations are compared.

First, let us look at the durations of affixes and bases in the different prosodic conditions. Figure 5.2 shows that seven of the 18 bars fall below the zero line: this means that in most cases, both affix durations and base durations are shorter than expected from their average segment duration.[3] However, if we compare affixes and bases, we see that there are differences in the amount they deviate from their average segment duration (significance brackets above the plots).

Starting with the Integrating category (INT; purple, dotted lines), we can see that integrating affixes behave as expected in all three corpora: they are consistently and significantly more lengthened than the bases to which they attach. In the ProsodicWord category (PW; blue, solid lines), too, affixes behave as expected in all three corpora (they are less lengthened than their bases). In the CliticGroup category (CG; orange, dashed lines), affixes are less lengthened than their bases in all three corpora, while they would have been expected to be more lengthened.

Second, let us examine the contrasts between the prosodic categories within the respective domains of base and affix (significance brackets to the left and right of the plots, respectively). Let us look at the base condition first. We can see that in the Audio BNC, ProsodicWord bases are most lengthened. CliticGroup bases are less lengthened, and Integrating bases are least lengthened. Expressed in terms of the lengthening hierarchy formulated in **H** PROS (see again Section 2.3 and Table 2.1 in Section 2.1.3), the Audio BNC thus follows exactly the expected pattern ProsodicWord > CliticGroup > Integrating. However, two of the contrasts are not significant, so it is possible to formulate the more accurate hierarchy ProsodicWord = CliticGroup = Integrating (with ProsodicWord > Integrating). The QuakeBox and ONZE corpora, too, are consistent with the expected lengthening hierarchy. However, the contrast between the clitic-group-forming category and the integrating category in the two New Zealand corpora, does not reach significance. This results in the hierarchy ProsodicWord > CliticGroup = Integrating. Bases with prosodic-word-forming affixes are most lengthened, followed by bases with clitic-group-forming affixes and bases with integrating affixes.

Third, let us look at the affix condition. In the Audio BNC, integrating affixes are most lengthened, followed by prosodic-word-forming affixes and clitic-group-forming affixes. This is a different pattern from the expected one (which

---

[3] This is expected since derived words are, on average, longer than the average word. Hence, the segments of derived words should be pronounced shorter than they are on average, due to the compression effect discussed in Section 3.3.2 (Nooteboom 1972; Lindblom 1963).

is CliticGroup > Integrating > ProsodicWord). However, since, none of these contrasts are significant, the lengthening hierarchy is more accurately represented as Integrating = ProsodicWord = CliticGroup. In the QuakeBox corpus, Integrating affixes are most lengthened, followed by CliticGroup affixes and ProsodicWord affixes. The contrast between the integrating affixes and the other two affix types is significant, so that we are dealing with this hierarchy: Integrating > CliticGroup = ProsodicWord. Lastly, one can also observe deviations from the expected lengthening hierarchy for the ONZE corpus. The ONZE affixes are most lengthened in the Integrating condition, followed by the ProsodicWord condition and the CliticGroup condition. This results in the pattern Integrating > ProsodicWord = CliticGroup.

It is now possible to evaluate all the contrasts in terms of how the observed lengthening hierarchies overall fit with the expected hierarchies. Table 5.6 summarizes the significance levels for all measured contrasts I have discussed in the three corpora, color-coded for the direction of a given effect. For convenience, the last column of this table displays the directional changes in duration one would have expected based on the hypotheses outlined in Section 2.1.3. I set up the contrasts for this table so that in every cell, we expect more lengthening from the first condition (for example, base or CG) to the second condition (for example, affix or PW). More lengthening is indicated by purple (darker) shading. In cases where we observe less lengthening, I use blue (lighter) shading.

Overall, we can observe that many, but not all of the expectations are confirmed by the data. Out of the 27 expectations (cells), 13 are in line with the predictions, 5 contradict the predictions, and 9 do not reach significance. Prosodic contrasts within the base condition (Table 5.6, rows 4–6) are in line with the expectations, but two of the prosodic contrasts in the affix condition (row 7) go in the opposite direction from what was expected. A similar situation holds for the base-affix contrasts: the Integrating and ProsodicWord conditions (rows 2–3) behave as expected, while the CliticGroup condition (row 1) contradicts the expectations. The 9 non-significant contrasts all pertain to the prosodic category contrasts (rows 4–9). Overall, only 3 out of 9 rows are completely in line with the hypotheses.

Tab. 5.6: Overview of prosodic category effects in the different conditions. Purple (darker) shading indicates a positive change in duration from the first to the second category, blue (lighter) shading a negative change in duration. Abbreviations: PW for ProsodicWord, CG for CliticGroup, INT for Integrating.

Significance of ...	Condition		Audio BNC	QuakeBox	ONZE	Expected	Row no.
Base-affix contrasts	CG		base-affix***	base-affix**	base-affix***	base-affix	1
	INT		base-affix***	base-affix***	base-affix***	base-affix	2
	PW		affix-base***	affix-base***	affix-base***	affix-base	3
Prosodic category contrasts	base		CG-PW	CG-PW**	CG-PW*	CG-PW	4
			INT-PW*	INT-PW***	INT-PW*	INT-PW	5
			INT-CG	INT-CG	INT-CG	INT-CG	6
	affix		INT-CG	INT-CG**	INT-CG**	INT-CG	7
			PW-INT	PW-INT**	PW-INT**	PW-INT	8
			PW-CG	PW-CG	PW-CG	PW-CG	9

longer durations from first condition (e.g., base) to second condition (e.g., affix)

shorter durations from first condition (e.g., base) to second condition (e.g., affix)

Together with the findings for relative frequency, it is now possible to relate all findings to the hypotheses as follows. First, we saw earlier that **H** FREQ$_{RELATIVE}$ again (like in Chapter 4) is largely not supported, despite one effect in the expected direction in the Audio BNC: higher relative frequency is not associated with longer durations. Second, **H** PROS$_{FREQREL}$ is not supported either, as there was not a single significant interaction between RELATIVE FREQUENCY and PROSODIC CATEGORY: how integrated an affix is into prosodic word structure does not modulate whether higher relative frequency can protect against reduction. In both cases, there is very strong evidence for the respective null hypothesis. Third, based on the findings summarized in Table 5.6, quite a few contrasts between bases and affixes within the prosodic categories, as well as contrasts between the prosodic categories within the affix domain, do not behave as expected (**H** PROS): durations often do not pattern according to prosodic boundary strength. The prosodic category approach cannot explain the patterning of the durational differences satisfactorily. I will now proceed to discuss these findings in more detail, returning to the theoretical assumptions of segmentability and prosodic word structure.

5.3 Discussion

Three main findings emerge from the analysis: (1) **H** FREQ$_{\text{RELATIVE}}$ is largely not supported by the data (with one exception), (2) **H** PROS$_{\text{FREQREL}}$ is not supported by the data, and (3) the hypothesis complex **H** PROS is sometimes contradicted by the data.

First, **H** FREQ$_{\text{RELATIVE}}$ is not supported, with one exception: there is one expected, positive effect of relative frequency on duration in the Audio BNC. In this case, we observed longer durations the higher the relative frequency becomes (the more segmentable a derivative is). This one case seems to speak in favor of the idea that words are protected against reduction by morphological segmentability (Hay 2001, 2003). If we took this one effect seriously (which I am not convinced we should), this effect would also support the idea that the more meaningful a stretch of segments is, the more important it is for speakers to fully realize these segments so as to facilitate recognition by their interlocutors (MacKenzie & Tamminga 2021; Guy 1991; Labov 1989; Guy 1980). This would resonate with listener-oriented or communicative accounts, as well as with the speaker-oriented accounts of production ease (Jaeger & Buz 2017).

However, we observe mostly null effects. The present study is thus in line with the results of the larger-scale study in Chapter 4. With differently set-up models compared to that study, the present study shows again that segmentability effects often do not emerge. These results are again in line with previous studies in a way, inasmuch as they replicate the mixture of effects and null effects (Zuraw et al. 2020; Plag & Ben Hedia 2018; Zimmerer et al. 2014; Schuppler et al. 2012; Hay 2007; Pluymaekers et al. 2005b; Hay 2003; also see Hanique & Ernestus 2012). As discussed extensively in Section 4.3, the emergence or non-emergence of relative frequency effects might be related to the emergence of word frequency effects in general: the study in Chapter 4 could only observe a relative frequency effect in datasets that also feature a word frequency effect. It seems that whether relative frequency affects duration is mainly dependent on whether word frequency affects duration – and word frequency effects, too, fail to be observed (e.g., Bowden et al. 2010; Pluymaekers et al. 2005b, the present book). The fact that relative frequency effects only emerge in the presence of word frequency effects may indicate that we should discard relative frequency as a predictor of duration (see also again the discussion in Section 4.3).[4]

Second, **H** PROS$_{\text{FREQREL}}$ is not supported by the data. Prosodic word structure does not interact with relative frequency in any of the corpora. This means that whether an affix is more or less prosodically integrated does not influence how relative frequency affects duration. A segmentability protection against reduction, then, is not diminished by the lack of a strong prosodic boundary. This conclusion is indirectly also supported by previous studies. Affixes for which effects of relative frequency on duration have been found before are sometimes non-integrating affixes (e.g., *dis-* and *un-* in Plag & Ben Hedia 2018, *un-* in Hay 2007) and sometimes integrating affixes (e.g., *-ly* in Hay 2003). What is more, neither an integrating nor a non-integrating affix guarantees a relative frequency effect, as demonstrated by the null results for both integrating and non-integrating affixes (e.g., *-ly* and *in-* in Plag & Ben Hedia 2018, *un-* and *in-* in Ben Hedia & Plag 2017, *ont-*, *ver-*, and *-lijk* in Pluymaekers et al. 2005b). It thus seems that we need to look for further factors that might be responsible for the apparent arbitrariness of the emergence of relative frequency effects. Prosodic word structure is not the culprit.

Third, the lengthening hierarchy in **H** PROS is often not supported. It seems that the prosodic structure of complex words can neither explain the capricious nature of relative frequency effects on duration, nor can it satisfactorily explain durational variation as such. For the base-affix contrasts, the contrasts for the Integrating category and the ProsodicWord category show a consistent and predicted pattern (see again Table 5.6, second and third row). In the CliticGroup category, however, not a single contrast behaves as expected (first row). For the contrasts between prosodic categories, the patterns are more difficult to interpret due to many non-significant effects. As summarized in rows 4 through 6 in Table 5.6 and in Figure 5.2, base durations mostly follow the predicted pattern ProsodicWord > CliticGroup > Integrating: bases with prosodic-word-forming affixes are more lengthened than bases with clitic-group-forming affixes, which in turn are more lengthened than bases with integrating affixes (even though this often does not reach significance). In contrast, affix duration contrasts in

---

[4] I also tested for an effect of WORD FREQUENCY on DURATION DIFFERENCE for the three complete datasets of the present study, using the same model specifications as for the models reported in Section 5.2, eliminating RELATIVE FREQUENCY and its interactions. An effect of WORD FREQUENCY was present only in the QuakeBox corpus (t = −2.493, p = 0.014).

two cases contradict the expected pattern CliticGroup > Integrating > ProsodicWord (row 7 in Table 5.6).[5]

It is interesting that predictions for bases are never contradicted by the empirical data, whereas affixes sometimes produce the opposite behavior. The reasons for this difference between bases and affixes are not clear. Both the predictions for bases and the ones for affixes are based on the same underlying prosodic mechanisms assumed in the literature (although it must be noted, of course, that these mechanisms – from the number of prosodic levels to their definition – do not go unquestioned, see Turk & Shattuck-Hufnagel 2020 for an overview). Affixes are, of course, generally shorter in segments and consequently in duration than their bases, which an analysis of the affix-base ratio confirms in the present data. With fewer segments and shorter durations, there might be less potential to reduce or enhance, and thus less potential for effects to play out significantly. While this could explain why there few significant effects for affixes, this cannot explain why there are effects going in unexpected directions.

Prosodic structure, if understood in terms of boundary strength, then, is not able to consistently account for the durational differences in English derivatives. This is interesting given that some studies had previously suggested that the prosodic structure of complex words can explain some of their durational variation (Bergmann 2018; Sugahara & Turk 2009; Auer 2002; Sproat & Fujimura 1993). However, there are some important differences between these studies and the present one.

First, all these studies investigated specific segments and did not consider other durational domains. Prosodic boundary effects might explain more of the variation in a very small domain, like a single base-final segment, than of the variation in a larger domain, like an affix. Second, some of the studies compared different prosodic categories than I did. For example, Sproat & Fujimura (1993) compared compound boundaries to affix boundaries and to simplex words. The durational difference between a prosodic boundary in an affixed word and a non-affixed word might be greater than the difference between pro-

---

[5] It may be hypothesized that the fact that I find some significant effects that have no clear theoretical basis is the consequence of analyzing a sample with high variance, in this case natural speech. Plotting standardized effect sizes against their standard errors, I should find a funnel shape where the largest effects (both positive and negative) also have the largest standard errors, and as the standard errors decrease, the estimated effects should shrink to zero. This suspicion was not confirmed by the data; I could not find a clear pattern or strong correlation between standardized coefficients and standard errors (see the scripts at https://osf.io/-4h5f3/).

sodic boundaries in different types of affixed words. Third, some of the studies report that prosodic boundary effects only emerge in very specific conditions. For example, Sugahara & Turk (2009) find that stem-final rhymes in prosodic-word-forming suffixes are only lengthened at a slow speech rate, and Bergmann's (2018) segments in derivatives with prosodic-word-forming suffixes are only lengthened if they are infrequent. Fourth, most of the studies investigated elicited data, while I investigated conversational data. Fifth, some of the studies suffer from methodological issues. For example, Sugahara & Turk (2009) only used data from five speakers and did not fit any statistical models that included potentially influential covariates. Their durational effects of prosodic structure might disappear if the data were analyzed with more controlled statistical modeling.

Taken together with these caveats, the present results show that effects of the prosodic structure of complex words on duration are to be taken with much more caution than assumed. I thus join Pluymaekers et al. (2010: 523) in their conclusion that "contrary to received wisdom, morphological effects on fine phonetic detail cannot always be accounted for by prosodic structure."

With regard to the previous work that found evidence for pre-boundary lengthening in general (e.g., Klatt 1975; Vaissière 1983; Edwards & Beckman 1988; Beckman & Pierrehumbert 1986; Campbell 1990; Wightman et al. 1992), it must be noted that much of this evidence comes from boundaries that are higher in the prosodic hierarchy than the ones we investigated in this study. As explained in Section 2.1.3, prosodic boundaries, and thus lengthening, are expected to be stronger the higher these boundaries are ranked in the prosodic hierarchy. Hence, lengthening effects before higher-level boundaries (for example, phrase-final lengthening or utterance-final lengthening) might show more consistent patterns than lengthening before low-level boundaries (like foot boundaries or pword boundaries). This means that the present results do not necessarily have to be interpreted as refuting the prosodic account in general, but perhaps merely as demonstrating that effects become more unstable the lower we zoom in on the hierarchy. It may well be that in order to meaningfully observe prosodic lengthening effects, one needs to look at higher-level constituents. To detect effects of very small magnitude, even though we would lose some advantages of spontaneous speech data, future studies could also use an experimental setup. This way, one could manipulate only relative frequency and prosodic category without the variance introduced by real conversations.

Overall, the results of the present study show that neither relative frequency nor prosodic word structure are able to explain the data perfectly for all corpora. At least for speech articulation, the predictions of a prosodic account thus are not satisfactory. Of course, the fault for the contradictory contrasts may not necessarily lie in the prosodic predictions themselves, but might also be caused by other, external factors. For example, potential prosodic differences between the varieties represented in the corpora, differences in the forced alignment, or differences in dataset size and statistical power might all be factors that introduce unwanted variation. It is interesting, for instance, that the Audio BNC seems to differ in its behavior somewhat from the two New Zealand corpora, while the results from the two New Zealand corpora are virtually the same (see again Table 5.6).[6] However, since not all affixes are present in all corpora (cf. again the affix distribution across the corpora in Table 5.1), I was not able to test whether an interaction of PROSODIC CATEGORY with CORPUS in a single dataset would turn out significant or not. The differences between corpora might as well be a coincidence and should, in my opinion, be taken with a grain of salt.

One potentially important additional factor which needs to be discussed is syntactic position. In the present study, I did not control for part-of-speech factors. Which syntactic category a derivative belongs to, however, is related to prosodic structure. This is because derivatives of a certain morphological category occur more often in certain positions in the sentence, and thus occur more often in certain prosodic positions. For example, the suffix *-less* derives adjectives and therefore often occurs in prenominal position within a noun phrase or after a copula in predicative position. The suffix *-ness* derives nouns and will therefore often be found in noun phrase-final position. This may affect how these suffixes are pronounced in these contexts and in other contexts (Bybee 2017, 2002). In the present study, I investigated the effect of lower-level prosodic boundaries (foot boundaries, pword boundaries, and clitic group boundaries), but one would also expect duration to be affected by higher-level prosodic boundaries (such as phrase boundaries or utterance boundaries).

The present study did not control for effects of prosodic phrasing since the coding of prosodic phrasing with the natural conversation data as found in the present corpora is extremely difficult and highly problematic in terms of rater

---

[6] One might suggest that this may be related to affix stress. The affixes included in the Audio BNC were different than those included in the two New Zealand corpora, and some of them are stressed differently. However, it is not straightforwardly possible to incorporate stress as an additional variable, as it is partly nested with prosodic category. Which prosodic category an affix belongs to, after all, is defined partly based on affix stress. Therefore, indirectly, prosodic category already codes for stress. In addition, I already control for the affix as such by using random intercepts for AFFIX. I thus consider it both conceptually and mathematically problematic to test the influence of affix stress within the setup of the present study.

reliability. I believe, however, that potential effects of prosodic phrasing are not overly influential in this study for several reasons.

First, I investigated a large number of different affixes that belong to different part-of-speech categories simultaneously. It is not the case that in the present data, for instance, all prosodic-word-forming affixes derive nouns, whereas all integrating affixes derive adjectives. If this were the case, syntactic position could be considered an important potential confound. Instead, the affixes come from different syntactic categories even within prosodic categories. Clitic-group-forming affixes derive both nouns and adjectives; integrating affixes derive nouns, adjectives, and verbs; and prosodic-word-forming affixes derive nouns, adjectives, verbs, and even adverbs.

Second, the study in Chapter 4 presented an analysis investigating the tokens in one morphological category at a time, for all eight affixes separately. These category-internal analyses again indicated that relative frequency effects frequently fail to emerge, without any clear pattern between categories and within categories (comparing base durations, affix durations, and word durations). The results indicate, then, that relative frequency is neither a reliable predictor within nor across morphological categories, prosodic categories, or syntactic categories.

Finally, and crucially, phrase boundaries and utterance boundaries – just as other prosodic boundaries – cause the strongest lengthening of segments that are close to those boundaries, compared to those segments that are further away. In other words, lengthening effects weaken with increasing distance from the boundary. This has been shown in a number of acoustic and articulatory studies (e.g., Byrd et al. 2006; Shattuck-Hufnagel & Turk 1998; Cambier-Langeveld 1997; Berkovits 1994, 1993a, 1993b). Higher-level boundaries, thus, will affect word-final segment lengthening more than word-internal segment lengthening. This in turn means that the present predictions for base lengthening versus affix lengthening as well as the interpretation of the results would remain unchanged: I always expected a word-final element (bases in the case of prefixes, or affixes in the case of suffixes, respectively) to be lengthened more than the corresponding word-internal element. The presence of higher-level boundaries would only enhance that effect.

This study set out to investigate the influence of prosodic structure and relative frequency on the durational properties of complex words. In particular, I wanted to test whether prosodic structure can explain the inconsistency in the emergence of relative frequency effects on duration in previous studies. The data showed that it is possible to rule out prosodic word structure as a gatekeeper for relative frequency effects. Second, the study again demonstrated, like the larger-scale study in Chapter 4, that relative frequency effects can emerge, but mostly fail to emerge over a large set of affixes and a large number of tokens. Finally, I have presented evidence that word-internal prosodic boundaries fail to account consistently for durational differences. In many cases, with more strength and a higher position in the prosodic hierarchy, prosodic boundaries are indeed associated with more pre-boundary lengthening of morphological constituents. But in some other cases, this pattern does not hold – especially not for affixes.

Where do we go from here? One other possibility that has been suggested is that prosodic word effects may underlyingly be related to transitional probability effects (see Côté 2013; Aylett & Turk 2004). Patients who make few anticipatory speech errors often fail to apply cross-boundary phonology (Michel Lange et al. 2017), which would support this idea (discussed in more detail in Section 6.3). While Côté (2013) makes this suggestion based on the transitional probability between words, not morphemes, it is conceivable that the transitional probability of an affix might also affect duration. The next chapter will report a study testing the effects of *conditional affix probability*, the probability of the affix given the preceding linguistic element. This measure captures the transitional probability between morphemes. Unfortunately, this measure is very strongly correlated with relative frequency, which makes it impossible to include both measures in the same model. However, the effects of conditional affix probability can be tested separately from relative frequency. In addition, the next study will also test for effects of *semantic information load*. Both measures are assumed to reflect the informativeness of an affix.

6 Affix informativeness

The present study is the final study taking a decompositional perspective. In it, I investigate whether the informativeness of an affix is correlated with acoustic enhancement or reduction. As described in Section 2.1.4, for the present study, it was decided to analyze two measures as operationalizations of informativeness, conditional affix probability and affix-specific semantic information load. It was hypothesized that higher conditional affix probability (lower informativeness) should be associated with shorter durations (**H** INF$_{PROB}$), while higher semantic information load of the affix (more informativeness) should be associated with longer durations (**H** INF$_{SEM}$). As variables, I will refer to these measures as CONDITIONAL AFFIX PROBABILITY and SEMANTIC INFORMATION LOAD, respectively. I will now describe the coding of these two predictors of interest.

6.1 Method

CONDITIONAL AFFIX PROBABILITY
As explained in Section 2.1.4, *conditional affix probability* C_{aff} measures the probability of the affix B given the probability of the preceding linguistic item A (equation and table with examples repeated here for convenience). In the case of prefixes, this preceding item is the previous word, and in the case of suffixes, it is the base to which the suffix attaches.

$$C_{aff} = \frac{p(AB)}{p(A)} \tag{6.1}$$

Tab. 6.1: Review: Example cases for the measurement of *conditional affix probability*. For suffixes, the derived word constitutes a base-affix bigram, whereas for prefixes, the bigram consists of the prefix and the preceding word in the utterance.

example of measurement for suffixes		example of measurement for prefixes		
A	B	A	B	C
random	-ize	her	pre-	determination

To estimate the conditional probabilities of the suffixes, I obtained frequency counts from COCA in the same way as described for the variable WORD FREQUENCY in Section 3.3.2. I then divided the frequency of the word $p(AB)$ by the frequency of the base word $p(A)$.

To estimate the conditional probabilities for prefixes, I did not use COCA, but took the frequencies from the respective corpus of speech data (the Audio BNC, the QuakeBox corpus, or the ONZE corpus, respectively). For the frequency of a prefix $p(B)$, this was necessary because this prefix frequency cannot as easily be obtained from COCA, as one will also count false positive results where the supposed prefix string is, in fact, nonmorphemic. It was therefore decided to take the lists of words from the three speech corpora that were already cleaned of false prefixes, i.e., that only contain true prefix/preceding-word bigrams. For the frequency of the preceding word in isolation $p(A)$, using the respective corpus of speech data instead of COCA was necessary because the speech corpora differ in size compared to each other and to COCA. It was therefore considered important to use the same respective corpus for $p(A)$ that was used for $p(B)$ in order to not distort the relative probabilities of preceding word and prefix. I then divided the frequency of the prefix/preceding-word bigram $p(AB)$ by the frequency of the preceding word $p(A)$. As explained in Section 2.1.4, it is expected that the higher the CONDITIONAL AFFIX PROBABILITY, the shorter the duration will become. I log-transformed the variable before it entered the models.

SEMANTIC INFORMATION LOAD

As explained in Section 2.1.4, this variable measures how much an affix contributes to the meaning of a derivative. Following Ben Hedia (2019), I evaluated all affixes for different criteria by consulting the pertinent literature (Plag 2018; Bauer et al. 2013). These criteria were: *clearness of semantic meaning*, *type of base* (free vs. bound root), *semantic transparency*, and *productivity*. For a detailed description of these criteria for each affix, the reader is again referred to Section 3.1. Unlike Ben Hedia (2019), I decided however to systematize the classification by coding how well the affixes fulfilled each criterion on 5-point Likert scales to create a semantic information load score. I considered this necessary because the present study investigates many more affixes than Ben Hedia (2019), which need to be compared as systematically as possible. The 5-point scales thus coded how much the affixes differ in each criterion. An overview of the scales is given in Table 6.2.

Tab. 6.2: Criteria for the classification of affixes according to semantic information load.

criterion	1	2	3	4	5
semantics	no lexical meaning	–	–	–	clear single meaning
type of base	bases are never free	–	–	–	bases are always free
transparency	opaque	–	–	–	very transparent
productivity	unproductive	–	–	–	highly productive

Which score was assigned to each affix criteria on these scales depended on the description of the affix in the literature. For instance, the affix *dis-* is described as "marginally productive" (Bauer et al. 2013: 361) and therefore received a productivity score of 2, while the affix *-ness* is described as "perhaps the most productive suffix of English" (Plag 2018: 92) and therefore received a productivity score of 5. To give another example, the vast majority of *un*-derivatives are described as "completely transparent in meaning" (Bauer et al. 2013: 371), so *un-* received a transparency score of 5, while *-ment*-derivatives are sometimes semantically opaque (e.g., *government*, Bauer et al. 2013: 162), so *-ment* received a transparency score of only 3. For a complete description of each affix and its characteristics, refer again to Section 3.1.

Tab. 6.3: Hierarchy of affixes according to the semantic information load score, sorted from highest to lowest.

affix	semantics	type of base	transparency	productivity	total score
-ness	4	5	5	5	19
un-	5	5	5	4	19
-less	5	4	5	4	18
re-	5	5	5	3	18
pre-	4	4	3	4	15
in-	5	4	3	3	15
-able	3	4	3	5	15
dis-	5	4	3	2	14
-ize	3	4	3	3	13
-ation	3	4	3	2	12
-ment	3	4	3	2	12
-ity	3	3	3	2	11

The resulting values were summed up, creating a unique semantic information load score for each affix. The affixes can be ranked according to this score so that the hierarchy in Table 6.3 emerges. As explained in Section 2.1.4, it is expected that the higher the semantic information load, the longer the duration should be.

It is important to note that this kind of coding is not unproblematic. This is because it brings along two potential sources of unreliability. The first of these sources is the literature used for reference. For the present study, it was made sure that the survey of affixes is based on pertinent and authoritative sources (Plag 2018; Bauer et al. 2013). However, a different study may choose different sources which use a different phrasing in their description of affixes, leading to minor differences in the scores assigned to each affix. The second potential source of unreliability is the coder. To assign the scores, the prose descriptions of affixes from the literature need to be translated into numbers. Different coders may exhibit variation in the way they interpret these descriptions and convert them into scores. For instance, they may differ in which values they assign to adverbs such as "marginally" or "completely" (cf. examples above). It is unlikely that such differences would result in an affix hierarchy that is completely different from the one in Table 6.3. However, when interpreting results, it must be kept in mind that minor differences in the ranking may determine whether an effect turns out "significant" or not in individual cases.

The two informativeness variables described above were analyzed in different ways. SEMANTIC INFORMATION LOAD is an affix-specific measure. Therefore, it is only possible to perform an across-category analysis. I build three models in each corpus study, one for each response variable (WORD DURATION DIFFERENCE, AFFIX DURATION DIFFERENCE, and BASE DURATION DIFFERENCE).

The variable CONDITIONAL AFFIX PROBABILITY, on the other hand, is a word-based measure. Therefore, like for the frequency measure analysis in Chapter 4, I performed an across-category analysis as well as category-internal analyses for each corpus. Again, the category-internal analyses investigated one morphological category at a time. I investigated all three durational domains: the duration of the derived word (WORD DURATION DIFFERENCE), the duration of the affix (AFFIX DURATION DIFFERENCE), and the duration of the derivative's base word (BASE DURATION DIFFERENCE). This means that for the category-internal analyses, there were 3 x 8 models – three response variables and eight affixes – per corpus. The interpretation for the category-internal analyses will be limited to effects below a more conservative significance threshold of $p < .001$ (see explanation in Section 4.1).

The across-category analysis investigated multiple morphological categories simultaneously. However, instead of investigating the whole dataset from each corpus at once (i.e., including all morphological categories, like in Chapter 4), it was decided to analyze prefixes and suffixes separately. One reason for this is that CONDITIONAL AFFIX PROBABILITY taps into different frequential properties depending on whether it is calculated for prefixed or for suffixed words. As explained above, for prefixes it is calculated based on the frequency of the preceding word and of the affix, while for suffixes it is calculated based on the frequency of the base and of the affix. A second reason is that the distribution of CONDITIONAL AFFIX PROBABILITY indicates clear differences between prefixes and suffixes. This second reason will be illustrated further below in Section 6.2.1.

Both variables (CONDITIONAL AFFIX PROBABILITY and SEMANTIC INFORMATION LOAD) were investigated with multiple linear regression models. Model creation, criticism, and simplification followed the procedure described in Section 3.4. For the number of observations lost during trimming in each model, refer to the materials at https://osf.io/4h5f3/. The initial models included the respective informativeness measure (either CONDITIONAL AFFIX PROBABILITY or SEMANTIC INFORMATION LOAD) fitted to the respective durational response variable (either WORD DURATION DIFFERENCE, AFFIX DURATION DIFFERENCE, or BASE DURATION DIFFERENCE). In addition, each maximal model included the following covariates (for a detailed description of these variables, the reader is referred back to Section 3.3):

SPEECH RATE	The number of syllables in a window of ±1 second around the target derivative divided by the duration of that window.
NUMBER OF SYLLABLES	The number of syllables of the target derivative.
WORD FREQUENCY	The log-transformed wordform frequency of the target derivative from COCA.
BIGRAM FREQUENCY	The log-transformed frequency of the target derivative occurring together with the word following it in COCA.
BIPHONE PROBABILITY	The sum of all biphone probabilities (the likelihood of two phonemes occurring together in English) in a target derivative divided by the number of segments.
SUBCORPUS	The subcorpus of the ONZE corpus (used only for the models with ONZE corpus datasets).

6.2 Results

In this section, I will report the results for the two informativeness measures. I will start with conditional affix probability in Section 6.2.1, before examining semantic information load in Section 6.2.2.

6.2.1 Conditional affix probability

Let us start with the category-internal models. Table 6.4 provides an overview that is structured in the same way as the frequency effects overview in Table 4.1, Section 4.2.1. Columns refer to the response variable DURATION DIFFERENCE (for the WORD, the AFFIX, and the BASE), rows to the predictor CONDITIONAL AFFIX PROBABILITY, and effect cells are grouped by affix and corpus. Purple cells (darker shade) indicate effects at p < .001 in the expected direction, blue cells (lighter shade) in the unexpected direction.

Tab. 6.4: Overview of category-internal effects of CONDITIONAL AFFIX PROBABILITY with a conservative threshold of p < .001 in all three corpora, grouped by affix. Purple cells (darker shade) mark models with probability effects in the expected direction (shorter durations for increasing CONDITIONAL AFFIX PROBABILITY). Blue cells (lighter shade) indicate prob-ability effects in the opposite direction from what was expected. Empty cells indicate that there was no significant effect at the p < .001 level.

DURATION DIFFERENCE	WORD DUR	AFFIX DUR	BASE DUR	WORD DUR	AFFIX DUR	BASE DUR	WORD DUR	AFFIX DUR	BASE DUR	WORD DUR	AFFIX DUR	BASE DUR
Audio BNC												
affix	-ness			-ize			-ation			dis-		
COND AFFIX PROBABILITY								🟦				
affix	-less			pre-			un-			in-		
COND AFFIX PROBABILITY												
QuakeBox												
affix	-ness			-ity			-ation			dis-		
COND AFFIX PROBABILITY					🟦							
affix	-able			-ment			un-			re-		
COND AFFIX PROBABILITY	🟦		🟦									
ONZE												
affix	-ness			-ity			-ation			dis-		
COND AFFIX PROBABILITY						🟪						
affix	-able			-ment			un-			re-		
COND AFFIX PROBABILITY	🟦											

■ p < .001 expected direction (negative effect on duration)
■ p < .001 unexpected direction (positive effect on duration)

To recap, it was expected with H INF$_{PROB}$ that with increasing CONDITIONAL AFFIX PROBABILITY, durations would decrease. We can observe in Table 6.4 that out of 72 possible effects, 7 emerge as significant. Most of these (six out of seven) are unexpected. Whenever CONDITIONAL AFFIX PROBABILITY significantly affects acoustic duration, it mostly does so positively – a higher probability of the affix given its preceding linguistic unit is associated with longer durations (of the base, the affix, or the word). This is the case for different affixes, different corpora, and different domains of durational measurement: the duration of *-ation*-affixed bases in the Audio BNC, the duration of the affix *-ity* and of *-able* derivatives and *-able* bases in the QuakeBox corpus, and the duration of the affix *-able* and its derivatives in the ONZE corpus all increase with higher probability. Only the duration of bases affixed with *-ity* in the ONZE corpus decreases with higher probability. Given the number of models, it could be argued that this one expected effect can be neglected.

Reliable informativeness effects, if we operationalize informativeness as conditional affix probability, fail to emerge in most cases. Can we formulate any generalizations as to when they emerge? It seems that similarly to the frequency effects (Chapter 4), there is no clear pattern regarding the affix, the corpora, the domain of durational measurement, or the dataset size. However, all the affixes for which effects emerge are suffixes (-*ation*, -*ity*, -*able*). This will be discussed further below. In addition, the two New Zealand corpora are more similar to each other than to the British English corpus. For both the QuakeBox corpus and the ONZE corpus, CONDITIONAL AFFIX PROBABILITY displays effects for -*able* and -*ity*, whereas the Audio BNC features only an effect for -*ation*. Given that the effects are so few in number, however, I do not consider it justifiable to attribute this to any systematic difference between the varieties of English.

The category-internal analyses do not support the hypothesis that CONDITIONAL AFFIX PROBABILITY correlates with acoustic reduction. Before moving on to SEMANTIC INFORMATION LOAD, let us look at the across-category analyses. Let us first examine the distribution of CONDITIONAL AFFIX PROBABILITY across prefixes and suffixes.

Figure 6.1, for all three corpora, shows the distribution of CONDITIONAL AFFIX PROBABILITY by the type of affix (blue or dark shade for prefixes, orange or light shade for suffixes), plotted against BASE DURATION DIFFERENCE. We can see that the distribution of prefix probabilities and the distribution of suffix probabilities hardly overlaps; the probability of prefixes is always lower than that of suffixes. This makes sense: the occurrence of a base that can take a specific suffix makes the subsequent appearance of that suffix much more likely, while prefixes occur word-initially and can be preceded by virtually any word (and are thus generally not as predictable).

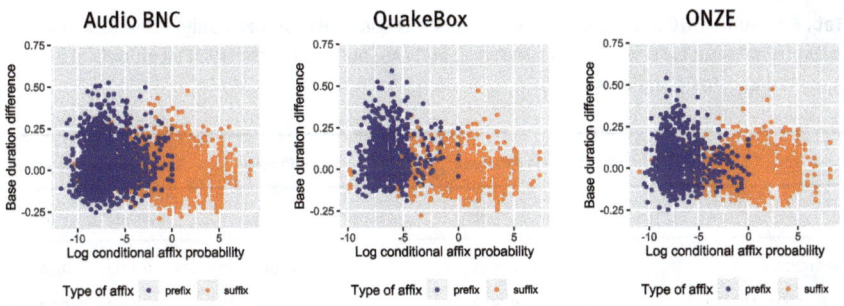

Fig. 6.1: Distribution of CONDITIONAL AFFIX PROBABILITY by type of affix (prefix or suffix) plotted against BASE DURATION DIFFERENCE in the three investigated corpora.

It was found during modeling that this distribution may obscure effects of CONDITIONAL AFFIX PROBABILITY for some domains of durational measurement, such as BASE DURATION DIFFERENCE (plotted on the y-axis in Figure 6.1). In these cases, both prefixes and suffixes can display the same effects in their own datasets (for example, the base durations of both prefixes and suffixes may each increase with higher probability), while the whole dataset behaves differently across prefixes and suffixes (for example, base durations may decrease with higher probability). In other words, probability may have a positive effect on duration for prefixed bases and a positive effect for suffixed bases, but a negative effect if both prefixes and suffixes are jointly included in the data. These inconsistencies are due to the distribution of CONDITIONAL AFFIX PROBABILITY we can see in Figure 6.1. Durations may appear to be shorter with higher probability in the whole dataset because suffixes are more probable than prefixes and have shorter durations overall. The individual effects for prefixes and suffixes, however, would each play out in their own data range. To not obscure any potential effects of CONDITIONAL AFFIX PROBABILITY by generalizing over the two types of affix, it therefore makes sense to create separate models for prefixes and suffixes.[1]

---

[1] Instead of creating separate models for each type of affix, it is also possible to include an interaction between CONDITIONAL AFFIX PROBABILITY and TYPE OF AFFIX. However, since the probability of prefixes is always lower than that of suffixes (see again the distribution in Figure 6.1), these two predictors exhibit increased collinearity. It was therefore decided not to include this interaction, but to model prefixes and suffixes separately. For the interested reader, I provide the models which jointly include prefixes and suffixes (both with and without the interaction) in the supplementary materials at https://osf.io/4h5f3/. The effects in these models generally turn out to be inconsistent.

Tab. 6.5: Audio BNC models with CONDITIONAL AFFIX PROBABILITY (prefixes only) fitted to WORD DURATION DIFFERENCE, AFFIX DURATION DIFFERENCE, and BASE DURATION DIFFERENCE. Full models are documented at https://osf.io/4h5f3/.

	Word duration difference			Affix duration difference			Base duration difference		
	Estimate	SE		Estimate	SE		Estimate	SE	
Intercept	0.3823	0.0165	***	0.1298	0.0062	***	0.2912	0.0128	***
CONDITIONAL AFFIX PROB	0.0033	0.0013	**				0.0033	0.0011	**
SPEECH RATE	-0.0578	0.0018	***	-0.0152	0.0008	***	-0.0434	0.0016	***
WORD FREQUENCY	-0.0035	0.0011	**	-0.0022	0.0005	***			
NUM OF SYLLABLES 3	0.0153	0.0064	*	-0.0152	0.0028	***	0.0279	0.0057	***
NUM OF SYLLABLES 4	0.0299	0.0066	***	-0.0142	0.0029	***	0.0419	0.0059	***
NUM OF SYLLABLES 5	0.0545	0.0085	***	-0.0175	0.0036	***	0.0695	0.0075	***
NUM OF SYLLABLES 6	0.0848	0.0291	**	-0.0214	0.0126		0.0891	0.0258	***
BIGRAM FREQUENCY							-0.0029	0.0008	***
BIPHONE PROBABILITY				-3.8109	0.4560	***			
N	1983			1982			1985		
R^2	0.3465			0.2277			0.2842		

Let us start with the prefixes. Recall that the prefixes are *pre-*, *dis-*, *un-*, and *in-* in the Audio BNC, and *dis-*, *un-*, and *re-* in the New Zealand corpora. Table 6.5 (for the Audio BNC), Table 6.6 (for the QuakeBox corpus), and Table 6.7 (for the ONZE corpus) report the final prefix models fitted to each DURATION DIFFERENCE variable. Empty cells indicate that the variable was removed during model simplification (see Section 3.4). In addition to the tables, Figure 6.2 provides plots of the effects of interest from these models (i.e., the effect of CONDITIONAL AFFIX PROBABILITY on the DURATION DIFFERENCE of the word, the affix, and the base) for all three corpora. In these figures, the first row presents the panels for the Audio BNC, the second row for the QuakeBox corpus, and the third row for the ONZE corpus. The y-axis represents (for each column from left to right) WORD DURATION DIFFERENCE, AFFIX DURATION DIFFERENCE, and BASE DURATION DIFFERENCE, respectively. The x-axis represents CONDITIONAL AFFIX PROBABILITY. If CONDITIONAL AFFIX PROBABILITY yields a significant effect, the significance level is marked with asterisks on the label (p: * < .05, ** < .01, *** < .001).

Tab. 6.6: QuakeBox models with CONDITIONAL AFFIX PROBABILITY (prefixes only) fitted to WORD DURATION DIFFERENCE, AFFIX DURATION DIFFERENCE, and BASE DURATION DIFFERENCE. Full models are documented at https://osf.io/4h5f3/.

	Word duration difference			Affix duration difference			Base duration difference		
	Estimate	SE		Estimate	SE		Estimate	SE	
Intercept	0.3892	0.0182	***	0.0727	0.0115	***	0.2899	0.0233	***
CONDITIONAL AFFIX PROB				-0.0037	0.0009	***			
SPEECH RATE	-0.0689	0.0033	***	-0.0129	0.0012	***	-0.0546	0.0028	***
WORD FREQUENCY				-0.0063	0.0010	***	0.0080	0.0024	**
NUM OF SYLLABLES 3	0.0100	0.0093		-0.0068	0.0034	*	0.0101	0.0077	
NUM OF SYLLABLES 4	0.0094	0.0103		-0.0235	0.0038	***	0.0180	0.0086	*
NUM OF SYLLABLES 5	0.1157	0.0159	***	0.0001	0.0059		0.1009	0.0132	***
NUM OF SYLLABLES 6	0.0604	0.0433		-0.0543	0.0156	***	0.1117	0.0357	**
BIGRAM FREQUENCY	-0.0054	0.0016	***				-0.0054	0.0014	***
BIPHONE PROBABILITY				-2.0531	0.8012	*			
N	844			824			815		
R²	0.3718			0.2511			0.3520		

The tables (Table 6.5, Table 6.6, and Table 6.7) show that the covariates generally behave as expected. WORD FREQUENCY, BIPHONE PROBABILITY, and BIGRAM FREQUENCY, if significant, have a negative effect on duration, as does SPEECH RATE. The NUMBER OF SYLLABLES is mostly (though not always) estimated to have a positive effect on duration. The subcorpora of the ONZE corpus additionally account for some of the variance in the ONZE models (Table 6.7).

Let us now examine the predictor of interest, CONDITIONAL AFFIX PROBABILITY. The tables and Figure 6.2 show that even in these larger datasets of multiple morphological categories, this predictor is not always predictive of duration. In four out of nine cases, it was removed from the models due to non-significance (in the AFFIX DURATION DIFFERENCE models of the Audio BNC and the ONZE corpus, Table 6.5 and Table 6.7, and in the WORD DURATION DIFFERENCE model and the BASE DURATION DIFFERENCE model of the QuakeBox corpus, Table 6.6). This lack of predictiveness can also be seen at a glance from Figure 6.2, where light blue regression lines represent non-significant effects from the maximal models.

Tab. 6.7: ONZE models with CONDITIONAL AFFIX PROBABILITY (prefixes only) fitted to WORD DURATION DIFFERENCE, AFFIX DURATION DIFFERENCE, and BASE DURATION DIFFERENCE. Full models are documented at https://osf.io/4h5f3/.

	Word duration difference			Affix duration difference			Base duration difference		
	Estimate	SE		Estimate	SE		Estimate	SE	
Intercept	0.2257	0.0374	***	0.1075	0.0089	***	0.1713	0.0379	***
CONDITIONAL AFFIX PROB	-0.0046	0.0019	*				-0.0036	0.0017	*
SPEECH RATE	-0.0597	0.0031	***	-0.0136	0.0011	***	-0.0475	0.0028	***
WORD FREQUENCY				-0.0057	0.0007	***	0.0039	0.0018	*
NUM OF SYLLABLES 3	0.0075	0.0079		-0.0083	0.0030	**	0.0049	0.0073	
NUM OF SYLLABLES 4	0.0200	0.0093	*	-0.0112	0.0034	**	0.0191	0.0086	*
NUM OF SYLLABLES 5	0.0861	0.0193	***	-0.0156	0.0072	*	0.0765	0.0177	***
NUM OF SYLLABLES 6	0.1856	0.0461	***	-0.0125	0.0170		0.1776	0.0427	***
SUBCORPUS 2014	0.1725	0.0426	***				0.1233	0.0390	**
SUBCORPUS CC	0.0488	0.0300					0.0568	0.0274	*
SUBCORPUS Darfield	0.0669	0.0310	*				0.0647	0.0282	*
SUBCORPUS IA	0.0905	0.0304	**				0.0955	0.0277	***
SUBCORPUS MU	0.0641	0.0304	*				0.0654	0.0277	*
SUBCORPUS SOHP	0.0830	0.0311	**				0.0606	0.0304	*
SUBCORPUS Southland	0.0441	0.0389					0.0556	0.0354	
N	934			905			933		
R^2	0.3711			0.2156			0.3124		

Turning to the significant effects, in the AFFIX DURATION DIFFERENCE model of the QuakeBox corpus (Table 6.6 and Figure 6.2, second row, second column) as well as in the WORD DURATION DIFFERENCE model and the BASE DURATION DIFFERENCE model of the ONZE corpus (Table 6.7 and Figure 6.2, last row, first and third panel), CONDITIONAL AFFIX PROBABILITY is associated with shorter durations, as expected. In the two other models where this predictor turned out significant, higher CONDITIONAL AFFIX PROBABILITY is associated with longer durations (Table 6.5 and Figure 6.2, first row, first and third panel). This is unexpected. Overall, we can observe that the effect of CONDITIONAL AFFIX PROBABILITY on duration is neither robust in its significance nor consistent in its direction.

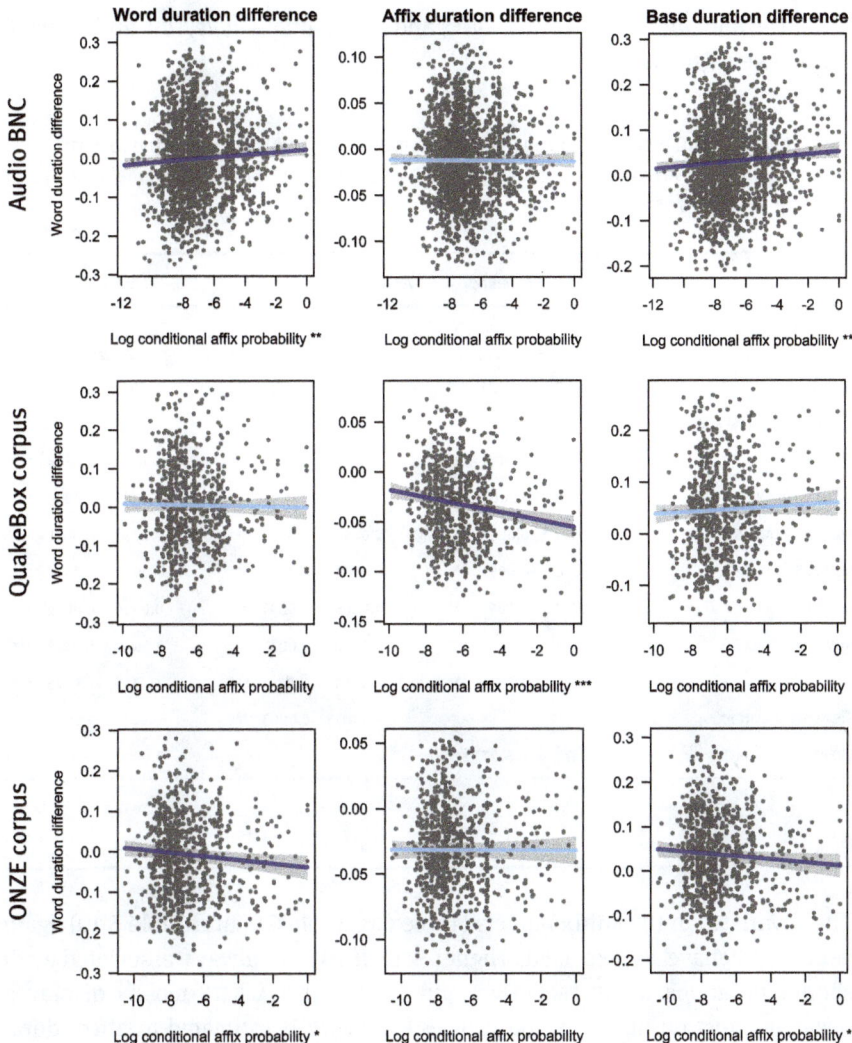

Fig. 6.2: Effects of CONDITIONAL AFFIX PROBABILITY for prefixes in the three corpora. Significance is marked with asterisks and indicating by the shading of the regression line: dark blue for significant effects, light blue for non-significant effects. Non-significant effects are taken from the maximal models.

Let us now examine the results for the suffixes. Table 6.8, Table 6.9, and Table 6.10 (for each corpus, respectively) as well as Figure 6.3 present the models and the plotted effects of interest for suffixes only. Recall that the suffixes are *-ness*,

-less, *-ize*, and *-ation* in the Audio BNC, and *-ness*, *-ation*, *-able*, *-ity*, and *-ment* in the two New Zealand corpora.

Tab. 6.8: Audio BNC models with CONDITIONAL AFFIX PROBABILITY (suffixes only) fitted to WORD DURATION DIFFERENCE, AFFIX DURATION DIFFERENCE, and BASE DURATION DIFFERENCE. Full models are documented at https://osf.io/4h5f3/.

	Word duration difference			Affix duration difference			Base duration difference		
	Estimate	SE		Estimate	SE		Estimate	SE	
Intercept	0.3669	0.0111	***	0.1801	0.0051	***	0.1931	0.0079	***
CONDITIONAL AFFIX PROB	0.0015	0.0007	*				0.0017	0.0005	**
SPEECH RATE	-0.0632	0.0011	***	-0.0349	0.0008	***	-0.0271	0.0008	***
WORD FREQUENCY	-0.0048	0.0009	***				-0.0053	0.0006	***
NUM OF SYLLABLES 3	0.0591	0.0053	***	0.0446	0.0035	***	0.0050	0.0037	
NUM OF SYLLABLES 4	0.0676	0.0053	***	0.0368	0.0029	***	0.0066	0.0037	
NUM OF SYLLABLES 5	0.1072	0.0055	***	0.0466	0.0034	***	0.0324	0.0039	***
NUM OF SYLLABLES 6	0.1533	0.0111	***	0.0502	0.0070	***	0.0640	0.0077	***
NUM OF SYLLABLES 7	0.2806	0.0304	***	0.1078	0.0201	***	0.1545	0.0225	***
BIGRAM FREQUENCY				-0.0011	0.0003	***	0.0012	0.0003	***
BIPHONE PROBABILITY	-2.9877	0.8127	***				-3.0063	0.5723	***
N	5051			5031			5042		
R^2	0.4301			0.3207			0.2451		

The covariates in the suffix models (Table 6.8, Table 6.9, and Table 6.10) again generally behave as expected. Higher SPEECH RATE is always associated with shorter durations. WORD FREQUENCY and BIPHONE PROBABILITY mostly display a negative effect on duration, too. BIGRAM FREQUENCY is estimated to affect durations positively as well as negatively (recall however that this instability is not due to collinearity, as all diagnostics were satisfactory). The NUMBER OF SYLLABLES mostly has a positive effect on duration. Finally, the SUBCORPUS variable again accounts for some variance in the ONZE data (Table 6.10).

Let us now turn to the predictor of interest. For suffixes, CONDITIONAL AFFIX PROBABILITY yields six significant effects out of nine possible cases. No effect could be detected in the AFFIX DURATION DIFFERENCE model of the Audio BNC data (Table 6.8 and Figure 6.3, first row, second panel) and in the WORD DURATION DIFFERENCE and BASE DURATION DIFFERENCE model of the ONZE corpus data (Table 6.10 and Figure 6.3, last row, first and third panel). All other effects are significant (visible in the tables and from the dark blue regression lines in Figure 6.3). However, these effects differ with regard to their direction. The effects on WORD DURATION DIFFERENCE and on BASE DURATION DIFFERENCE (first and last column of Figure 6.3) are positive, which is unexpected. Higher suffix probability is associated with longer durations of base words and their derivatives. The effects on AFFIX DURATION DIFFERENCE, on the other hand (second column of Figure 6.3), are negative, which is expected. Higher suffix probability is associated with shorter suffix durations.

Tab. 6.9: QuakeBox models with CONDITIONAL AFFIX PROBABILITY (suffixes only) fitted to WORD DURATION DIFFERENCE, AFFIX DURATION DIFFERENCE, and BASE DURATION DIFFERENCE. Full models are documented at https://osf.io/4h5f3/.

	Word duration difference			Affix duration difference			Base duration difference		
	Estimate	SE		Estimate	SE		Estimate	SE	
Intercept	0.4407	0.0228	***	0.1193	0.0164	***	0.2361	0.0132	***
CONDITIONAL AFFIX PROB	0.0037	0.0014	**	-0.0027	0.0010	**	0.0034	0.0008	***
SPEECH RATE	-0.0686	0.0022	***	-0.0357	0.0016	***	-0.0264	0.0013	***
WORD FREQUENCY	-0.0123	0.0021	***	0.0043	0.0015	**	-0.0151	0.0012	***
NUM OF SYLLABLES 3	0.0154	0.0100		0.0321	0.0072	***	-0.0078	0.0056	
NUM OF SYLLABLES 4	0.1061	0.0095	***	0.1093	0.0068	***	0.0099	0.0055	
NUM OF SYLLABLES 5	0.1277	0.0111	***	0.1173	0.0080	***	0.0345	0.0064	***
NUM OF SYLLABLES 6	0.1468	0.0237	***	0.1338	0.0168	***	0.0285	0.0141	*
BIGRAM FREQUENCY				-0.0018	0.0006	**	0.0030	0.0005	***
BIPHONE PROBABILITY	-4.5910	1.3988	**	-3.4699	0.9958	***			
N	1762			1707			1718		
R^2	0.4240			0.3343			0.3184		

What do we make of this? It seems that both for prefixes and for suffixes, effects of CONDITIONAL AFFIX PROBABILITY are unreliable in their predictiveness and in their direction. Overall, for both prefixes and suffixes, there are null effects. This is despite the larger datasets in the across-category models compared to the category-internal models (which provide more statistical power), and despite allowing for a higher alpha level of $p < .05$ to consider an effect "significant," compared to the alpha level of $p < .001$ in the category-internal models. For the effects that do emerge as significant, they differ in their direction. Many effects do not play out according to the expectation that higher probability should lead to shorter durations, but some of them do. No convincing pattern can be detected across the models with regard to when CONDITIONAL AFFIX PROBABILITY affects durations positively, and when it does so negatively.

Tab. 6.10: ONZE models with CONDITIONAL AFFIX PROBABILITY (suffixes only) fitted to WORD DURATION DIFFERENCE, AFFIX DURATION DIFFERENCE, and BASE DURATION DIFFERENCE. Full models are documented at https://osf.io/4h5f3/.

	Word duration difference			Affix duration difference			Base duration difference		
	Estimate	SE		Estimate	SE		Estimate	SE	
Intercept	0.3401	0.0242	***	0.1136	0.0130	***	0.1492	0.0155	***
CONDITIONAL AFFIX PROB				-0.0038	0.0008	***			
SPEECH RATE	-0.0569	0.0017	***	-0.0290	0.0012	***	-0.0249	0.0011	***
WORD FREQUENCY	-0.0059	0.0012	***	0.0034	0.0011	**	-0.0053	0.0008	***
NUM OF SYLLABLES 3	0.0308	0.0087	***	0.0178	0.0066	**	0.0075	0.0056	
NUM OF SYLLABLES 4	0.1055	0.0083	***	0.0778	0.0063	***	0.0277	0.0053	***
NUM OF SYLLABLES 5	0.1428	0.0094	***	0.0980	0.0071	***	0.0445	0.0060	***
NUM OF SYLLABLES 6	0.1624	0.0161	***	0.1136	0.0118	***	0.0693	0.0104	***
SUBCORPUS 2014	0.0043	0.0261					0.0262	0.0166	
SUBCORPUS CC	-0.0186	0.0190					-0.0039	0.0120	
SUBCORPUS Darfield	0.0189	0.0193					0.0036	0.0123	
SUBCORPUS IA	0.0076	0.0194					0.0190	0.0123	
SUBCORPUS MU	-0.0087	0.0192					0.0048	0.0122	
SUBCORPUS SOHP	0.0432	0.0196	*				0.0298	0.0124	*
SUBCORPUS Southland	-0.0096	0.0215					0.0170	0.0137	
BIGRAM FREQUENCY				-0.0015	0.0005	**	0.0014	0.0005	**
BIPHONE PROBABILITY	-9.1440	0.9672	***	-5.7216	0.6943	***	-1.9136	0.6161	**
N	2609			2533			2602		
R^2	0.4478			0.3271			0.2627		

For the suffix dataset, the direction of effect seems to be related to the domain of durational measurement. Higher-probability suffixes are themselves mostly produced with shorter durations, while their bases are mostly lengthened (the latter being also reflected in the duration of the whole word). However, for prefixes, the picture is much less clear. This is because for prefixes, there are major differences between the corpora. With rising affix probability, words and bases are sometimes longer (e.g., in the Audio BNC) and sometimes shorter (e.g., in the ONZE corpus). Affixes are shortened in one case. I will discuss the implications of these findings in Section 6.3. Let us now look at the second informativeness measure, SEMANTIC INFORMATION LOAD.

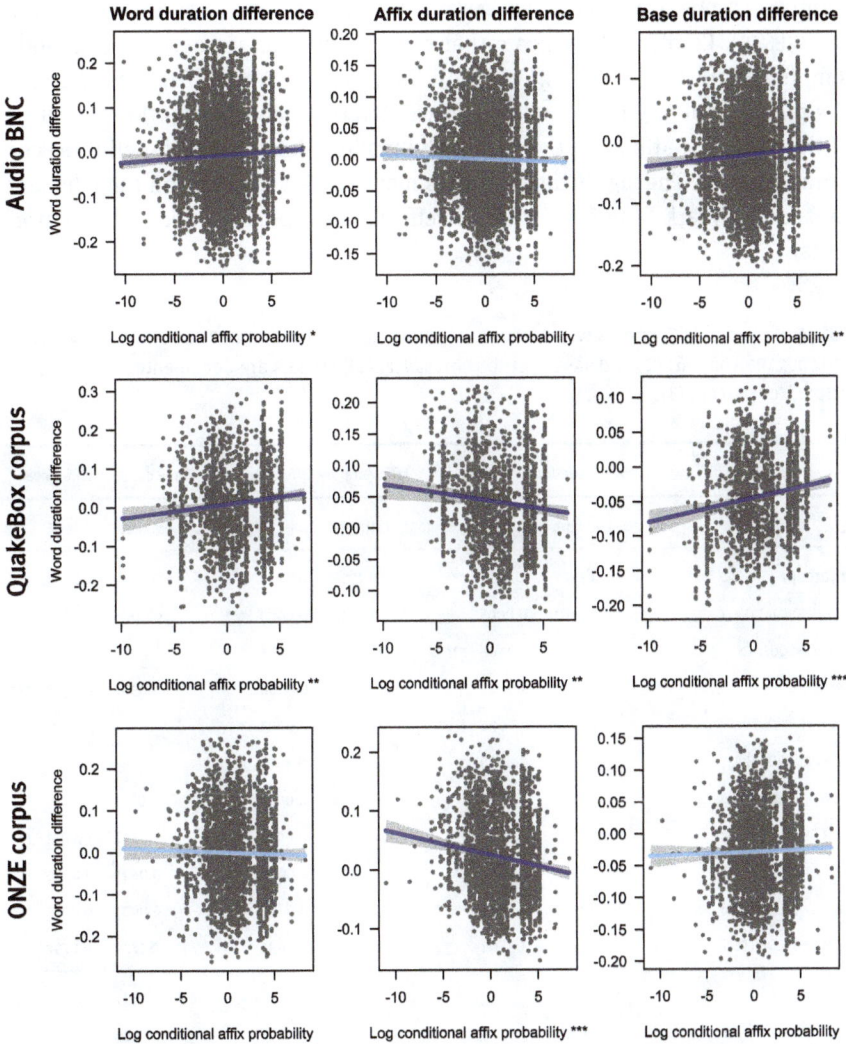

Fig. 6.3: Effects of CONDITIONAL AFFIX PROBABILITY for suffixes in the three corpora. Significance is marked with asterisks and indicating by the shading of the regression line: dark blue for significant effects, light blue for non-significant effects. Non-significant effects are taken from the maximal models.

6.2.2 Semantic information load

Table 6.11 (for the Audio BNC), Table 6.12 (for the QuakeBox corpus), and Table 6.13 (for the ONZE corpus) report the final models with SEMANTIC INFORMATION LOAD effects on the different durational response variables (columns from left to right: WORD DURATION DIFFERENCE, AFFIX DURATION DIFFERENCE, and BASE DURATION DIFFERENCE). Empty cells indicate that the variable was removed during model simplification (see Section 3.4). In addition, Figure 6.4 visualizes the effects of the predictor of interest, SEMANTIC INFORMATION LOAD, on the DURATION DIFFERENCE of the word, the affix, and the base (columns from left to right) for all three corpora (in rows). The significance level is marked with asterisks on the label and by shading (dark blue for significant effects, light blue for non-significant effects).

Tab. 6.11: Audio BNC models with SEMANTIC INFORMATION LOAD fitted to WORD DURATION DIFFERENCE, AFFIX DURATION DIFFERENCE, and BASE DURATION DIFFERENCE. Full models are documented at https://osf.io/4h5f3/.

	Word duration difference			Affix duration difference			Base duration difference		
	Estimate	SE		Estimate	SE		Estimate	SE	
INTERCEPT	0.3407	0.0131	***	0.1954	0.0081	***	0.0799	0.0094	***
SEM INFORMATION LOAD	0.0011	0.0005	*	-0.0014	0.0003	***	0.0066	0.0004	***
WORD FREQUENCY	-0.0034	0.0006	***	-0.0009	0.0004	*	-0.0029	0.0005	***
SPEECH RATE	-0.0617	0.0009	***	-0.0283	0.0006	***	-0.0307	0.0007	***
BIGRAM FREQUENCY	-0.0009	0.0004	*	-0.0007	0.0003	*			
BIPHONE PROBABILITY	-1.4379	0.6483	*	-2.6605	0.4001	***			
NUM OF SYLLABLES 3	0.0469	0.0041	***	0.0163	0.0025	***	0.0321	0.0031	***
NUM OF SYLLABLES 4	0.0578	0.0041	***	0.0145	0.0025	***	0.0380	0.0031	***
NUM OF SYLLABLES 5	0.0932	0.0046	***	0.0198	0.0029	***	0.0625	0.0036	***
NUM OF SYLLABLES 6	0.1372	0.0102	***	0.0188	0.0063	**	0.0937	0.0077	***
NUM OF SYLLABLES 7	0.2793	0.0311	***	0.0780	0.0191	***	0.1770	0.0237	***
N	7133			7099			7102		
R^2	0.4006			0.2627			0.2616		

We can see from the tables that the covariates generally behave as expected. SPEECH RATE has a negative effect on duration. If significant, WORD FREQUENCY, BIGRAM FREQUENCY, and BIPHONE PROBABILITY mostly affect duration negatively.

The NUMBER OF SYLLABLES, however, is mostly estimated to have a positive effect on duration. Some ONZE subcorpora account for durational variation as well.

Tab. 6.12: QuakeBox models with SEMANTIC INFORMATION LOAD fitted to WORD DURATION DIFFERENCE, AFFIX DURATION DIFFERENCE, and BASE DURATION DIFFERENCE. Full models are documented at https://osf.io/4h5f3/.

	Word duration difference		Affix duration difference		Base duration difference	
	Estimate	SE	Estimate	SE	Estimate	SE
Intercept	0.4778	0.0273 ***	0.2846	0.0139 ***	0.1021	0.0195 ***
SEM INFORMATION LOAD	-0.0023	0.0010 *	-0.0092	0.0006 ***	0.0091	0.0007 ***
WORD FREQUENCY	-0.0087	0.0013 ***			-0.0081	0.0009 ***
SPEECH RATE	-0.0688	0.0019 ***	-0.0249	0.0011 ***	-0.0357	0.0013 ***
BIPHONE PROBABILITY	-4.5957	1.3273 ***	-8.3864	0.8075 ***	4.6902	0.9441 ***
NUM OF SYLLABLES 3	-0.0034	0.0068	-0.0109	0.0042 **	0.0003	0.0049
NUM OF SYLLABLES 4	0.0618	0.0070 ***	0.0330	0.0043 ***	0.0215	0.0050 ***
NUM OF SYLLABLES 5	0.0978	0.0094 ***	0.0344	0.0057 ***	0.0613	0.0067 ***
NUM OF SYLLABLES 6	0.0952	0.0212 ***	0.0375	0.0130 **	0.0497	0.0154 **
N	2603		2514		2541	
R^2	0.3911		0.2940		0.3588	

Turning to the predictor of interest, SEMANTIC INFORMATION LOAD, we can see from the tables and figures that in all cases but one, this predictor affects durations significantly. The one case where it fails to do so is WORD DURATION DIFFERENCE in the ONZE corpus (Table 6.13 and Figure 6.4, last row, first panel). In the other 8 models, SEMANTIC INFORMATION LOAD is estimated to be significantly correlated with duration. However, the effects differ in their direction. The duration of words in the Audio BNC (Figure 6.4, first row, first panel) and the duration of bases in all three corpora (Figure 6.4, last row) are positively affected by SEMANTIC INFORMATION LOAD. That is, the more semantically informative an affix is, the longer the duration of its host word and of the base to which it attaches. This is in accordance with hypothesis **H** INF$_{SEM}$. However, the duration of words in the QuakeBox corpus (Figure 6.4, second row, first panel) and the duration of affixes in all three corpora (Figure 6.4, second row) is negatively affected by SEMANTIC INFORMATION LOAD. That is, the more semantically informative an affix is, the shorter the duration of its host word and of the affix itself becomes. This is unexpected.

Tab. 6.13: ONZE models with SEMANTIC INFORMATION LOAD fitted to WORD DURATION DIFFERENCE, AFFIX DURATION DIFFERENCE, and BASE DURATION DIFFERENCE. Full models are documented at https://osf.io/4h5f3/.

	Word duration difference			Affix duration difference			Base duration difference		
	Estimate	SE		Estimate	SE		Estimate	SE	
Intercept	0.3612	0.0202	***	0.2334	0.0169	***	0.0849	0.0188	***
SEM INFORMATION LOAD				-0.0039	0.0005	***	0.0062	0.0006	***
WORD FREQUENCY	-0.0049	0.0010	***	-0.0031	0.0006	***	-0.0029	0.0007	***
SPEECH RATE	-0.0576	0.0015	***	-0.0213	0.0009	***	-0.0306	0.0011	***
SUBCORPUS 2014	0.0479	0.0226	*	0.0041	0.0141		0.0392	0.0167	*
SUBCORPUS CC	-0.0051	0.0163		-0.0203	0.0102	*	-0.0004	0.0121	
SUBCORPUS Darfield	0.0298	0.0167		0.0034	0.0104		0.0123	0.0123	
SUBCORPUS IA	0.0292	0.0167		-0.0113	0.0104		0.0298	0.0123	*
SUBCORPUS MU	0.0106	0.0165		-0.0146	0.0103		0.0123	0.0122	
SUBCORPUS SOHP	0.0524	0.0169	**	0.0084	0.0106		0.0342	0.0124	**
SUBCORPUS Southland	0.0079	0.0189		-0.0307	0.0118	**	0.0180	0.0139	
BIPHONE PROBABILITY	-9.0155	0.8630	***	-7.5103	0.5819	***			
NUM OF SYLLABLES 3	-0.0026	0.0055		-0.0166	0.0036	***	0.0032	0.0043	
NUM OF SYLLABLES 4	0.0599	0.0054	***	0.0208	0.0039	***	0.0230	0.0045	***
NUM OF SYLLABLES 5	0.1011	0.0071	***	0.0349	0.0051	***	0.0451	0.0058	***
NUM OF SYLLABLES 6	0.1270	0.0146	***	0.0522	0.0094	***	0.0747	0.0110	***
N	3623			3505			3608		
R^2	0.4106			0.3005			0.2832		

Can we make sense of these findings? For the present models, we can generalize that more informative affixes become shorter, while their bases become longer. Because of this, it may be speculated that these two effects cancel out effects on the duration of the word as a whole. In fact, the two opposite effects on WORD DURATION DIFFERENCE (positive in the Audio BNC, negative in the QuakeBox corpus) are weaker than the other effects. In addition, in the ONZE corpus, the effect on WORD DURATION DIFFERENCE is non-significant. While this may be the case, it does not explain why affixes should become shorter the more informative they are. **H** INF$_{SEM}$ predicts all constituents (word, affix, and base) to behave the same with regard to informativeness, i.e., to become longer with increasing information load. This will be discussed further in Section 6.3 below.

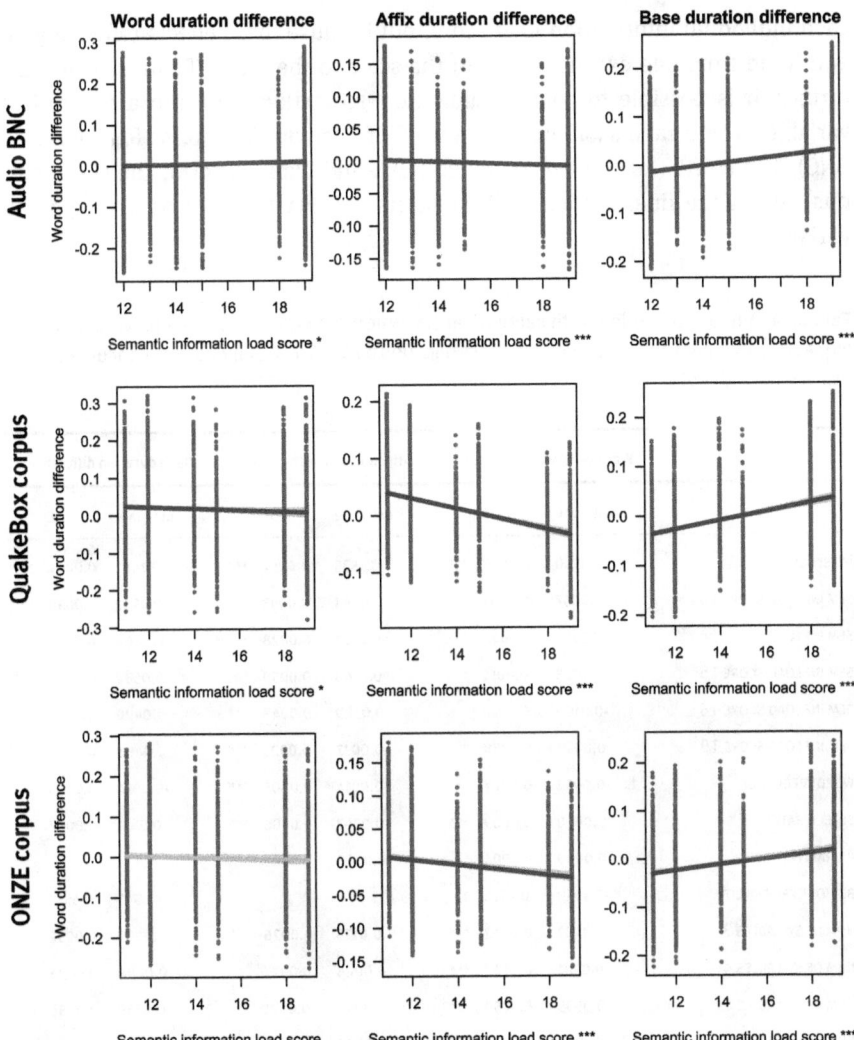

Fig. 6.4: Effects of SEMANTIC INFORMATION LOAD in the three corpora. Significance is marked with asterisks and indicating by the shading of the regression line: dark blue for significant effects, light blue for non-significant effects. Non-significant effects are taken from the maximal models.

One may also examine the behavior of SEMANTIC INFORMATION LOAD in more detail by investigating the patterning of the individual scores in the proposed hierarchy of affixes (see again Table 6.3). It may be the case that the effects come about not because of a constant and reliable increase or decrease in duration by each individual information load score, but because these effects reflect a general trend from one extreme point of the scale to the other. To investigate this further, it is possible to convert SEMANTIC INFORMATION LOAD into a categorical variable, where each score value is a level of a factor. Table 6.14 (for the Audio BNC), Table 6.15 (for the QuakeBox corpus), and Table 6.16 (for the ONZE corpus) report the final models with SEMANTIC INFORMATION LOAD as a categorical variable.

Tab. 6.14: Audio BNC models with categorical SEMANTIC INFORMATION LOAD fitted to WORD DURATION DIFFERENCE, AFFIX DURATION DIFFERENCE, and BASE DURATION DIFFERENCE. Full models are documented at https://osf.io/4h5f3/.

	Word duration difference			Affix duration difference			Base duration difference		
	Estimate	SE		Estimate	SE		Estimate	SE	
Intercept	0.3560	0.0092	***	0.1835	0.0054	***	0.1461	0.0069	***
SEM INF LOAD SCORE 13	0.0057	0.0053		-0.0043	0.0033		0.0261	0.0040	***
SEM INF LOAD SCORE 14	0.0172	0.0048	***	-0.0291	0.0028	***	0.0664	0.0036	***
SEM INF LOAD SCORE 15	0.0125	0.0051	*	-0.0164	0.0030	***	0.0582	0.0039	***
SEM INF LOAD SCORE 18	-0.0100	0.0077		-0.0389	0.0048	***	0.0490	0.0058	***
SEM INF LOAD SCORE 19	0.0096	0.0038	*	0.0077	0.0013	***	0.0488	0.0029	***
WORD FREQUENCY	-0.0032	0.0007	***	-0.0014	0.0004	***	-0.0014	0.0005	**
SPEECH RATE	-0.0620	0.0009	***	-0.0283	0.0006	***	-0.0315	0.0007	***
BIGRAM FREQUENCY	-0.0009	0.0004	*	-0.0008	0.0003	**			
BIPHONE PROBABILITY	-2.3050	0.7395	**				-2.6345	0.5575	***
NUM OF SYLLABLES 3	0.0437	0.0042	***	0.0125	0.0026	***	0.0299	0.0032	***
NUM OF SYLLABLES 4	0.0581	0.0045	***	0.0044	0.0027		0.0484	0.0034	***
NUM OF SYLLABLES 5	0.0935	0.0050	***	0.0099	0.0031	**	0.0739	0.0038	***
NUM OF SYLLABLES 6	0.1376	0.0104	***	0.0093	0.0064		0.1074	0.0078	***
NUM OF SYLLABLES 7	0.2810	0.0311	***	0.0670	0.0191	***	0.1981	0.0234	***
N	7128			7102			7100		
R^2	0.4040			0.2745			0.2905		

From the coefficients in the tables, we can see that in relation to the reference level of SEMANTIC INFORMATION LOAD, which is always the lowest score (12 for the Audio BNC model in Table 6.14, and 11 for the QuakeBox and ONZE models in Table 6.15 and Table 6.16), durations sometimes increase and sometimes decrease with a higher score. That is, when the affix becomes more informative in the sense of having a higher semantic information load, durations may increase or decrease. Sometimes these changes do not reach significance. In general, how many of these changes pattern according to the expectations? For a more convenient overview that enables us to see the answer at a glance, Figure 6.5 plots the effect for SEMANTIC INFORMATION LOAD as a categorical variable for all three corpora and durational domains.

Tab. 6.15: QuakeBox models with categorical SEMANTIC INFORMATION LOAD fitted to WORD DURATION DIFFERENCE, AFFIX DURATION DIFFERENCE, and BASE DURATION DIFFERENCE. Full models are documented at https://osf.io/4h5f3/.

	Word duration difference			Affix duration difference			Base duration difference		
	Estimate	SE		Estimate	SE		Estimate	SE	
Intercept	0.4737	0.0199	***	0.2572	0.0119	***	0.2047	0.0132	***
SEM INF LOAD SCORE 12	-0.0242	0.0065	***	-0.0718	0.0039	***	0.0063	0.0044	
SEM INF LOAD SCORE 14	0.0124	0.0104		-0.0892	0.0061	***	0.0787	0.0073	***
SEM INF LOAD SCORE 15	-0.0555	0.0102	***	-0.0559	0.0061	***	-0.0187	0.0067	**
SEM INF LOAD SCORE 18	-0.0181	0.0104		-0.0992	0.0061	***	0.0740	0.0067	***
SEM INF LOAD SCORE 19	-0.0386	0.0096	***	-0.1240	0.0057	***	0.0557	0.0060	***
WORD FREQUENCY	-0.0087	0.0014	***	-0.0020	0.0008	*	-0.0076	0.0010	***
SPEECH RATE	-0.0692	0.0019	***	-0.0275	0.0011	***	-0.0340	0.0013	***
BIPHONE PROBABILITY	-6.8702	1.3852	***	-8.4251	0.8167	***			
NUM OF SYLLABLES 3	0.0047	0.0072		-0.0008	0.0042		0.0100	0.0050	*
NUM OF SYLLABLES 4	0.0671	0.0075	***	0.0252	0.0044	***	0.0306	0.0052	***
NUM OF SYLLABLES 5	0.0946	0.0098	***	0.0277	0.0058	***	0.0634	0.0066	***
NUM OF SYLLABLES 6	0.0928	0.0214	***	0.0188	0.0125		0.0567	0.0152	***
N	2604			2514			2539		
R^2	0.4036			0.3681			0.3929		

Tab. 6.16: ONZE models with categorical SEMANTIC INFORMATION LOAD fitted to WORD DURATION DIFFERENCE, AFFIX DURATION DIFFERENCE, and BASE DURATION DIFFERENCE. Full models are documented at https://osf.io/4h5f3/.

	Word duration difference			Affix duration difference			Base duration difference		
	Estimate	SE		Estimate	SE		Estimate	SE	
Intercept	0.4032	0.0229	***	0.2654	0.0100	***	0.1345	0.0162	***
SEM INF LOAD SCORE 12	-0.0375	0.0058	***	-0.0786	0.0036	***	-0.0009	0.0042	
SEM INF LOAD SCORE 14	-0.0011	0.0086		-0.0717	0.0052	***	0.0530	0.0063	***
SEM INF LOAD SCORE 15	-0.0425	0.0083	***	-0.0484	0.0051	***	-0.0033	0.0058	
SEM INF LOAD SCORE 18	-0.0204	0.0087	*	-0.0762	0.0053	***	0.0648	0.0063	***
SEM INF LOAD SCORE 19	-0.0565	0.0086	***	-0.1086	0.0052	***	0.0416	0.0058	***
WORD FREQUENCY	-0.0043	0.0011	***	-0.0024	0.0007	***	-0.0024	0.0007	**
SPEECH RATE	-0.0582	0.0015	***	-0.0247	0.0009	***	-0.0305	0.0011	***
SUBCORPUS 2014	0.0403	0.0224					0.0432	0.0164	**
SUBCORPUS CC	0.0028	0.0161					0.0053	0.0118	
SUBCORPUS Darfield	0.0335	0.0164	*				0.0161	0.0121	
SUBCORPUS IA	0.0378	0.0164	*				0.0354	0.0121	**
SUBCORPUS MU	0.0164	0.0162					0.0170	0.0120	
SUBCORPUS SOHP	0.0551	0.0166	***				0.0366	0.0122	**
SUBCORPUS Southland	0.0176	0.0186					0.0253	0.0137	
BIGRAM FREQUENCY	-0.0012	0.0006	*	-0.0012	0.0004	**			
BIPHONE PROBABILITY	-12.1792	0.9590	***	-9.3775	0.5877	***			
NUM OF SYLLABLES 3	0.0021	0.0061		-0.0088	0.0037	*	0.0129	0.0045	**
NUM OF SYLLABLES 4	0.0548	0.0067	***	0.0143	0.0040	***	0.0363	0.0047	***
NUM OF SYLLABLES 5	0.0906	0.0085	***	0.0250	0.0051	***	0.0592	0.0059	***
NUM OF SYLLABLES 6	0.1151	0.0152	***	0.0277	0.0093	**	0.0866	0.0110	***
N	3614			3528			3604		
R^2	0.4271			0.3634			0.3108		

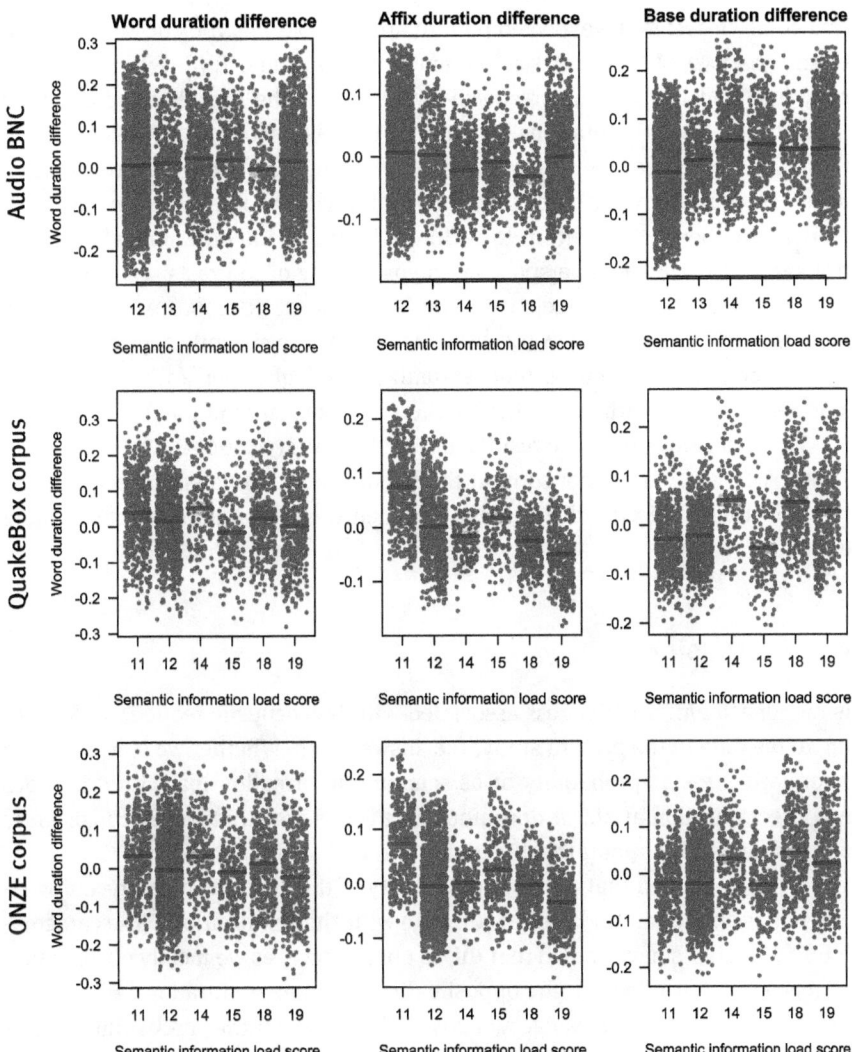

Fig. 6.5: Effects of SEMANTIC INFORMATION LOAD as a categorical variable.

We can see from the contrasts in each plot that the positive and negative effects found in the gradient models are due to a general trend rather than a consistent increase or decrease in duration for each step of the hierarchy. In none of the categorical models, we can observe a consistent pattern that the higher the value of SEMANTIC INFORMATION LOAD, the longer the durations become (and neither can we observe a consistent pattern in the opposite direction). The cases that come closest to the expected pattern are the WORD DURATION DIFFERENCE model and the BASE DURATION DIFFERENCE model in the Audio BNC (Figure 6.5, first row, first and last column, respectively). Here, in the first three score levels (from 12 to 13 to 14), durations increase. In the BASE DURATION DIFFERENCE model, these three steps are significant contrasts (see Table 6.14). However, this pattern does not continue with higher semantic information load scores in the same models. Neither is this pattern to be found in any of the other models. In fact, from an informativeness perspective, the patterning of contrasts seems random. In general, neither the models with gradient SEMANTIC INFORMATION LOAD nor the models with categorical SEMANTIC INFORMATION LOAD consistently support the idea that higher informativeness (conceptualized as higher semantic information load) is associated with less reduction (i.e., with shorter durations).

To foreshadow, both the results for CONDITIONAL AFFIX PROBABILITY and SEMANTIC INFORMATION LOAD do not support the hypotheses formulated in Section 2.1.4. It is now time to discuss the findings and their theoretical implications in more detail.

6.3 Discussion

Is higher affix informativeness associated with less acoustic reduction? According to the data in the present study, the answer is no. Whether we conceptualize informativeness as probability or as semantic information load, it either does not affect duration at all, or does not affect it in a way that would consistently and convincingly support the directional claim of the hypotheses.

H INF_{PROB} claimed that a higher probability of the affix given its preceding element (less informativity) should correlate with shorter durations. The category-internal analyses have shown that this is not the case, as we mostly observe null effects and a few effects in the opposite direction (longer durations with higher probability). The across-category analyses have shown that probability effects vary according to the type of affix (prefix versus suffix), the domain of durational measurement, and according to corpus. Prefixes are generally estimated to be less probable than suffixes, which is why these two types of affix were analyzed separately. The individual datasets of prefixes and suffixes, however, still show internal inconsistencies in significance and direction of effects. This variety of effects is observable even though all models were constructed in the same way and did not indicate collinearity issues (see again Section 3.4). Together, this potpourri of effects is highly unconvincing to me with regard to whether we should believe that affix informativeness (as operationalized here) truly works against acoustic reduction.

H INF_{SEM} claimed that the more loaded with semantic information an affix is (as gauged by the clearness of its semantics, its type of base, its semantic transparency, and its productivity), i.e., the more informative it is, the less reduction should occur. This is often not the case. With increasing semantic information load, we did sometimes observe longer durations, mainly of bases, when treating the predictor of interest as gradient. But sometimes, we also observed shorter durations, mainly of affixes. This different behavior of bases versus affixes cannot be explained by the rationale underlying the informativeness hypothesis H INF_{SEM}. As explained in Section 2.1.4, more meaningful units should be more resistant to reduction, since for particularly important constituents, speakers prioritize making themselves understood over minimizing articulatory effort. This should hold for affixes just as it does for bases. One could even argue that since SEMANTIC INFORMATION LOAD encodes properties of the affix rather than of the base, if anything it should be the affix that becomes more resistant to reduction with higher informativeness. However, this is not borne out by the data of the present study. In addition, treating the information load score as categorical and examining the individual contrasts between the scores revealed a seemingly random patterning of durations. This pattern cannot be ascribed to affix idiosyncrasies in phonological length, as this was controlled for by the response variable (duration difference based on baseline segment duration). Of course, it is important to keep in mind that the semantic information load hierarchy is vulnerable to intra-coder differences and depends on the literature used for coding (as explained in Section 6.1). However, for the present study, we must conclude that higher affix informativeness (as operationalized here) does not convincingly lead to less reduction, i.e., longer durations. Neither words with more unexpectable affixes nor words with more meaningful affixes are more resistant to reduction.

What does this imply in the context of previous research, as well as in the context of the previous findings of this book? Several previous studies have found informativeness measures of various kinds to be predictive for both speech comprehension and speech production, including effects of acoustic reduction of more informative items (see, e.g., Ben Hedia 2019; Hanique et al. 2013; Hanique & Ernestus 2012; Schuppler et al. 2012; Pluymaekers et al. 2010; Bell et al. 2009; Pluymaekers et al. 2005a; Jurafsky et al. 2001; Kuperman et al. 2007; Aylett & Turk 2004). However, as illustrated in detail in Section 2.1.4, these studies operationalize informativeness in vastly different ways and are often not concerned with affix informativeness, but with the informativeness of whole words or even n-grams. Ben Hedia's (2019) study, which did attempt to operationalize the informativeness of affixes, is also characterized by differences compared to the present study. For instance, Ben Hedia (2019) used fewer affixes, and she did not systematically code a semantic information load score, but instead formulated a semantic information load hierarchy without numerical coding. Moreover, informativeness was not operationalized as conditional probability in her study. In an attempt to address the question highlighted in Ben Hedia (2019) of how to compare the syntagmatic probability of derivational prefixes, the present study used conditional affix probability as a usage-based alternative to a comparison of derivational functions. However, this operationalization is apparently not successful. Together, the null results and different directions of effects in the present study thus do not necessarily contradict previous research. They are, however, informative (no pun intended) with regard to which measures may not be worth pursuing if one is interested in operationalizing informativeness.

The results of the present study are also interesting when compared to the other studies so far included in this book. In the previous sections, I have discussed that frequency (Section 2.1.4), morphological segmentability (Section 4.3), as well as prosodic structure (Section 5.3) are conceptually related to informativeness. Let us now explore the respective implications in more detail in this order, starting with frequency.

In Section 2.1.4, I have explained that the conceptual line between informativeness, frequency, and their respective connection to processing difficulty is not at all clear-cut. Not only are there many different ways to operationalize each of those notions, but they also seem to represent similar theoretical ideas. More informative units are supposedly more "costly" to access and process (Milin et al. 2009: 217). At the same time, more frequent units are supposedly easier to access and process. Informativeness and lexical frequency are thus characterized by a negative correlation. More frequent units are less informative, because they are more predictable. Hence, frequency and informativeness can be interpreted in the same way and might capture the same underlying force. With regard to duration, while highly frequent units should be more reduced, highly informative units should be less reduced, or enhanced. As the study in Chapter 4 hardly found any frequency effects on duration, it may thus not be surprising that there are mostly no informativeness effects either. Note, however, that the operationalization of informativeness as CONDITIONAL AFFIX PROBABILITY is closer in spirit to frequency than the operationalization of informativeness as SEMANTIC INFORMATION LOAD. While the metaphor of "informativeness" is ascribed to both measures, they may each capture different properties. This is because while CONDITIONAL AFFIX PROBABILITY is predictability-based (and calculated by using frequencies), SEMANTIC INFORMATION LOAD is estimated by qualitatively comparing semantic criteria (semantic meaning, type of base, semantic transparency, productivity). In addition, the present study investigated the informativeness of affixes, not of words or bases. Affix *frequency*, however, is generally not tested for in the literature (see footnote 4 in Section 2.1.1). In general, though, this study provides no support for theories which assume frequency/informativeness/predictability to modulate the lexical access speed of items from the mental lexicon (see Section 2.1.1, also see again Jaeger & Buz 2017 on the production ease account). Particularly the few effects that go in the opposite direction from what was expected (i.e., those that indicate more highly informative affixes and their bases to be pronounced shorter) speak against this idea. The findings do also not support the communicative account: in the present data, speakers do not enhance the duration of words whose affixes are more informative for the listener (Jaeger & Buz 2017).

Let us now examine the relationship between informativeness and segmentability. In Sections 4.3, I have discussed that morphological segmentability (relative frequency) is related to the idea of transitional probability. To recap, for segmentability, I have explained that a highly segmentable suffixed word features a low transition probability at the boundary. This is because a suffix is less likely to follow a base that occurs more frequently on its own than to follow a base that occurs more frequently in the suffixed derivative (note that for prefixes, this argument cannot be made straightforwardly due to their position preceding the base). A low probability of the transition cue at the boundary makes that transition very informative for a speaker, because its predictiveness for the word is very high. From this perspective, higher transitional probability goes together with less informativeness and lower segmentability. In other words, less segmentable words are less informative. With regard to duration, more informative words (more segmentable ones) should feature longer durations. This contradicts the learnability perspective outlined in Section 4.3. This perspective assumed a low transitional probability to be facilitatory for production, i.e., to be associated with shorter durations, because words with low transitional probabilities can be better learned and discriminated. However, the idea that more informative and segmentable words should be longer is in line with both the segmentability hypothesis **H** FREQ$_{\text{RELATIVE}}$ and with the informativeness hypothesis **H** INF$_{\text{PROB}}$ (and **H** INF$_{\text{SEM}}$ if we assume semantic criteria to gauge the same underlying mechanism of informativeness). In light of the fact that I was not able to detect segmentability effects on duration (see again the study in Chapter 4), it may not be surprising that I also do not find conclusive informativeness effects. Interestingly, in the category-internal models for CONDITIONAL AFFIX PROBABILITY, the affixes for which significant effects emerged were all suffixes, whereas no effects could be detected for prefixes. Since all but one of these effects were unexpectedly positive (longer durations with higher probabilities), one could even interpret this as an additional lack of support for a segmentability effect (or as additional support for the learnability perspective). I do not seriously intend to advocate these interpretations, however: rather, I mention this to make the point that the conceptual interrelatedness of such morphological and psycholinguistic measures enables the researcher to "explain away" unexpected findings by simply reinterpreting their measure and assigning to it another metaphor. I will discuss this highly problematic observation more extensively in the general discussion in Chapter 8.

In addition, recall that due to the way CONDITIONAL AFFIX PROBABILITY was operationalized (Sections 2.1.4 and 6.1), the probability of suffixes is equal to an inverse measure of RELATIVE FREQUENCY. For RELATIVE FREQUENCY, the frequency of the base was divided by the frequency of the word; for CONDITIONAL AFFIX PROBABILITY, the frequency of the word (conceptualized as morpheme bigram frequency) was divided by the frequency of the base. It is not at all surprising that such a measure would yield equally few significant effects as another measure that has already been shown to lack robust results (see Chapter 4).

Finally, let us examine the relationship between informativeness and prosodic structure. At the end of Section 5.3, I have hinted at the idea that stronger prosodic boundaries might be conceptualized as lower transitional probability. This idea can be found, for instance, in the Smooth Signal Redundancy Hypothesis (Aylett & Turk 2004). This hypothesis proposes that the mechanism behind the planning of prosodic structure is the pressure to evenly distribute throughout the utterance the likelihood that the listener recognizes a signal. This idea thus falls into the group of listener-oriented, communicative accounts (Jaeger & Buz 2017). The idea of Smooth Signal Redundancy states that when items are less predictable (more informative), then prosodic boundaries become stronger, and consequently durations become longer (see, e.g., Turk & Shattuck-Hufnagel 2020 for discussion). This is because for less predictable items, durations must be enhanced to make up for the lack of redundancy and to guarantee listener recognition.

This idea is supported by findings that indicate durations to be shorter and cross-boundary phonology to be more likely in items that are highly predictable. For example, Côté (2013) has suggested that words associated with high transitional probabilities are more likely to be subject to liaison in French (*liaison* refers to the insertion of an additional consonant, as in *plus utile* 'more useful': [ply] + [ytil] = [plyzytil]). In addition, Michel Lange et al. (2017) found that brain-damaged speakers who make few anticipatory speech errors more likely fail to apply cross-boundary phonology; in other words, they found that more anticipatory errors are associated with more liaison. If the transitional probability is low, speakers are worse in predicting the following phonological material and therefore are less likely to make anticipatory speech errors because they fail to plan ahead. In this case, they less often apply cross-boundary phonology (liaison); the "boundary" is therefore stronger. Thus, lower probability, or more informativity, according to this rationale, goes together with less prosodic integration. This would fit with the expectations from H PROS in Section 2.1.3, as both lower probability and less integration should be associated with less reduction, i.e., longer durations.

The study in Chapter 5 found that in many cases, prosodic boundaries as postulated from a traditional perspective of structural analysis (Raffelsiefen 2007, 1999) cannot account for durational variation in the expected way. The study in the present chapter can now extend this conclusion to prosodic boundaries as postulated from a usage-based probability perspective. One of the informativeness measures in the present study, CONDITIONAL AFFIX PROBABILITY, can be conceptualized as the transitional probability between the affix and whatever item precedes it (the base in the case of suffixes, and the preceding word in the case of prefixes). The results have shown that CONDITIONAL AFFIX PROBABILITY cannot satisfactorily account for the variation in acoustic duration. This is because there are many null effects and effects in unexpected directions that do not follow a clear pattern in terms of where they emerge. Transitional probability does not provide a better account of the data than prosodic categories.

From the perspective of transitional probability (both if viewed from a segmentability or prosodic angle), we can, however, make sense of the finding that the probability of prefixes was always lower than that of suffixes (see again Figure 6.1). An affix is much more probable and therefore predictable when it follows the base, as in this case the suffix of a derived word may be foreshadowed by the appearance of the base. However, the prefix of a derived word cannot be foreshadowed by its base, as the prefix precedes the base. This contrast between prefixes and suffixes will potentially be even stronger in less segmentable words: in these cases, suffixes will be even more predictable, given that the base occurs less often on its own and more often with its suffix. This connection between probability/predictability/informativeness and segmentability could be worthwhile to explore further in future studies.

Of course, similar to other measures in the decompositional perspective, there is one problem with the view of the present study on informativeness and probability: I investigated the informativeness of affixes, not of words, i.e., the rationale of the study hinges on the crucial assumption that we decompose words into affixes and bases. If affixes do not exist (i.e., if a "complex" word is perceived as a simplex word by a speaker or listener), then the probability of an affix may not play a role in processing. The frequency of bases, morphemic boundaries, the informativeness of affixes – what if these are not predictive because the constituents on which they are based have no cognitive reality in the first place? The non-decompositional perspective may offer an alternative approach, which may be able to explain some effects in an alternative way (for example, reconceptualize predictability as certainty based on associative strength). It is this alternative perspective that the next and final study will take.

7 Linear discriminative learning

To explore the non-decompositional perspective, it was decided to investigate measures derived from linear discriminative learning networks. As explained in Section 2.2.1, due to the explorative nature of the study, it was dispreferred to formulate concrete hypotheses regarding individual LDL-derived measures. Instead, I asked more generally with **Q** LDL$_{PREDICT}$ whether LDL-derived measures are comparable to traditional measures in their predictiveness for acoustic duration (WORD DURATION DIFFERENCE). In addition, **Q** LDL$_{INTERPRET}$ was formulated to guide the interpretation of effects. What do effects of LDL measures tell us about speech processing? They should be informative with regard to the interaction of cognitive processes and acoustic reduction. Finally, I asked with **Q** LDL$_{NETWORKS}$ whether there would be differences in the networks and in the durational effects of their measures between different semantic and morphological specifications of the network architectures.[1]

7.1 Method

The methodology consists of three main steps: first, selecting a subset of the speech data which provides the durational measurements (Section 7.1.1), second, building the LDL networks to retrieve LDL-derived predictors of interest (Sections 7.1.2 to 7.1.5) and third, devising regression models to predict derivative durations from various predictors (Section 7.1.6).

7.1.1 Dataset

The morphological categories selected for investigation in the present study are DIS, NESS, LESS, ATION, and IZE from the Audio BNC. This constitutes a subset of the total set of categories described in Section 3.1. Selecting a subset was necessary because not all morphological categories investigated in this book are attested in Baayen et al.'s (2019b) vector space (explained below). Again, it was made sure that the affixes associated with the remaining morphological categories still cover a wide spectrum of characteristics traditionally considered important for affix classification (see Section 3.1).

---

[1] An earlier version of the study in the present chapter was published in Stein & Plag (2021). It was only minimally altered for this book.

After reducing the Audio BNC dataset based on morphological categories, in a second step, the dataset was further reduced based on individual words to make it usable for LDL. To construct a linear discriminative learning network, it is necessary to obtain semantic vectors that represent the words' meanings (this will be explained in more detail in Section 7.1.3). For this, I made use of the vectors generated by Baayen et al. (2019b) from the TASA corpus (Landauer et al. 1998; Ivens & Koslin 1991). Baayen and colleagues used an algorithm to predict words in each sentence of the corpus from other words in that sentence. To make sure that I can use these semantic vectors for the present derivatives, I first reduced the speech dataset from the Audio BNC to those derivatives that are attested in TASA (losing 352 words). In a second step, I used the CELEX lexical database (Baayen et al. 1995) to obtain phonological transcriptions for the words in the dataset. These transcriptions are necessary for constructing the matrices. Since CELEX did not have transcriptions for all words, this step led to a slight reduction of the dataset (losing 9 words). In a final step, I excluded all derivatives (49 words) whose bases were already complex, i.e., all derivatives that have more than one derivational function (e.g., *stabilization, specification, attractiveness, disclosure, disagreement*). One reason for excluding these derivatives is that it is currently not clear how to build their semantic vectors. Another reason is that multi-affixed words in corpora are comparatively infrequent. Too infrequent derivatives might require a corpus even bigger than TASA from which to construct reliable semantic vectors.

Tab. 7.1: Overview of tokens and types per morphological category for LDL models from the Audio BNC. Counts represent initial numbers before excluding outliers during statistical modeling.

	Tokens	Types
DIS	233	35
NESS	344	49
LESS	145	31
ATION	3403	209
IZE	405	39

The final dataset of derivatives that entered the models comprised 4530 tokens and 363 types. Table 7.1 gives an overview of the data in each morphological category. As in the previous studies, further descriptive statistics of the datasets can be accessed at https://osf.io/4h5f3/.

7.1.2 Training data

The aim is to predict the durational patterning in the 4530-token dataset described above with measures derived from an LDL network. These measures can be calculated on the basis of a transformation matrix that maps a cue matrix C for forms onto a semantic matrix S for meanings (for comprehension), and the semantic matrix S onto the cue matrix C (for production). The basic building blocks used to construct the meaning dimensions in matrix S are referred to as *lexomes*. Lexomes are atomic units of meaning in an LDL network and serve as pointers to semantic vectors. In comprehension, they are also the 'outcomes' in the S matrix, which are predicted from the 'cues' in the C matrix. Lexomes can for example correspond to words (content lexomes, such as LEMON), but also to derivational or inflectional functions (function lexomes, such as NESS).

It is important to understand that function lexomes correspond to morphological categories but are not the same thing as morphemes. In LDL, morphological categories (like NESS) are coded as semantic vectors and are not units of form and meaning, but units of meaning only. LDL does not assume any fixed relationship between form and meaning. Meanings are dynamically mapped onto a stream of forms (overlapping triphones in this case, see Section 7.1.3), but never defined as being tied to strings that we would traditionally describe as being "morphemic". In other words, LDL's lexomes are pointers to meanings only, not to forms. Further below, I will explain how these lexomes and their vectors were obtained, how the matrices were constructed, and how these matrices were mapped onto each other.

As explained in Section 7.1.1, the dataset for the present study contained 363 unique derivatives (i.e., types). This dataset consists of all derivatives from the Audio BNC that are also attested in TASA. One problem with this dataset is that it would be rather unrealistic as training data for a discriminative network. This is because a speaker encounters far more than just a few hundred words during their lifetime, and not all these encountered words contain one of the five investigated morphological categories DIS, NESS, LESS, ATION, and IZE. It was therefore decided to merge this dataset with all words in TASA that had already been coded in Baayen et al. (2019b) for derivational functions (function lexomes) and phonological transcriptions (4880 more words). This dataset contained 897 derivatives with the 25 derivational function lexomes AGAIN, AGENT, DIS, EE, ENCE, FUL, IC, INSTRUMENT, ATION, ISH, IST, IVE, IZE, LESS, LY, MENT, MIS, NESS, NOT, ORDINAL, OUS, OUT, SUB, UNDO, and Y, as well as 3983 monomorphemic words. Derivational functions were coded irrespective of variation in affix spelling. Most of these words are not attested in the speech data of the present study and therefore not of interest for the durational modeling, but including them makes the training itself more realistic.

The resulting 5176 unique wordforms were then used for the C matrix, and the 5201 unique lexomes (comprising the vectors for the 5176 content lexomes and the 25 derivational function lexomes) were used for the S matrix. The next section illustrates what these matrices are and how they are constructed.

7.1.3 Matrices for form and meaning

In an LDL network, features of a word are represented by a vector for this word in a multidimensional space. Each word has a vector that specifies its form features and a vector that specifies its semantic features. Two matrices are therefore required: a cue matrix C for the words' forms and a semantic matrix S for the words' meanings.

Tab. 7.2: Schematic examples of a cue matrix C (left) and a semantic matrix S (right) for the words *cat, happiness, walk,* and *lemon*. Note that for the triphones in the C matrix, word boundaries are also counted, represented by a hash (#). The DISC phonetic alphabet is used for computer-readable transcription (Burnage 1990).

Schematic example of a C matrix						Schematic example of an S matrix				
	#k{	k{t	{t#	#h{	h{p		CAT	HAPPINESS	WALK	LEMON
k{t	1	1	1	0	0	k{t	0.00000	-6.24e-05	4.71e-05	-0.00013
h{pInIs	0	0	0	1	1	h{pInIs	-0.00011	0.000000	0.00019	-2.20e-05
w$k	0	0	0	0	0	w$k	0.00030	-0.000233	0.00000	-3.74E-05
lEm@n	0	0	0	0	0	lEm@n	-7.28e-05	-2.41e-07	-2.68e-05	0.00000

The cue matrix C contains in rows the words' phonological transcriptions, and in columns form indicators that are either present or absent in those words. As shown in Arnold et al. (2017) and Shafaei-Bajestan et al. (2020), it is possible to use real-valued features extracted directly from the speech signal instead of discrete features. In the present study, I used triphones as form indicators, following Baayen et al. (2019b). These triphones overlap and can be understood as proxies for transitions in the articulatory signal. As explained in Section 2.2.1, they are thus not to be understood as fixed symbolic chunks that "have" meaning. Each cell in the matrix codes in a binary fashion (1 for present or 0 for absent) whether the respective triphone string (specified in the column) occurs in the phonological transcription of the word (specified in the row). An example of the layout of the C matrix is given in Table 7.2 on the left-hand side. For the C matrix in this study, I used the 5176 unique wordforms mentioned in Section 7.1.2.

The semantic matrix S contains in its rows the words' phonological transcriptions, and in its columns the semantic dimensions, or lexomes, with which the words are associated. In the present study, these lexomes correspond to interpretable linguistic items, such as words and derivational functions. Each cell in the S matrix contains a real number, which represents the association strength of a word (specified in the row) to a lexome (specified in the column). As mentioned in Section 2.2.1, this is an important difference of LDL compared to NDL, where word meanings are initially coded as binary-valued vectors similar to the cue matrix. LDL, on the other hand, starts out with real-valued association weights. An example of the layout of the S matrix is given in Table 7.2 on the right-hand side. For the S matrix in this study, I used the 5201 unique lexomes mentioned in Section 7.1.2.

Where do these association weights come from? In the present study, I used association weights that were generated from word co-occurrence in real language data. For this, Baayen et al. (2019b) trained an NDL network on the TASA corpus (Landauer et al. 1998; Ivens & Koslin 1991). This NDL network operated on an established learning algorithm (Widrow & Hoff 1960) that incrementally learns association strengths between lexomes. In such an approach, words in a sentence are predicted from the words in that sentence. While the network goes through the sentences in the corpus, the associations strengths of the lexomes with each other are continuously adjusted over time. As language learning is about learning which connections are relevant, the association strength of lexomes that often occur together will be strengthened. As discriminative learning is also about unlearning connections that are irrelevant, similarly, the association strength of lexomes will be weakened each time they do not occur together. For the implementational and mathematical details of this procedure and for the validation of the resulting semantic vector space, the reader is referred to Baayen et al. (2019b). Importantly for the present study, Baayen and colleagues included lexomes not only for words, but also for derivational functions corresponding to suffixes and prefixes. This enables the researcher to build LDL networks that take into account morphological categories shared between derivatives (in addition to an LDL network that does not take these into account and treats all words as idiosyncratic, i.e., as having a unique semantics that is not related to the semantics of constituents below the word level).

The so-called *lexome-to-lexome matrix* resulting from this learning process is a vector space in which each lexome vector represents a certain association with the meanings of all other lexomes. According to the idea that "you shall know a word by the company it keeps" (Firth 1957, see again Section 2.2.1), each value in the vector of a lexome represents the association strength of this lexome to the meaning of another lexome in TASA. Following Baayen et al. (2019b), I used a version of their lexome-to-lexome matrix that was trimmed to about five thousand dimensions and whose main diagonal was set to zero.[2] From this lexome-to-lexome matrix, I extracted the vectors for the 5201 unique lexomes (described in Section 7.1.2), which I then used for the S matrix.

As foreshadowed in Section 2.2.1, for the present study, I built three different LDL networks that differ in what kind of explicit semantic and morphological information they are provided with. I will call these three networks the *Idiosyncratic Network*, the *Morphology Network*, and the *Base Network*. For each of these networks we need a matrix S and a matrix C. I will refer to the matrices of the Idiosyncratic Network as matrix S_I and matrix C_I, to the matrices of the Morphology Network as matrix S_M and matrix C_M, and to the matrices of the Base Network as matrix S_B and matrix C_B. Let me now explain the purpose and construction of these three networks in more detail.

The Idiosyncratic Network with matrices S_I and C_I does not include any information about morphological category and treats all derivatives as idiosyncratic. The Idiosyncratic Network considered only the semantic vector of the derivative lexome (e.g., only the vector for HAPPINESS, which can be represented as $\overrightarrow{happiness}$). This vector was taken as is from the lexome-to-lexome matrix and straightforwardly entered matrix S_I for each word. This way, the vector contains only idiosyncratic information, and no information about any shared morphological category. In this case, both forms and meanings are maximally non-decompositional.

The Morphology Network with matrices S_M and C_M used vectors that include semantic information about the derivative and about the morphological category it belongs to. This operationalization is still non-decompositional, but it makes explicit the semantic similarity between words of one morphological category, i.e., the abstraction of or analogy between whole words (see Section

---

[2] The main diagonal of a lexome-to-lexome matrix represents the association strengths of each word to itself. Each word occurring in a sentence naturally predicts itself very well to occur in that sentence, but this value is not very informative about the word's relation to other words. Baayen et al. (2019b) therefore argue that when the researcher is interested in semantic similarity, they should replace these values with zero values.

2.2). Mathematically, this network made use of the semantic vector of the content lexome of the derivative (e.g., the vector for HAPPINESS, i.e., $\overrightarrow{happiness}$) and the semantic vector of the corresponding derivational function lexome (e.g., the vector for NESS, which can be represented as $\overrightarrow{NESS}$).[3] I took both these vectors from the lexome-to-lexome matrix, and the sum of these two vectors entered matrix S_M for each word. That is, the semantic vector associated with the word *happiness* was the sum of the vectors for HAPPINESS and NESS: $\overrightarrow{happiness} + \overrightarrow{NESS}$. This way, the resulting vector contains idiosyncratic information, but also information about the morphological category it shares with other derivatives. Thus, we are dealing with a non-decompositional operationalization that explicitly codes for the semantic similarity between words of one morphological category. While it is also conceivable to add to the vector of NESS the vector of HAPPY (instead of HAPPINESS), taking HAPPINESS better reflects the fact that derived words most often still carry some idiosyncratic meaning, i.e., signify more than merely the sum of their parts. The combination of HAPPINESS and NESS, thus, takes into account the morphological category NESS that the word shares with other derivatives, but still acknowledges that English derivatives are not characterized by strictly compositional semantics.

Finally, the Base Network with matrices S_B and C_B uses vectors that include semantic information about the base word (instead of the derivative) and about the morphological category. This network still refrains from the classic sign-based, morphemic view because its forms are still represented subsymbolically, i.e., non-decompositionally. However, this network is *semantically* compositional because it assumes the semantics of a derivational function to be added to the semantics of a base word. Mathematically, the Base Network uses the semantic vectors of the content lexomes of the bases of derived words and the vectors of the derivational function lexomes. That is, instead of adding the derivational lexome vector to the lexome vector of the derivative as in the Morphology Network, in the Base Network I added the derivational lexome vector to the content lexome vector of the derivative's base. For instance, the semantic vector associated with the word *happiness* in matrix S_B is the sum of the vectors for HAPPY and NESS: $\overrightarrow{happy} + \overrightarrow{NESS}$. This way, the resulting vector contains information about the morphological category it shares with other derivatives, like in the Morphology Network. But unlike the Morphology Network, it contains no idiosyncratic information at all. The meaning of complex words in the Base Network is assumed (against our better knowledge) to be strictly compositional.

---

[3] Note that the form matrices C_I, C_M, and C_B are identical, as the networks only differ in their construction of semantic vectors, not of form vectors.

While the forms in the network are still non-decompositional, and the network is therefore irreconcilable with the decompositional perspective (especially with the sign-based view), its semantics are compositional. In principle, this property makes this network unattractive and less suitable for predicting word durations from the non-decompositional perspective, but it can be fruitfully used to gain further insights into the differences between architectures.

We now have three matrices (for each morphological setup respectively) of the layout shown in Table 7.2. We have the C matrix, containing information about form, and the S matrix, containing information about meaning. These matrices can now be mapped onto each other.

7.1.4 Comprehension and production mapping

In speech comprehension, a speaker encounters a form and needs to arrive at the corresponding meaning. Therefore, for comprehension we calculate a transformation matrix F which maps the semantic matrix S onto the cue matrix C, so that

$$CF = S. \tag{7.1}$$

In speech production, on the other hand, a speaker starts out with a meaning and needs to find the right form to express this meaning. Therefore, for production we calculate a transformation matrix G which maps the cue matrix C onto the semantic matrix S, so that

$$SG = C. \tag{7.2}$$

Mathematically, the transformation matrices F and G can be calculated by multiplying the generalized inverse (Penrose 1955; Moore 1920) of C with S (for comprehension) and the generalized inverse of S with C (for production). The transformations are visually illustrated in Figure 7.1.

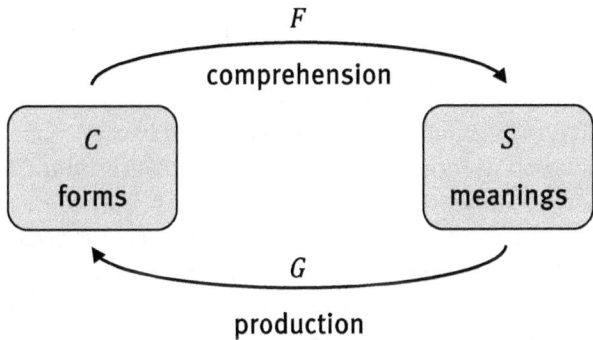

Fig. 7.1: Comprehension and production mapping, adapted from Baayen et al. (2019b). For comprehension, transformation matrix F transforms the cue matrix C into the semantic matrix S. For production, transformation matrix G transforms the semantic matrix S into the cue matrix C.

As soon as we have obtained the transformation matrices, we can use them to estimate what forms and meanings the network would predict. For this, we calculate the predicted matrices $\hat{S}$ and $\hat{C}$. For comprehension, we multiply the form matrix C with the transformation matrix F, i.e., we solve $\hat{S} = CF$. For production, we multiply the semantic matrix S with the transformation matrix G, i.e., we solve $\hat{C} = SG$. It is important to keep in mind that the mappings are simple linear transformations that are achieved by matrix multiplication (for an introduction in the context of LDL, see Baayen et al. 2019b). It is possible to think of the transformation matrices F and G as coefficients in linear regression, which try to approximate the target matrix but will not produce exactly the same values. This is true especially for large datasets like in the present study. The predicted matrices $\hat{S}$ and $\hat{C}$ are thus not exactly the same as the original matrices S and C.

One challenge with using mappings of triphone chunks of sublexical form onto meaning is that while we can predict which triphones are in a word, we have no information about their order (Baayen et al. 2019b). The present implementation of LDL addresses this challenge by ordering the triphones into target wordforms. Concatenating the triphones is possible because the triphones overlap (compare again the C matrix in Table 7.2). To properly order the triphones, LDL uses an algorithm based on graph theory from the igraph package (Csardi & Nepusz 2006). Which triphones are selected is based on their transitional probabilities, i.e., the support each triphone receives in the network from its predicted semantic vector. The most highly supported triphones will be selected, eventually forming an articulatory 'path' trough the maze of triphones. This results in the predicted word form. An toy example of such a path for the word *lawless* is given below in Section 7.1.5.

We can also use the predicted matrices to evaluate model accuracy. To see how well the model predicts the semantics of an individual word in comprehension, we can multiply an observed form vector c from the cue matrix with the transformation matrix F to obtain a predicted semantic vector $\hat{s}$. We can then see how similar this predicted semantic vector $\hat{s}$ is to the target semantic vector s. For production, in turn, we can multiply an observed meaning vector s from the semantic matrix with the transformation matrix G to obtain the predicted form vector $\hat{c}$, which represents the estimated support for the triphones. We can then see how similar this predicted form vector $\hat{c}$ is to the target form vector c. If the correlation between the estimated vector and the targeted vector, i.e., between $\hat{s}$ and s or between $\hat{c}$ and c, respectively, is the highest among the correlations, a meaning or form is correctly recognized or produced. The overall percentage of correctly recognized meanings or forms is referred to as comprehension accuracy and production accuracy, respectively.

To obtain the mappings, I used the learn_comprehension() and learn_production() functions from the R package WpmWithLDL (Baayen et al. 2019a). Accuracy estimations were obtained with the functions accuracy_comprehension() and accuracy_production(). Finally, the measures of interest that I use to predict the durations were extracted from the networks with the help of the comprehension_measures() function and the production_measures() function. While the present study models word durations, which are the result of speech production, both speech production and speech comprehension mappings produce relevant measures for the analysis of production data. This is because the emergent structure of the learner's lexicon is determined both by the association of forms with meanings and of meanings with forms. In LDL, like in human learning, production and comprehension are inextricably linked to each other (see Baayen et al. 2019b for discussion, and Chuang et al. 2020 for another study following this rationale). I will now describe these measures in more detail.

7.1.5 LDL variables

As described above, many potentially useful LDL measures can be extracted automatically from the matrices by the package WpmWithLDL (Baayen et al. 2019a). However, some of the variables provided by this package capture similar things and are strongly correlated with each other. Careful variable selection, and sometimes adaptation, was therefore necessary. Below I illustrate the selection and explain the conceptual dimensions each variable aims to capture.

MEAN WORD SUPPORT

MEAN WORD SUPPORT is a measure that I introduce to capture how well supported on average transitions from one triphone to the next are in the production of a word. Taken together, these transitions are referred to as an articulatory 'path' (see again Section 7.1.4). MEAN WORD SUPPORT is calculated based on the variable PATH SUM from the package WpmWithLDL. PATH SUM refers to the summed semantic support that a given predicted articulatory path receives from its corresponding predicted semantic vector $\hat{s}$, i.e., the path from one triphone to the next in the predicted form of a word. This is illustrated in Figure 7.2 with the toy example *lawless*.

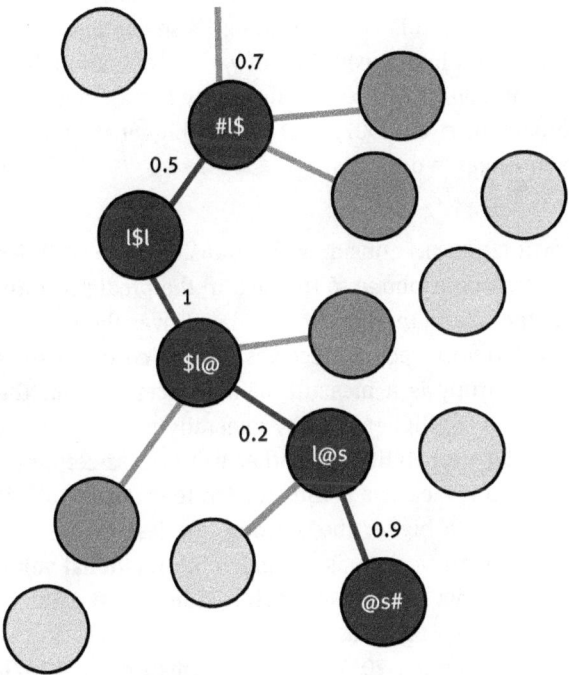

Fig. 7.2: Toy example of an articulatory path for the word *lawless*. Each connection between a triphone node is assigned a probability of being selected against other triphones.

Each node in the path, i.e., each triphone, has a certain probability of being selected against all the other possible triphones when trying to produce a word based on its semantics. The maximum value per transition is therefore 1, i.e., a hundred percent probability of being selected. However, with longer words, there are also more transitions. For example, if a word's form is perfectly predicted across all triphone transitions, but there are five such transitions, PATH SUM would take the value 5. Thus, the problem with PATH SUM is that it increases not only with higher support, but also with increasing segmental length of words. This would not be ideal as a measure of semantic support when modeling durations, since durations naturally increase with longer words. The interpretation of PATH SUM as a measure for mere semantic support would be difficult. Therefore, it was decided to divide each value of PATH SUM, i.e., each summed support of a word's path, by the number of path nodes in a word. This new variable MEAN WORD SUPPORT controls for path length and only reflects the average transition support in each word. MEAN WORD SUPPORT can be read as a metaphor for certainty. The higher the average transition probabilities in a word, the more certain the speaker is in pronouncing this word based on its semantics. Based on previous studies that have found higher certainty of various operationalizations to be associated with lengthening (Tucker et al. 2019a; Tomaschek et al. 2019; Cohen 2015, 2014; Kuperman et al. 2007), words with higher MEAN WORD SUPPORT can be expected to be longer in duration.

PATH ENTROPIES

Like MEAN WORD SUPPORT, PATH ENTROPIES considers the transition probabilities between nodes in the path from one triphone to the next in the predicted form of a word. PATH ENTROPIES is the Shannon entropy calculated over the support that a given path in the predicted form vector $\hat{c}$ receives from its corresponding predicted semantic vector $\hat{s}$. Entropy is a measure of the uncertainty in the choice of one of several alternatives. Higher entropy generally means a larger number of possibilities of similar probabilities, in other words, less certainty. Similarly to MEAN WORD SUPPORT, this measure is thus related to certainty, albeit in a conceptually different way. The higher the entropy, the less certain the speaker is in producing a word, because there is not much informational value in the path support differences. Higher PATH ENTROPIES thus indicate more uncertainty. Based on the above-mentioned previous studies on certainty (Tucker et al. 2019a; Tomaschek et al. 2019; Cohen 2015, 2014; Kuperman et al. 2007), words with higher PATH ENTROPIES can thus be expected to be shorter.

SEMANTIC VECTOR LENGTH

SEMANTIC VECTOR LENGTH refers to the L1 distance, also known as taxicab distance, Manhattan distance, or city-block distance, of $\hat{s}$. It thus measures the length of the predicted semantic vector by summing the vector's absolute values. It was decided to use the L1 distance instead of the correlated L2 distance, as the former does not lose information by smoothing over the city-block distance. The longer the predicted semantic vector becomes, the stronger the links to other lexomes become. SEMANTIC VECTOR LENGTH can thus be understood as a measure of semantic activation diversity. It is the extent to which a given word predicts other words. As a result, it can also be understood as a measure of polysemy. The more semantic dimensions a speaker is active on for a word and the more other meanings the word can predict, the more collocational relations it has and the more varied and confusable the meanings of this word are (cf. Tucker et al. 2019a, also cf. the notion of "sense uncertainty" in Filipović Đurđević & Kostić 2021). Following Tucker et al. (2019a), words with higher activation diversity can be expected to be shorter: the speaker is more uncertain when more meanings are activated and therefore invests less energy in maintaining the signal.

SEMANTIC DENSITY
SEMANTIC DENSITY refers to the mean correlation of $\hat{s}$ with the semantic vectors of its top 8 neighbors' semantic vectors. A strong average correlation of the estimated semantic vector with the vectors of its neighbors means that the neighboring words are semantically very similar to the word in question. The higher the density, the more semantically similar these words are. SEMANTIC DENSITY applied to derived words is thus an important measure of semantic transparency: Words in a dissimilar neighborhood are idiosyncratic and their meaning is not predictable. Words in a semantically similar neighborhood are semantically transparent, i.e., mathematically shifted in the same direction. It is currently unclear whether one should expect a facilitatory or inhibitory effect of measures related to semantic transparency on duration. I explore this question in more detail in the discussion in Section 7.3.

TARGET CORRELATION
TARGET CORRELATION refers to the correlation between a word's predicted semantic vector $\hat{s}$ and the word's target semantic vector s. This is a measure for how accurate the network is in predicting meaning based on form. The closer the predicted meaning to the actual targeted meaning, the more successful is the model, and the better is the learner in making the correct connection between form and meaning. Being better in making the correct connection between form and meaning could be expected to have a facilitatory effect in both comprehension and production, i.e., in the present case, to lead to shorter durations.

7.1.6 Modeling word durations

As mentioned above, the present study explored the predictiveness of measures for the duration of the derived word as a whole, i.e., for WORD DURATION DIFFERENCE. Due to the distributional properties of the words in the present dataset, it was decided to fit both standard multiple linear regression models and mixed-effects regression models to the data. In the dataset, there are many types that are attested only once, which precludes the use of mixed-effects regression.[4] Having many single observations for one type involves the danger that certain word types may become too influential in the model. Mixed-effects regression, on the other hand, can prevent certain word types from being too influential in the model but necessitates the exclusion of items for which no repeated measurements are available. For the present study, it was decided to address this problem by fitting and documenting both types of model.

Model creation, criticism, and simplification followed the procedure described in Section 3.4. For the standard regression models, the trimming resulted in a loss of 82 observations (1.8 % of the data) for the model based on the Idiosyncratic Network, and 74 observations (1.6 % of the data) for the models based on the Morphology Network and the Base Network. For the mixed models, I only included word types that occurred more than once (reducing the dataset from 363 to 261 types, or from 4530 to 4358 observations). The trimming procedure for the mixed models resulted in a loss of 71 observations (1.6 % of the data) for the models based on the Idiosyncratic Network and the Base Network, and 70 observations (1.6 % of the data) for the model based on the Morphology Network.

Conceptually, it is desirable to not have any traditional linguistic covariates in the models that are not derived from the network, such as lexical frequencies, neighborhood densities, or bigram frequencies. It is important to build models instead that contain LDL-derived variables only. This is because, first, the present study is interested in how well an LDL network fares on its own in predicting speech production. Second, many traditional covariates bring along implicit assumptions that LDL does not want to make, such as the existence of discrete phonemic and morphemic units. Third, it is unclear how these traditional measures contribute to learning and processing. At the same time, however, the traditional measures might tap into properties of the linguistic signal that are

---

[4] I provide plots illustrating the frequency distribution in the data in the supplementary materials at https://osf.io/4h5f3/.

picked up in a discriminative learning process. Hence, LDL measures often correlate with traditional measures.[5]

The models of interest therefore only include LDL-derived variables (described in Section 7.1.5), with one exception: the one important non-LDL variable that needs to be taken into account is SPEECH RATE. This variable was described in Section 3.3.2 and is defined as:

SPEECH RATE
: The number of syllables in a window of ±1 second around the target derivative divided by the duration of that window.

How fast we speak is an influence that is beyond the control of the network. The initial models were thus fitted including all the variables described in Section 7.1.5 plus SPEECH RATE.

In addition, I built models with just non-LDL variables (I have described these variables in Section 3.3.2). This is to compare the explanatory power of the LDL-derived models with traditional models used in morpho-phonetic research. These models included the following predictors (for a detailed description of these variables, the reader is referred back to Section 3.3):

SPEECH RATE
: The number of syllables in a window of ±1 second around the target derivative divided by the duration of that window.

WORD FREQUENCY
: The log-transformed wordform frequency of the target derivative from COCA.

RELATIVE FREQUENCY
: The wordform frequency of the base word divided by the wordform frequency of the derivative from COCA, log-transformed. Higher values indicate more segmentability.

BIGRAM FREQUENCY
: The log-transformed frequency of the target derivative occurring together with the word following it in COCA.

---

[5] Correlation matrices and variable clustering trees for both LDL-derived variables and traditional variables are documented at https://osf.io/4h5f3/.

BIPHONE PROBABILITY The sum of all biphone probabilities (the likelihood of two phonemes occurring together in English) in a target derivative divided by the number of segments.

AFFIX Coding which affix is included in the derivative.

7.2 Results

Before investigating the models predicting acoustic duration, let us first compare the three networks to each other in their accuracy and similarity of the estimated semantic matrices.

7.2.1 General comparison of the networks

Network accuracy was generally satisfactory, with comprehension accuracies at 81 %, 82 %, and 83 % for the Idiosyncratic Network, the Morphology Network, and the Base Network, respectively, and production accuracies at 99 %, 99 %, and 98 %, respectively.

Let us now compare the predicted semantic matrices $\hat{S}$ of the three networks. This can be done by calculating the correlation of each predicted semantic vector $\hat{s}$ from one network with its corresponding predicted semantic vector $\hat{s}$ from the other two networks, and then taking the mean of these correlations for all words. Comparing the semantic vectors $\hat{s}_I$ of the Idiosyncratic Network to the semantic vectors $\widehat{s_M}$ from the Morphology Network, I find that they are on average very weakly correlated: the mean correlation between the vectors of the $\widehat{S_I}$ matrix and the $\widehat{S_M}$ matrix was r = .08. This means that the matrices are rather different. Likewise, the mean correlation between the vectors of the $\widehat{S_I}$ matrix and the $\widehat{S_B}$ matrix is weak (r = .1).

However, the mean correlation between the vectors of the $\widehat{S_M}$ matrix and the $\widehat{S_B}$ matrix is extremely high (r = .9). This indicates that it is probably the information about derivational function that differentiates the semantic vectors of the Idiosyncratic Network from the semantic vectors of the other two networks. Morphological category matters.

7.2.2 Predicting durations with LDL variables

Let us now turn to the regression models predicting duration. Table 7.3 and Table 7.4 report the final models regressing WORD DURATION DIFFERENCE against the LDL-derived variables and SPEECH RATE.

Tab. 7.3: Final standard regression LDL models reporting effects on WORD DURATION DIFFERENCE with variables from the three networks. Full models are documented at https://osf.io/4h5f3/.

	Idiosyncratic Network model		Morphology Network model		Base Network model	
	Estimate	SE	Estimate	SE	Estimate	SE
Intercept	0.216901	0.026210 ***	0.090708	0.025887 ***	0.408246	0.029999 ***
MEAN WORD SUPPORT	0.170726	0.023507 ***	0.250262	0.020700 ***	0.050723	0.012716 ***
PATH ENTROPIES	-0.008688	0.002242 ***	-0.008442	0.002309 ***	-0.009342	0.002259 ***
SEMANTIC DENSITY	-0.043545	0.008925 ***	0.033868	0.012372 **	-0.093906	0.025844 ***
SPEECH RATE	-0.058757	0.001148 ***	-0.058602	0.001159 ***	-0.058702	0.001171 ***
N	4448		4456		4456	
R^2 adjusted	0.3778		0.3742		0.3623	

Tab. 7.4: Final mixed-effects LDL models reporting effects on WORD DURATION DIFFERENCE with variables from the three networks. Full models are documented at https://osf.io/4h5f3/.

	Idiosyncratic Network model		Morphology Network model		Base Network model	
	Estimate	SE	Estimate	SE	Estimate	SE
Intercept	1.328e-01	4.601e-02 **	2.146e-01	6.024e-02 ***	2.595e-01	2.510e-02 ***
MEAN WORD SUPPORT	2.722e-01	4.600e-02 ***	2.535e-01	4.572e-02 ***	1.211e-01	2.654e-02 ***
PATH ENTROPIES	-1.173e-02	5.625e-03 *	-1.163e-02	5.633e-03 *		
SEM VECTOR LENGTH	-1.606e-02	6.860e-03 *	-3.294e-02	1.550e-02 *		
SPEECH RATE	-5.944e-02	1.116e-03 ***	-5.937e-02	1.116e-03 ***	-5.936e-02	1.117e-03 ***
N	4357		4358		4357	
R^2 marginal	0.3690016		0.3638608		0.3487138	
R^2 conditional	0.5198377		0.5168201		0.5200542	

The model in Table 7.3 reports the results of the standard regression models. As we can see, of the LDL-derived variables, MEAN WORD SUPPORT, SEMANTIC DENSITY, and PATH ENTROPIES significantly affect duration in the regression models of all three networks. In addition, SPEECH RATE is significant in all three models. The variables SEMANTIC VECTOR LENGTH and TARGET CORRELATION, on the other hand, did not reach significance and were therefore excluded from these final models.

The model in Table 7.4 reports the results of the mixed models. These models are very similar to the standard regression models, with two important differences. The variables MEAN WORD SUPPORT and SPEECH RATE display the same effects as in the standard models. PATH ENTROPIES also displays the same effects for the Idiosyncratic Network and the Morphology Network (it was only marginally significant for the Base Network and therefore excluded). However, SEMANTIC DENSITY does not reach significance in the mixed models. Instead, there is a significant effect of SEMANTIC VECTOR LENGTH in the models derived from the Idiosyncratic Network and the Morphology Network, but not in the Base Network.

Before looking at the effects of individual variables, let us first examine how much variation is actually explained by the models. Table 7.3 and Table 7.4 show that for all three networks in both types of model, the R^2 of the fixed effects is between .36 and .37, i.e., about 36–37 % of the variance in duration is explained by the predictors (the marginal R^2 of the mixed model for the Base Network is an exception, being slightly lower with about 35 %). To put this number into perspective, I compared the explained variance of the LDL-derived models to that of a model containing "traditional" predictor variables. These variables are traditionally used in morpho-phonetic corpus studies of duration, and have been used in the studies in previous chapters of the present book. I fitted a standard linear regression model and a mixed model including the traditional predictors WORD FREQUENCY, RELATIVE FREQUENCY, BIGRAM FREQUENCY, BIPHONE PROBABILITY, AFFIX, and SPEECH RATE from Section 3.3.2. These variables were fitted to the response variable WORD DURATION DIFFERENCE. Some observations were lost during trimming (80 observations, or 1.8 % of the data, for the standard model, and 74 observations, or 1.7 % of the data, for the mixed model). For the sake of comparing the explanatory power of individual predictors, I did not remove non-significant variables from the models. The models are summarized in Table 7.5.

Tab. 7.5: Traditional models with non-LDL predictors. Both a standard linear regression model and a mixed-effects regression model are fitted to WORD DURATION DIFFERENCE. Full models and ANOVAs are documented at https://osf.io/4h5f3/.

	Traditional standard regression model			Traditional mixed-effects model		
	Estimate	SE		Estimate	SE	
Intercept	3.888e-01	8.345e-03	***	4.159e-01	1.106e-02	***
WORD FREQUENCY	4.970e-08	3.764e-08		-2.608e-07	2.328e-07	
RELATIVE FREQUENCY	-2.136e-05	4.166e-05		-1.446e-05	8.931e-05	
BIGRAM FREQUENCY	-6.542e-07	6.293e-07		7.978e-07	6.382e-07	
BIPHONE PROBABILITY	-5.188e+00	8.872e-01	***	-7.167e+00	1.545e+00	***
AFFIXation						
dis	8.145e-03	6.700e-03		-1.405e-03	1.438e-02	
ize	-2.316e-02	5.251e-03	***	-1.491e-02	1.377e-02	
less	-5.749e-02	8.226e-03	***	-7.569e-02	1.524e-02	***
ness	-5.473e-02	5.700e-03	***	-3.630e-02	1.295e-02	**
SPEECH RATE	-5.893e-02	1.163e-03	***	-5.986e-02	1.116e-03	***
N	4450			4354		
R^2 adjusted/marginal	0.3731			0.3705799		
R^2 conditional				0.5344904		

WORD FREQUENCY, RELATIVE FREQUENCY, and BIGRAM FREQUENCY were not significant in the models, while BIPHONE PROBABILITY, some levels of AFFIX, and SPEECH RATE were. We can see that about the same proportion of the variance is explained by the traditional models (R^2 = .37).

Partitioning how much each of the predictors contributes to the proportion of explained variance, using the lmg metric (Lindeman et al. 1980) from the relaimpo package (Grömping 2006) and the calc.relip.mm function (Beręsewicz 2015) reveals that in both the traditional models and the LDL models, by far most of the variance is explained by SPEECH RATE (which alone explains about 35 % of the total variance in the standard regression models and about 20 % in the mixed models). This is shown in Table 7.6.

The variables of interest MEAN WORD SUPPORT, PATH ENTROPIES, SEMANTIC DENSITY, and SEMANTIC VECTOR LENGTH are all comparable in their explanatory power to the categorical AFFIX variable and BIPHONE PROBABILITY, and often better than the three frequency measures WORD FREQUENCY, RELATIVE FREQUENCY, and BIGRAM FREQUENCY. While the small differences in the explained variance between the LDL-derived variables and the traditional variables after factoring out the contribution of SPEECH RATE are not large enough to truly say which set of variables is "better," they clearly show that they are in the same ballpark. We can thus say that LDL-derived variables can compete against traditional variables from morpho-phonetic studies.

Tab. 7.6: Relative importance of variables in the LDL models and traditional model for the overall explained variance (marginal variance for mixed models).

	Idiosyncratic Network		Morphology Network		Base Network		Traditional model	
	lm	lmer	lm	lmer	lm	lmer	lm	lmer
MEAN WORD SUPPORT	0.0089	0.1649	0.0148	0.0956	0.0025	0.1641		
PATH ENTROPIES	0.0023	0.0031	0.0023	0.0017	0.0030			
SEMANTIC DENSITY	0.0067		0.0020		0.0014			
SEMANTIC VECTOR LENGTH		0.0064		0.0399				
SPEECH RATE	0.3605	0.1946	0.3556	0.2266	0.3559	0.1845	0.3561	0.2140
WORD FREQUENCY							0.0007	0.0065
RELATIVE FREQUENCY							0.0006	0.0044
BIGRAM FREQUENCY							0.0007	0.0034
BIPHONE PROBABILITY							0.0025	0.1178
AFFIX							0.0136	0.0246
total variance explained	0.3778	0.3690	0.3742	0.3639	0.3623	0.3487	0.3731	0.3706

We can now take a closer look at the effects of each of the variables. Figure 7.3 (for the standard regression models) and Figure 7.4 (for the mixed models) plot the effects of the LDL-derived variables and SPEECH RATE on duration. Figure 7.5 displays the density distributions of the variables in all three networks. I will discuss the two variables relating to certainty in the articulatory path first (MEAN WORD SUPPORT and PATH ENTROPIES), followed by a discussion of the two variables relating to the semantic relations between words (SEMANTIC DENSITY and SEMANTIC VECTOR LENGTH). The covariate SPEECH RATE and the variable TARGET CORRELATION will not be further discussed, as SPEECH RATE behaves as expected (see the bottom rows of Figure 7.3 and Figure 7.4) and TARGET CORRELATION was not significant in any of the models.

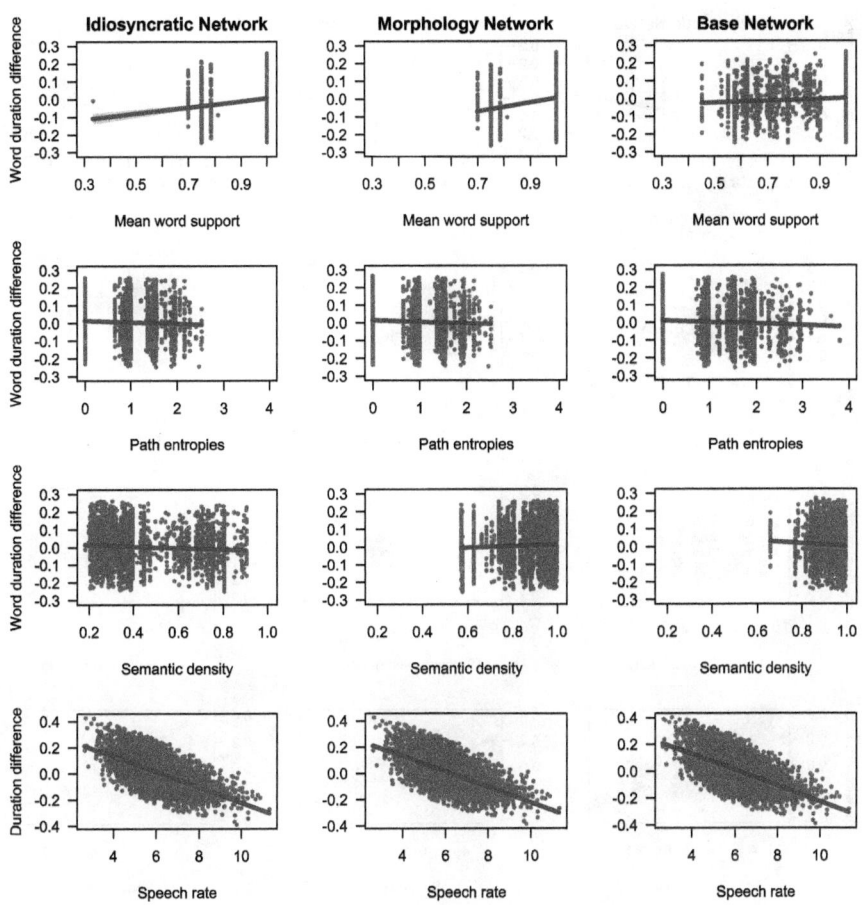

Fig. 7.3: Effects on WORD DURATION DIFFERENCE in the standard linear regression LDL models for the Idiosyncratic Network variables (left column), the Morphology Network variables (middle column), and the Base Network variables (right column).

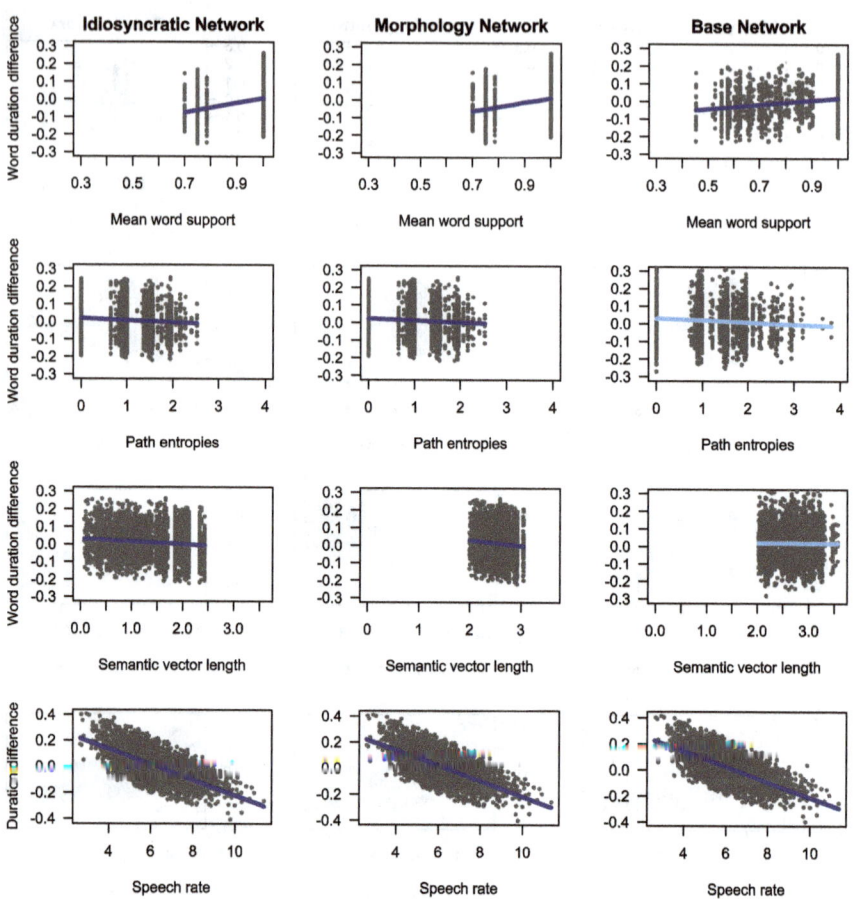

Fig. 7.4: Effects on WORD DURATION DIFFERENCE in the mixed-effects regression LDL models for the Idiosyncratic Network variables (left column), the Morphology Network variables (middle column), and the Base Network variables (right column). Dark blue regression lines indicate significant effects from the final models, light blue regression lines indicate non-significant effects from the maximal models.

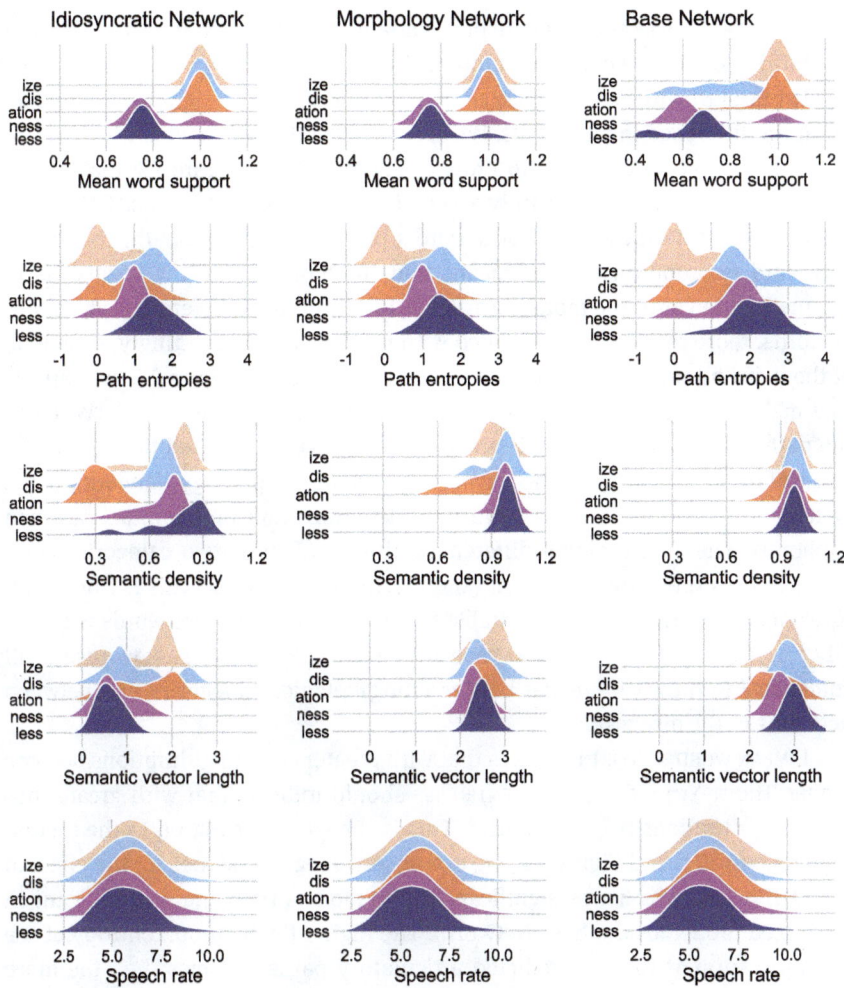

Fig. 7.5: Density distributions of variables by derivational function in the Idiosyncratic Network models (left column), the Morphology Network models (middle column), and the Base Network models (right column). Note that in the first two panels in the top row, the density curves around 1.0 are calculated over a single value.

7.2.2.1 Mean word support and path entropies

As explained in Section 7.1.5, the two variables MEAN WORD SUPPORT and PATH ENTROPIES both reflect properties of the semantic support for the predicted articulatory path, and they both tap into articulatory certainty. Given that the way these variables are calculated, MEAN WORD SUPPORT is a measure of certainty, while PATH ENTROPIES is a measure of uncertainty, they should mirror each other by showing opposite effects on duration. This is the case.

Let us start with MEAN WORD SUPPORT. This variable has a significant effect on duration difference in all models. We can see from the coefficients in as well as from its positive slope in the top row of Figure 7.3 and Figure 7.4 that higher MEAN WORD SUPPORT is significantly associated with longer durations. The higher the average semantic support of a word's predicted triphone path, the longer this word is pronounced. This means that the more certain the speaker is in producing the word, the more the articulation is durationally enhanced. In other words, more certainty is associated with lengthening. Interestingly, if we look at the distribution of MEAN WORD SUPPORT in the top row of Figure 7.5, we can see that mainly two derivational functions are responsible for this effect: Whereas the paths of IZE and ATION words are always very well supported (as well as the paths of DIS in the Idiosyncratic Network and in the Morphology Network), paths of NESS and LESS words often feature weaker transition probabilities between triphones. The distributional differences of each of these two categories compared to the others are significant (Mann-Whitney, $p < .001$). This is true for all three networks. However, it is notable that the mean support of words is generally lower in the Base Network, especially for IZE, NESS, and LESS words. I will come back to these differences between morphological categories and between networks in the discussion.

If MEAN WORD SUPPORT indicates that with greater certainty, durations become longer, the next predictor PATH ENTROPIES should indicate that with greater uncertainty, durations become shorter. This is the case. Moving on to the second row in Figure 7.3 and Figure 7.4, we can observe negative slopes for the effect of PATH ENTROPIES, which was significant in the models (marginally significant in the mixed model for the Base Network). The higher the Shannon entropy of the semantic support for the predicted articulatory paths becomes, i.e., the more variation of support there is in the system, the shorter the durations are. More uncertainty is associated with reduction. In other words, a speaker's lower certainty in production means the articulatory signal is less strengthened or less enhanced. Again, there are differences between morphological categories in all three networks. For example, words with IZE are characterized by more diverse and informative support values, while the other categories often feature more entropic support across the paths, especially LESS and DIS. All differences in the distributions are significant at $p < .001$, except for the non-significant difference between LESS and DIS in the Idiosyncratic Network and the Morphology Network, and the difference between NESS and DIS in the Base Network.

7.2.2.2 Semantic density and semantic vector length

Let us now look at the two variables that capture the semantic relations to other words, SEMANTIC DENSITY and SEMANTIC VECTOR LENGTH.

SEMANTIC DENSITY is significant in the standard regression models, but did not reach significance in the mixed models. Its coefficients in Table 7.3 show that while it has a negative effect on duration when derived from the Idiosyncratic Network and the Base Network, it has a positive effect on duration when derived from the Morphology Network. This is illustrated in the third row of Figure 7.3. For the Idiosyncratic Network and the Base Network, the stronger an estimated semantic vector correlates with its neighbors, the shorter the duration of a word becomes. For the Morphology Network, the stronger an estimated semantic vector correlates with the semantic vectors of its neighbors, the longer the duration of a word becomes. High-density words live in a space more semantically close to other words, i.e., they can be said to be less idiosyncratic and, due to their being derived words, more semantically transparent. Higher transparency can thus lead to both lengthening and shortening, depending on how the network is constructed.

Investigating the distribution of this variable, one can observe that SEMANTIC DENSITY shows differences between the networks. The datapoints in Figure 7.3 and the distributions in Figure 7.5 show that density is lowest in the Idiosyncratic Network, higher in the Morphology Network, and highest in the Base Network. This means that density increases with the amount of morphological structure I encode in the networks. SEMANTIC DENSITY also shows differences between derivational functions. Especially in the Idiosyncratic Network, this difference is very pronounced. This is again illustrated in Figure 7.5 (third row, first column). Words with LESS and IZE have particularly high densities, whereas densities are lower for DIS and NESS words, and lowest for ATION words. All of the distributions are significantly different from each other at $p < .001$. The fact that these morphological categories cluster so distinctly is particularly surprising, given that the Idiosyncratic Network was not provided with any vectors for these categories. I will return to the peculiar behavior of this variable in the discussion.

Turning to the second semantic variable, we can see that SEMANTIC DENSITY is replaced by SEMANTIC VECTOR LENGTH in the mixed models: SEMANTIC VECTOR LENGTH, while not significant in the standard regression models, reaches significance in the mixed models for the Idiosyncratic Network and the Morphology Network (Table 7.4 and third row in Figure 7.4). When derived from these networks, SEMANTIC VECTOR LENGTH has a negative effect on duration. Recalling that this variable captures activation diversity, one can say that being active on more semantic dimensions as a speaker has a facilitatory effect in production. The more collocational relations a word has to other words and the more meanings are activated, the shorter it is pronounced.

Investigating the distribution of SEMANTIC VECTOR LENGTH (Figure 7.5, fourth row), we can observe that the estimated semantic vectors are generally longer in the Morphology Network and the Base Network than in the Idiosyncratic Network. Not only are they longer on average, they also cluster more closely together in terms of their length: the L1 distance in the Morphology Network and the Base Network covers a range from about 2 to 3, while in the Idiosyncratic Network, it is spread out across a range from about 0 to 2.5. One reason for this may be purely mathematical: The vectors in the two networks with information about the morphological category can often be longer because the vector for the derivational function lexome is added to the vector of the derived word's content lexome. However, the vectors are not just generally longer in these networks, but the spread of the datapoints is also narrower. This indicates that the words cluster more closely together. Since SEMANTIC VECTOR LENGTH can represent activation diversity, this is expected: If words share a morphological function with other words, they become more similar to each other, hence are more likely to be semantically active when a member of their category is accessed. In the Idiosyncratic Network, words do not explicitly share a morphological category, hence members of a given category are not as likely to be co-activated. Again, the distributions show that vector lengths cluster differently depending on derivational function, meaning that different morphological categories are characterized by different degrees of semantic activation diversity.

It is interesting to note that when modeling durations, it is the Base Network that seems to behave differently from the other two networks, even though it shares with the Morphology Network its property of having information about morphological categories. The mixed model based on the variables from the Base Network is the least successful, as two predictors that are significant in the other networks (PATH ENTROPIES and SEMANTIC VECTOR LENGTH) do not reach significance in the Base Network. In Section 7.1.3, I have already discussed that the Base Network is conceptually unappealing and theoretically flawed from a non-decompositional perspective, as it wrongly assumes that the meaning of a derived word is strictly composed of the meaning of its base word and the meaning of the affix. I now find that it also seems to perform less optimal in modeling durations. Importantly, it is surprising that the Base Network shows a facilitatory effect of SEMANTIC DENSITY similar to the Idiosyncratic Network, instead of behaving like the Morphology Network, i.e., showing an inhibitory effect. This is despite the fact that the distribution of SEMANTIC DENSITY is very similar in the

Base Network and in the Morphology Network, but very different in the Idiosyncratic Network (see again Figure 7.5, third row). Moreover, it was the $\widehat{S_M}$ matrix and the $\widehat{S_B}$ matrix that are extremely correlated with each other (see Section 7.2.1) and not at all correlated with the $\widehat{S_I}$ matrix.

Exploring the aberrant behavior of the Base Network further, I investigated the semantic space of the Base Network in more detail and found that the clustering of words in the semantic space is detrimental.

Tab. 7.7: Extract from the closest semantic neighbors of DIS words in the three LDL networks.

Word	Phones	Neighbors						
Idiosyncratic Network								
disarm	dIs,m	mayday	quint	wham	mambo	cranky	nosy	blankly
disband	dIsb{nd	mayday	quint	blankly	wham	mambo	cranky	pippin
discard	dIsk,d	disarray	distaste	discredit	disgrace	discomfort	awl	disobey
discharge	dIsJ,=	dislike	dishonest	distrust	disagree	discomfort	disgrace	discontent
disclose	dIskl5z	mayday	quint	mambo	wham	blankly	nosy	shit
discount	dIsk6nt	dishonest	discomfort	disgrace	discontent	distrust	distaste	disguise
discourse	dIsk$s	disarray	distaste	discredit	disgrace	discomfort	disparity	dislodge
disease	dIziz	discover	disappear	disorder	discharge	dislike	discount	disagree
disgrace	dIsgr1s	distaste	discomfort	disarray	discredit	disobey	dislodge	disparity
disguise	dIsg2z	discomfort	disgrace	distaste	disarray	dishonest	discontent	discredit
dislike	dIsl2k	dishonest	discomfort	disgrace	distrust	discontent	distaste	disguise
Morphology Network								
disarm	dIs,m	disunity	disown	disband	disarray	discredit	disparity	disobey
disband	dIsb{nd	disunity	disown	disarm	disarray	discredit	disobey	disparity
discard	dIsk,d	discomfort	disgrace	distaste	dishonest	disarray	discontent	dislodge
discharge	dIsJ,=	dislike	dishonest	distrust	disagree	discomfort	disgrace	discontent
disclose	dIskl5z	disarray	disown	disarm	discredit	disunity	disband	disparity
discount	dIsk6nt	discomfort	dishonest	disgrace	dislike	disagree	distrust	disguise
discourse	dIsk$s	discomfort	disgrace	distaste	dishonest	discontent	disarray	disregard
disease	dIziz	discover	disappear	disorder	discharge	dislike	discount	disagree
disgrace	dIsgr1s	distaste	discomfort	disarray	discredit	disobey	dislodge	disparity
disguise	dIsg2z	discomfort	disgrace	distaste	disarray	dishonest	discontent	discredit
dislike	dIsl2k	discomfort	dishonest	disgrace	distrust	disagree	discontent	disguise

Word	Phones	Neighbors						
Base Network								
disarm	dIs,m	disguise	disparity	disgust	disarray	dislike	disobedience	displace
disband	dIsb{nd	disguise	disparity	disarray	disgust	dislike	displace	disobedience
discard	dIsk,d	disguise	disparity	disgust	disarray	disobedience	dislike	displace
discharge	dIsJ,=	disguise	disparity	disgust	disarray	dislike	disobedience	dishonest
disclose	dIskl5z	disguise	disparity	disgust	disarray	dislike	disobedience	dislodge
discount	dIsk6nt	disguise	disparity	disgust	disarray	disobedience	dislike	dishonest
discourse	dIsk$s	disguise	disparity	disgust	disarray	displace	disobedience	dishonest
disease	dIziz	disguise	disparity	disgust	disarray	disobedience	dislike	dishonest
disgrace	dIsgr1s	disguise	disparity	disgust	disarray	dislike	disobedience	dishonest
disguise	dIsg2z	disparity	disgust	disarray	disobedience	dislike	dishonest	dislodge
dislike	dIsl2k	disguise	disparity	disgust	disarray	disobedience	dislodge	dishonest

This is exemplified in Table 7.7, which shows an extract from the list of closest semantic neighbors to words with DIS in the three networks. Quite expectedly, the Idiosyncratic Network features a lower number of DIS words as neighbors of target DIS words than the other two networks. And there are more neighbors featuring DIS in the Base Network than in the Morphology Network. This increase in the number of DIS words as neighbors across the three networks mirrors the increasing role of explicit morphological information encoded in these networks. There is an important difference, however, between the Morphology Network and the Base Network. While in the Morphology Network, the DIS neighbors consist of many different word types with DIS, in the Base Network these are very often exactly the same word types.

A type analysis of the neighbors for all morphological categories in the three networks confirms this impression: Figure 7.6 shows that the Base Network is characterized by the least diverse neighbor space of the three networks, and that this is true for every investigated morphological function.

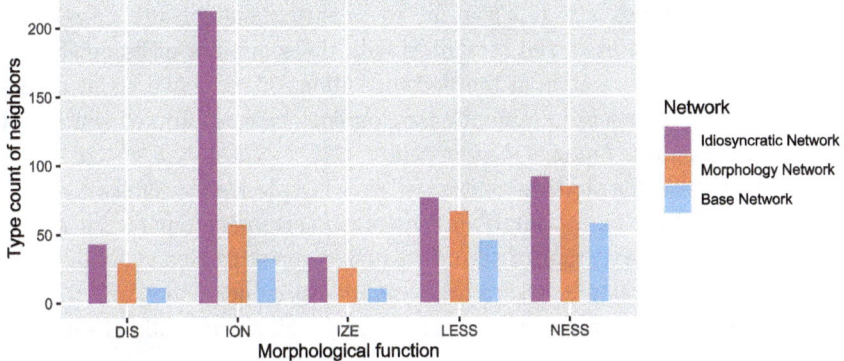

Fig. 7.6: Type count of top 8 neighbors by network and morphological function.

Given this behavior, it is thus no longer surprising that measures derived from the Base Network might behave strangely or not display effects. I conclude that the Base Network is not only theoretically the least appealing of the three networks from the non-decompositional perspective, but that these problems also lead to an empirically unattractive model.

7.3 Discussion

The present study explored the non-decompositional perspective by using linear discriminative learning networks. It investigated whether LDL-derived measures are predictive for acoustic duration (**Q** LDL$_{PREDICT}$), what their effects tell us about speech production (**Q** LDL$_{INTERPRET}$), and which differences we can find between different morphological operationalizations of meaning (**Q** LDL$_{NETWORKS}$).

Three key findings emerge from the analysis. First, all LDL networks achieve high learning accuracy and the proportion of variance in duration explained by the LDL-derived predictors is comparable to that explained by traditional predictors (**Q** LDL$_{PREDICT}$). Second, the effects of LDL measures seem to highlight specific patterns of speech production. For example, they suggest that words are lengthened in speech production when the semantic support of the word's predicted articulatory path is stronger (i.e., when certainty is higher), mirroring findings of some previous discriminative studies (**Q** LDL$_{INTERPRET}$). Third, there are differences, but also similarities between the three networks (**Q** LDL$_{NETWORKS}$). Importantly, even though I did not provide the Idiosyncratic Network with any vectors encoding the morphological category a word belongs to, these categories still emerge from the network. For instance, the different morphological categories are reflected in the distributions of the correlation strength of a word's predicted semantics with the semantics of its neighbors. This corresponds to what from the decompositional perspective could be described as the differences in semantic transparency between affixed words. Let me now discuss these findings in more detail.

For **Q** LDL$_{PREDICT}$, the study demonstrated that LDL-derived variables can successfully predict derivative durations. The mean semantic support of a word's articulatory path, the entropy of a word's path supports, the mean correlation of a word's predicted semantics with the semantics of its neighbors, and the distance of the semantic vector in the semantic space all significantly affect duration. I have also shown that these measures explain a reasonable proportion of the durational variance, in the sense that their contribution to the explained variance is comparable to the contribution of traditional linguistic variables used in corpus studies of duration (see, for instance, the studies in previous chapters of this book). The present study thus contributes to the growing literature that demonstrates that LDL is a promising alternative approach to speech production that can explain the variation in fine phonetic detail found in different kinds of words, be they simplex, complex, or non-words (e.g., Schmitz et al. 2021b; Chuang et al. 2020; Baayen et al. 2019b).

Regarding the question what the effects of LDL-derived variables can tell us about speech production (**Q** LDL$_{INTERPRET}$), the study finds that two important concepts relevant for production are the certainty in the association of form with meaning and the semantic relations of words to other words. The positive effects of MEAN WORD SUPPORT and the negative effects of PATH ENTROPIES on duration both indicate that generally, higher certainty in the association of form and meaning is associated with longer durations. The better an articulatory path is on average semantically supported, and the less these supports vary over the path, the more strengthened the articulation becomes. It is important to note that the metaphor of "certainty" which is ascribed to these measures can generate two opposing expectations, both of which are intuitive in their own way. On the one hand, it could be assumed that the more certain a speaker is, the more strengthened the signal will be, leading to longer durations. This may be because a speaker invests more energy in maintaining duration when they are certain, and less energy when they are uncertain, in order to not prolong a state of uncertainty (Tucker et al. 2019a). On the other hand, it could be assumed that the more certain a speaker is, the more efficient they can articulate, leading to shorter durations. This may be because more certainty could enable a speaker to select the correct path or execute an articulation more quickly. The present results provide support for the first interpretation rather than the second one.

This interpretation is in line with the findings for other measures that have been interpreted with reference to the concept of certainty. Tomaschek et al. (2019), for instance, found that with higher functional certainty, gauged by the support for a word's inflectional lexome and the word's overall baseline support, segment durations of different types of English final S are lengthened. Kuperman et al. (2007) found that with higher certainty, gauged by the paradigmatic support (probability) of Dutch compound interfixes, these interfixes are realized longer. Cohen (2014) found that higher certainty, gauged by the paradigmatic probability of English suffixes, is associated with phonetic enhancement, i.e., again with longer durations. Cohen (2015) found that higher paradigmatic support can also enhance Russian vowels. Tucker et al. (2019a) found that with higher support for tense and regularity (more certainty), acoustic duration of stem vowels increases, and with greater activation diversity (more uncertainty), acoustic duration decreases. In sum, regarding the question whether certainty has an effect of enhancement or reduction, recent evidence – including the present study – points towards enhancement.

The significant effects of SEMANTIC DENSITY and of SEMANTIC VECTOR LENGTH indicate that a second relevant factor in the production of derivatives is the semantic relation of a word to other words. Starting with SEMANTIC DENSITY, depending on the architecture of the network, the average semantic similarity of a word's neighbors to this word can lead to both longer and shorter durations. If the network has information about the semantics of the morphological category of the derivative and of the derivative itself, higher densities are associated with longer durations. If the network has no such information and treats all words as idiosyncratic, or if the network has information about the morphological category and the semantics of the derivative's base word, higher densities are associated with shorter durations. In order to get a better understanding of this somewhat puzzling finding, three observations are helpful.

Let us first compare the Idiosyncratic Network and the Morphology Network. We can see in the datapoints in Figure 7.3 as well as in the density plots in Figure 7.5 that SEMANTIC DENSITY is distributed very differently when derived from the Idiosyncratic Network than when derived from the Morphology Network (both the model results and the distributions are plotted on the same x-axis scale, respectively, for easier comparison). For the Idiosyncratic Network, there are hardly any datapoints above 0.8 and the vast majority of datapoints have density values below 0.4. For the Morphology Network, on the other hand, the vast majority of datapoints show densities above 0.8. At the conceptual level this makes sense: One would expect words sharing the semantics of their morphological category to be closer to their neighboring words, i.e., to be more transparent and less idiosyncratic. This means that if the model has information about morphological categories, density should be generally higher. This is the case. In contrast, words in the Idiosyncratic Network are generally more dissimilar to each other because they do not share the semantic information that comes with belonging to a particular morphological category. This difference between the two networks is also illustrated by the example of DIS neighbors in Table 7.7, which shows that in the Morphology Network, a larger proportion of nearest neighbors comes from the morphological category of the target word.

Returning to the relation between SEMANTIC DENSITY and duration, we can now see in Figure 7.3 that the contradictory effects happen at different ends of the distribution. The negative effect found in the Idiosyncratic Network is carried by the low-density words, while the positive effect of semantic density on duration is carried by the high-density words. The positive effect of densities above 0.8 is even visible in the Idiosyncratic Network: the residuals in that range are clearly skewed towards higher durations. If one attempts an interpretation of the relation of SEMANTIC DENSITY and word duration across these two networks, it is possible to say that the shortest durations are found in the middle of the semantic density range. Having many close semantic relatives slows down articulation, and so does having very few relatives.

What about SEMANTIC DENSITY in the Base Network? SEMANTIC DENSITY in this network is distributed similarly to the Morphology Network, yet the effect is similar to the Idiosyncratic Network, as it negatively affects duration. However, the exploration of the type diversity in the semantic space of the networks in Section 7.2.2.2 has shown that the neighbors that are behind these semantic densities are not at all diverse in the Base Network. This was true to such an extent that for the DIS words, for example, the Base Network considered the same few words (especially *disguise, disparity, disgust, disarray*) to be the closest neighbors for the vast majority of the target words. I consider this clustering to be rather unrealistic. Most likely, it is the consequence of the questionable premise of strict semantic compositionality underlying this network architecture discussed earlier. Overall, I conclude that the effect of SEMANTIC DENSITY in this network is not interpretable.

The question remains how we can understand the opposite effects of SEMANTIC DENSITY in the Idiosyncratic Network and the Morphology Network. If the interpretation that SEMANTIC DENSITY captures semantic transparency is correct, one would expect higher densities to lead to longer durations. From a decompositional perspective, more transparent words should be more protected against phonetic reduction because they feature a stronger morphological "boundary," i.e., they are more decomposable (see Section 2.1.2). Assuming that the theoretical concept of a morphological boundary and the similarity of a word to its neighboring words capture the same underlying dimension of semantic transparency, it should still be possible to replicate this effect. However, it is not entirely clear why a higher degree of semantic transparency would lead to lengthening from a non-decompositional perspective. Given that a higher semantic transparency means that more words will be more strongly activated, one would rather expect durations to shorten. This is because semantic activation diversity has been found to be associated with reduction (Tucker et al. 2019a). This reduction in speech production is mirrored in reaction time experiments that have found shorter reaction times with larger morphological family sizes (Bertram et al. 2000a; Schreuder & Baayen 1997). This family size effect has been interpreted as a semantic effect arising through activation spreading between morphologically related words. Interestingly, in the study by Bertram et al. (2000a) the effect was restricted to transparent family members. This is an indication that the effect may not be as linear as standardly assumed.

A non-linear, U-shaped effect of transparency on reaction times was observed by Plag & Baayen (2009). These authors demonstrated that suffixes that are either very easily segmentable or hardly segmentable have lower processing costs (as gauged by shorter reaction times in lexical decision) than suffixes in the middle of the segmentability range. Plag & Baayen (2009) interpreted this as an effect of the opposing forces of storage and computation. Assuming that the high-density words in the present study are those that are easily segmentable, while the low-density words are the ones that are not segmentable, one can come up with the tentative interpretation that the short durations in the midrange of density are a reflection of the higher processing costs incurred by the forms in the middle of the segmentability scale. One problem with this account is, however, that higher processing costs in lexical decision seem to be correlated with shorter durations in production, but with longer latencies in comprehension. This contradiction can only be solved if we know more about the specific processing differences between production and comprehension, or about the specific processing stages involved in lexical decision versus freely generated conversational speech. I leave this issue to be explored in future studies.

The second variable capturing the semantic relation between words that this study has shown to be able to successfully predict duration is SEMANTIC VECTOR LENGTH. Compared to SEMANTIC DENSITY, the effect of SEMANTIC VECTOR LENGTH is more straightforward to interpret. A longer semantic vector, i.e., a higher activation diversity, is associated with shorter duration. Tucker et al. (2019a) argue that the more semantic dimensions a speaker is active on for a word, the more confusable the meanings of this word are. When more meanings are activated and these meanings are more confusable, the speaker is more uncertain and therefore invests less energy in maintaining the signal. In this account, the finding that words with higher activation diversity are shorter is thus expected. This result is in line with other studies finding higher activation diversity to be associated with reduction (Schmitz et al. 2021b; Tomaschek et al. 2019; Tucker et al. 2019a).

Let me now return to the role of morphological information in the networks (**Q** LDL_{NETWORKS}). Importantly, the results for the two semantic variables show that differences between morphological categories can emerge even from the network without explicit information about derivational functions. For example, semantic density is significantly higher for words with the derivational functions NESS, LESS, and DIS than for words with ATION. This is in accordance with traditional descriptions of the semantic transparency of affixes, which posit *-ness*, *-less* and *dis-* as producing mostly transparent derivatives, while words with *-ation* are assumed to be less transparent (see again Section 3.1; Bauer et al. 2013; Plag 2018). Only IZE does not fit that pattern, as many IZE words are characterized by high densities but are considered about as transparent as *-ation* (however, *-ize* is considered to be more productive than *-ation*). Another interesting example of this is the distribution of SEMANTIC VECTOR LENGTH. The longer the vector of a word, the higher its semantic activation diversity becomes and the more collocational relations it has to other words, i.e., the more polysemous it is. The average vector length was highest for IZE and ATION words. This reflects traditional descriptions of *-ize* and *-ation* having highly multifaceted semantics (cf. the locative, ornative, causative, resultative, inchoative, performative or similative meaning of *-ize*, and the meanings of *-ation* denoting events, states, locations, products or means; Bauer et al. 2013; Plag 2018). The affixes *-less*, *dis-*, and to a lesser extent *-ness*, on the other hand, have comparatively clearer and narrower semantics. In sum, these differences between morphological categories in the Idiosyncratic Network demonstrate that LDL can discriminate derivational functions from sublexical and contextual cues alone.

There are several potential future directions for discriminative learning studies on the phonetics of derived words. First, it would be interesting to model the durations of more derivational functions in a larger dataset (e.g., those used in the studies reported in previous chapters of this book). Investigating more than the five morphological categories of the present study might reveal further important differences between these categories. Second, one issue that future studies could resolve concerns the response variable. In a corpus study of duration with different word types, it is essential to control for phonological length. This is why instead of duration, it was decided to model WORD DURATION

DIFFERENCE, i.e., the residuals of a model regressing a word's absolute duration against the sum of its average segment durations (see Section 3.3.1). However, for an LDL implementation, this response variable is not optimal, since strictly speaking it still implicitly assumes segmental structure. It would be desirable to control for segmental makeup without actually having to refer to segments. Third, it could be fruitful to investigate how best to construct vectors for words with multiple derivational functions. This would enable us to gain more insight into the complex interplay of morphological categories. And, finally, I think that to further test how well LDL can predict durations when the semantics of derivatives are strictly compositional (like in the Base Network), one interesting avenue for future research would be to use vectors that already assume this compositionality when generating lexome-to-lexome vectors. That is, while in the present study I used lexome vectors that Baayen et al. (2019b) generated by using the Widrow-Hoff algorithm to predict function lexomes in addition to content lexomes for words in a sentence, it is conceivable to use vectors generated by predicting function lexomes in addition to content lexomes for *bases* in a sentence. The lexome vector $\overrightarrow{happy}$, for instance, would then capture relations to contextual lexomes surrounding the word *happiness* as well. Similarly, one could generate vectors of derived words to use in the Idiosyncratic Network that do not capture cues of any functional lexomes by refraining from coding them altogether in the training data. I leave this interesting option to be explored in future studies.

The present study has shown in an explorative fashion that measures derived from linear discriminative learning networks can predict acoustic duration and that morphological structure can emerge without making explicit the analogies between words sharing their derivational function. However, the study also raises questions about how the measures found to be predictive relate to the decompositional measures explored in this book (Chapters 4–6). How can we interpret these results in the overall dichotomy between the decompositional perspective and the non-decompositional perspective? I will address these questions in the following chapter.

8 General discussion

This book has explored the units and mechanisms of speech production by investigating the role that morphological structure plays for the phonetic properties of derived words. For this purpose, it has grouped approaches to morphology and language processing into two perspectives: the decompositional perspective and the non-decompositional perspective. It is a fallacy to regard these two perspectives as homogeneous families of theories, and one must be careful not to construct a strawman out of traditional approaches which vastly differ in their understanding of language processing and structure (cf. Acquaviva et al. 2020). Nonetheless, it has been possible to identify different types of testable predictors associated with the two basic distinctive ideas underlying this binary grouping: for decompositional approaches, the idea that words can be analyzed as, decomposed into, computed from, and stored as smaller morphological units; for non-decompositional approaches, the idea that words are the basic units of analysis and that the mental lexicon may not even be a place of storage, but one of association strengths.

This book does not "test" which of these two perspectives is "better." No book, and indeed no single study of any scope, can do that. Answers to such a general question can only be approached over time by a large and growing body of research. The results and line of argumentation so far may suggest to the reader that, due to the unsuccessfulness of the decompositional measures and the apparent success of the LDL networks, I want to argue that a non-decompositional discriminative learning perspective is empirically superior to decompositional approaches. But based on the present studies, it is not possible to make this argument. For instance, in the present book the decompositional measures were tested on far more observations, more corpora, and with more models than the LDL-derived measures. Measures derived from discriminative learning networks may as well turn out to be similarly unsuccessful in future replications. Larger-scale studies that systematically explore how reliably effects emerge across a large number of models, like the ones for the frequency and informativeness measures in this book, are required to test effects of LDL-derived measures on acoustic duration more comprehensively. This book can argue for theoretical advantages and disadvantages of both perspectives based on the findings and discussions of the present work. However, at this point it cannot argue for a pure *empirical* advantage of the non-decompositional perspective.

In addition, before I discuss the results for the two perspectives in more detail, I would like to remind the reader that the general observation of the decompositional measures as being "unsuccessful" rests on the fact that the present studies observe null effects. But, as discussed in Section 5.2, the problem with the NHST framework is that null effects cannot be interpreted as evidence *against* the hypotheses. Null effects do not contradict the hypotheses, they merely do not support them. In one study (Chapter 5), I have used the BIC approximation to the Bayes Factor to quantify the evidence for the null in order to mitigate against this problem, but this strategy was not implemented in all studies. It would be wise to keep in mind the old saying that the absence of evidence is not the evidence of absence. On a more general note, relying only on arbitrary thresholds of statistical "significance" when interpreting whether differences in the data are meaningful has to be seen critically (see, e.g., Wasserstein et al. 2019 for discussion). In many cases, the present studies were intentionally more conservative with regard to the threshold, but the threshold is still arbitrary, and it is not entirely clear how one would define what is "conservative" or "meaningful." In addition, whether p-values emerge as significant is subject to all kinds of decisions within the available researcher degrees of freedom: differences in power between subsets of the data, the fact that I used linear models instead of allowing for nonlinear or wiggly effects, the selection of covariates from the potentially hundreds of possible covariates that would be conceivable, and more.

However, the studies in Chapters 4 and 6 have also demonstrated a major advantage of the present methodology, which is the fact that the unreliability of effects can only emerge in a large-scale approach to modeling. Typically, studies only look at one or a few models. If they find a significant effect, they conclude that this effect must exist. In the worst case, this narrow focus can be exploited with p-hacking or HARKing. However, in testing many models and reporting all of them transparently, the researcher can make a more honest assessment about the robustness of an effect. A massive modeling approach, provided that the study is presented as exploratory and the models are reported transparently, is thus more conservative in the sense that the occasional $p < .05$ or even $p < .001$ is less at risk of being overinterpreted. While the robustness of effects can also be evaluated across many different individual studies, this is often more difficult, as these studies will feature different methodologies. Within the present studies, the variables and model specifications were largely kept constant, using the same covariates, the same operationalization of the durational response variable (carefully controlled for phonological length by regressing the observed duration against a baseline duration), and the same procedure of model criticism.

While null effects are difficult to interpret, the results for the decompositional perspective show that many effects are much more unreliable than the literature sometimes seems to suggest. Base frequency effects largely fail to emerge, providing no support for the idea that words are stored and accessed in a decomposed fashion. But whole-word frequency effects are likewise less robust than assumed, providing no convincing support for undecomposed whole-word storage and access. Relative frequency, supposedly capturing morphological segmentability, is highly unreliable in predicting duration, as hinted at by previous studies. In addition, the data suggested that the emergence of relative frequency effects is strongly linked to the emergence of word frequency effects. Effects of relative frequency are almost only observable in datasets with a word frequency effect, suggesting that relative frequency is unnecessary as a separate predictor. The inconsistency of relative frequency effects on duration was further investigated in relation to prosodic structure, but prosodic structure does not seem to modulate whether relative frequency affects duration or not. In addition, durations did not pattern according to a hierarchy of prosodic boundaries, calling into question the status of word-internal prosodic structure in phonological theory and in models of speech production. The durational evidence for these boundaries is not convincing. Finally, the durational variation could not be explained convincingly by two operationalizations of affix informativeness, conditional affix probability and semantic information load. Null results, as well as different directions of effects between affixes, affix types, domains of durational measurement, and corpora, cast doubt on the reliability of these measures.

What do we make of this? Of course, the seemingly random patterning of effects between affixes could mean that each affix has its own idiosyncratic phonology, phonetics, and processing: no affix behaves like another. This would be very unsatisfying, as we would like to find generalizations, and at the same time nonsensical from a theoretical perspective. Measures supposedly tapping into speech processing, like frequency, segmentability, and informativeness, are supposed to be general mechanisms at work in comprehension and production. The patterning we observe between affixes might be "random" in the sense of "yet unexplained," but it might also be a meaningless artifact. One more productive approach that was taken in the present book was to ask, if decompositional measures cannot explain the durational variation we observe, whether there are alternative approaches that can. We may not necessarily need boundaries (morphological or prosodic) to model phonetic detail in speech production. Even if some decompositional measures had turned out to be highly predictive and their effects to be ubiquitous, these effects should not have been taken as final explanations. Rather, they provoke the question of which mechanisms could provide interpretations for the effects (cf. Divjak 2019: 268).

As an alternative to decompositional measures, this study modeled speech production as the result of a dynamic discriminative learning process, where relations between form and meaning are constantly recalibrated based on the speaker's experience. This approach, linear discriminative learning, does not rely on morphemic or prosodic boundaries, but estimates the strength of associations between sound and meaning based on their discriminative potential. A study using LDL-derived measures demonstrated that some of these measures can successfully predict derivative durations. The results suggested that more semantic certainty in pronunciation is associated with acoustic enhancement, i.e., longer durations, which was found to be consistent with some previous studies of paradigmatic probability and semantic support measures. In addition, semantic activation diversity was found to be associated with acoustic reduction.

The LDL study revealed that the results partly seem to depend on the type of semantic compositionality, or amount of explicit morphology, encoded in the network architecture. In discriminative models, morphological structure "can emerge through self-organization of unstructured input" (Pirrelli et al. 2020: 25). But it is important to understand while the input is unstructured, the coding of meaning in the present LDL implementation, as well as in other LDL implementations, may guide the network towards a certain semantic structure. This is because Baayen et al.'s (2019b) semantic vector space was constructed by learning associations of lexomes not only to content lexomes (like HAPPINESS and HAPPY), but also to function lexomes (like NESS). As discussed in Section 7.3, it could be interesting to see what would happen if one refrained from coding functions in the generation of lexome-to-lexome vectors. This way, the algorithm would not be able to capture any relations to contextual function lexomes at all. Likewise, one could decide to code for content lexomes of bases only and not of derived words, if one wanted to make the derivatives in the Base Network even less idiosyncratic. In Baayen et al.'s (2019b) implementation, base lexomes captured only the contextual lexomes in environments where the bases occurred on their own, but not in environments where they occurred inside of a derived word.

Despite this, the present LDL implementation clearly highlighted the consequences of whether the semantics of a morphological category are explicitly specified as vectors or not, and whether these semantics are added to the meaning of the derivative or the base. The Base Network, in which the semantics of a derivational function were added to the semantics of a base word, was demonstrated to be not only theoretically, but also empirically unattractive. The Base Network further emphasized the importance of a nuanced view on the decompositional and the non-decompositional perspective. This is because it showed how the idea of decompositionality can be applied to different levels of linguistic analysis: forms in discriminative learning are always non-decompositional, but the semantics may be operationalized as being decompositional. The decompositionality of only the semantics still makes LDL stand in contrast to a semiotic, sign-based view on morphemes, where both form and meaning are decomposed into form-meaning units. However, some parallels might be made to decompositional theories which take a separationist view on morphemes. As explained in Section 2.1, this view assumes the morpheme to have no independent lexical existence, but to be an anchor for morphosyntactic and semantic features dissociated from morphophonological exponents. Morphophonological exponent units may be incompatible with LDL. But the compositional semantics of the Base Network could be interpreted as the abstract morphosyntactic and semantic units of a placeholder morpheme. Given that the grammatical/semantic information is not being "spelled out" by predetermined exponents but rather mapped to a continuous stream of forms, this analogy is however questionable. It remains unclear what theoretical use the term "morpheme" would be left with (see Baayen et al. 2018 for more discussion).

Importantly, LDL-derived predictors were successful for the Morphology Network – which rendered morphological abstractions over words explicit by adding the meaning of a derivational function to the meaning of the derivative – but also for the Idiosyncratic Network. The vectors in the Idiosyncratic Network did not encode any analogies or regularities between morphologically related words. The success of this network shows that differences between morphological categories emerge from discriminative learning, even without explicitly providing the network with morphological information. This further strengthens the position of LDL as a promising theoretical alternative for speech production. Morphological functions can emerge as a by-product of a morpheme-free learning process: morphology is possible without morphemes. Given the many problems with the morpheme as a theoretical construct (see, e.g., Baayen et al. 2019b), this is a welcome finding. Finding morphological effects on phonetic realization need not lead to the conclusion that these effects must originate from morphemes. They can also emerge in the mapping of forms and meanings that have no information on morphology at all (see, for example, Baayen et al. 2011 et seq. for more examples of this). In addition, the present implementation has implications not just for morphemes, but also for phonemes. This is because the form matrices used as cues triphones that overlap. Thus, they do not encode distinct units, but serve as a proxy for a continuous speech signal. Just as the morpheme, phonemes are not necessarily self-evident as cognitive categories and provoke difficult questions. For example, do we really perceive all instances of a phoneme like /s/ as more similar to each other than to any other phoneme? Are there separate representations for different types of /s/, just like there are for different phonemes? Are there no phonemic representations at all?

Linguistics now wants to do more than just describe surface structures in linguistic data. It wants to know what the structures are that people use to produce, perceive, and comprehend language. In academia, we develop new theories by building on older ones, but therein lies the danger that by building psycholinguistic theories on structural theories, we transfer surface descriptions to claims about cognitive reality. As Divjak (2019: 247) puts it, "it is not because a phenomenon can be described in a certain way that the description is psychologically realistic, let alone real." Uncritically adapting categories from structural descriptions and then retroactively attempting to establish their cognitive existence may not be an ideal strategy. Instead, it may be better to start with insights from approaches already established in the fields of psychology and cognitive science, like learning theories, and then transferring these insights to linguistic data (Divjak 2019: 259).

Of course, non-decompositional approaches like discriminative learning models are not innocent of the cognitive fallacy either. Just as decompositional approaches transfer structural descriptions to cognitive reality, discriminative learning models, because they can model the data in a certain way, may be at risk of concluding that the model's architecture could therefore be how human memory works. This is true not only for discriminative learning, but also the premises from distributional semantics on which it builds. Many have argued for distributional semantic representations as psychologically valid (Acquaviva et al. 2020). The structure of such arguments is often similar to the one in decompositional approaches. I illustrate it below, following the classic rain example of the *affirming the consequent* fallacy (for a formalized version in the context of discriminative learning, see Baayen et al. 2018).

(1) If it is raining, then the ground is wet. The ground is wet. Therefore, it is raining.
(2) If morphemes exist, then we should observe some effect (e.g., base frequency or segmentability effects). We observe the effect. Therefore, morphemes exist.

(3) If the human lexicon is discriminative, then we should observe some effect (e.g., effects of LDL-derived measures). We observe the effect. Therefore, the human lexicon is discriminative.

In all three cases, the effects can also come from elsewhere. Someone may have spilled a bucket of water on the ground (1), base frequency or segmentability may underlyingly capture discriminative association strengths or transitional probabilities which do not require morphemes (2), and LDL-derived measures may vice versa underlyingly capture morphemic structure (3). The apparent success of LDL in this study and other studies does not allow us to infer that there is no cognitive plausibility to these structural units at all. Maybe humans still have them. If LDL is modeling rather how children learn languages, adult speakers may learn differently once they have explicit knowledge of morphemic structure. Such structure might also be acquired after-the-fact, when a speaker has seen enough words to start seeing analogies, or after learning about this structure explicitly. The morpheme might be epiphenomenal rather than superfluous. The only thing that the present LDL implementation does demonstrate is that such fixed units of form and meaning are at the very least not necessary for modeling speech data.

The *affirming the consequent* fallacy leads us to a more general problem, namely the problem that we do not really know what these decompositional and non-decompositional measures *are*. This problem has come up numerous times during the discussions of the findings from the four studies in the present book. Take frequency as an example: I have illustrated in Section 4.3 that it is unclear how humans would store and make use of "frequency" information in the first place. As we do not consciously count the words we encounter, how is it that we seem to instinctively keep track of their distributional properties? And how can we use this statistical information to perform accordingly? Finding an answer to this question requires a more general understanding of how memory and human consciousness work, which we currently do not have. Metaphors of information storage, or even frequency counters (like the *logogen* in Morton 1969), have increasingly been seen critically in different research fields, including linguistics. New models like LDL enable us to explain potential effects from a different angle that may be more compatible with evidence from other fields (for a discussion of frequency in light of learning models, see Baayen et al. 2016). We know from biology and neuroscience that learning essentially affects temporary electrical signals in the brain. Instead of a representation of static entities in a "lexicon" which are being "counted," a (linguistic) memory mechanism could thus rather be conceived of as a dynamic system of ongoing changes of synaptic connection strength, caused by the learning process (Ramón y Cajal 1894, Divjak 2019: 114). When the input and output of units occur together frequently, connections between them are strengthened, similarly to neuronal connections. In the Hebbian sense, "neurons that fire together wire together" (Hebb 1949). The stronger the wiring, the better and faster the signals can be transmitted. Consequently, for high-frequency units we observe effects of reaction time shortening and decreasing durations in pronunciation. This makes intuitive sense, but it is not clear whether such a network relation between linguistic form units and their meanings has the same ontological status as an actual neural network. In addition, theories would need to specify how exactly transmission speed would translate into articulatory reduction. Similar arguments can be made for other measures, like those related to morphological or prosodic boundaries. The jury is still out on the question of how exactly purported word-internal boundaries translate into articulatory gestures or acoustic properties. At which point do we start taking predictors for granted and ignore intermediate or preceding (e.g., articulatory or neurological) steps?

These ontological problems are exacerbated by the interrelatedness of the measures investigated in the present studies (as well as other measures). I have shown in the discussion sections of the respective chapters that if subjected to theoretical scrutiny, many of the predictors are conceptually inseparable. Let me now summarize this by bringing the interpretation of these measures together. Throughout this book I have touched on (at least) the following words which are used to describe some kinds of mechanisms of speech processing: "frequency," "segmentability," "transparency," "boundary strength," "phonological integration," "informativeness," "probability," "predictability," "certainty," and "entropy."

A potential circle of interpretation could go as follows: for frequency, I have illustrated that whole-word frequency can be interpreted as morphemic (base-affix) bigram frequency; base frequency and word frequency are closely related (Section 4.3). Base frequency and word frequency are naturally highly correlated with relative frequency, or segmentability. Segmentability is strongly related to semantic transparency (Section 2.1.2). In addition, if base frequency and word frequency are perfectly correlated, relative frequency is a constant, obscuring potential effects (see again the calculation of relative frequency in Section 2.1.2). Relative frequency, in turn, can be conceptualized as boundary strength, with stronger boundaries being associated with more phonological integration (Sections 2.1.2 and 2.1.3). Boundary strength can be conceptualized as transitional probability or predictability (Section 4.3). Transitional probability can be conceptualized as informativeness (Section 6.3), informativeness as predictability

(Section 2.1.4), predictability as frequency (Sections 2.1.1 and 2.1.4). Bridging the gap to LDL, the more predictable/probable/frequent/uninformative something is, the more certainty a speaker should display (Section 7.1.5). Certainty, in turn, is associated with less entropy (also Section 7.1.5).

In fact, there is no way to know for sure if all of these measures could be capturing the same underlying force, as we do not know the cognitive difference between them. The fact that each of these measures can be operationalized in various ways (e.g., informativeness as probability or semantic information load, uncertainty as syntagmatic uncertainty or paradigmatic uncertainty, entropy as path entropy or paradigm entropy) only makes this worse. In addition, many other morphological and psycholinguistic variables that the present studies did not focus on could be added to this list of conceptually related predictors (e.g., neighborhood density, family size, age of acquisition, and more, also see again Baayen et al. 2016), as well as some of the covariates used in the present studies (particularly bigram frequency and biphone probability). This is a theoretical problem, but also a statistical one. As Divjak (2019: 256) observes, researchers need the predictor variables in their linear regression models to be as orthogonal as possible lest they cause multicollinearity problems. The conceptual interrelatedness of these predictors makes it even harder to justify decisions to remove their redundancy (which may not be desirable).

For acoustic duration, in many cases these measures and their predictions go hand in hand. For example, the more frequent, the more predictable, the more probable, and the less informative a linguistic item, the shorter should its duration become. But sometimes, we have also seen that the directions of the predictions do not coincide. For example, higher frequency, higher predictability and probability, and lower informativeness are associated with more certainty. But more certainty is sometimes hypothesized to lead to longer durations (e.g., Tucker et al. 2019a), while higher values of the other measures are hypothesized to lead to shorter durations (see previous chapters). I have also illustrated that this depends on the interpretation of individual predictors. For instance, higher relative frequency may be conceptualized as lower transitional probability (Section 4.3). From a learnability perspective, lower transitional probabilities should make the item highly discriminable and facilitate articulation, leading to shorter durations. But from a predictability or informativeness perspective, lower transitional probabilities should be less predictable and more informative, leading to longer durations. In turn, less predictability means that the speaker may be more uncertain, which would again predict shorter durations. These are just some examples of the connections we can make between the predictors in the present studies and others, and of how these connections enrich, but also complicate the generation of hypotheses and the interpretation of effects.

When we do research, we might, for all practical purposes, pretend that there is an objectively measurable reality beyond what we perceive. But it is not a novel idea that the phenomena we attempt to unveil are ultimately formed as much by our linguistic descriptions of them as they are by whatever might underlie these descriptions. Our variables, research objects, and categories of analysis are, first and foremost, social and linguistic constructs. Which conclusions we draw generally depends on which words we choose to use in our descriptions, rather than on some ontological truth. The somewhat paradoxical task of describing language with language, in particular, is therefore a truly humbling experience. This does not only hold true for the words that we use for predictors, like "certainty," "informativeness," or "frequency," but also for words we use to describe effects on duration. Take, for instance, the difference between words like "enhancement," "reduction," "facilitation," and "inhibition" that are used in the literature (and the present book). To say that when a speaker is highly uncertain, we should observe a "facilitatory" effect on duration, is not intuitive. Why should uncertainty make a task easier? However, to say that when a speaker is uncertain, durations should be less "enhanced" makes intuitively more sense. An uncertain speaker is less confident, uncertainty thus makes it more difficult to enhance the signal. This is despite the fact that in both cases, what is being described are simply shorter durations. In the end, "we should be mindful of the conceptual 'trap' laid out by the metaphors used to guide inquiry about memory" (Divjak 2019: 108).

Does this mean that the inquiry about memory and speech processing is hopeless? Of course not. In fact, I think openly acknowledging the fact that we ultimately work with metaphors enables us to better distance ourselves from established notions, subject them to critical scrutiny, and explore new ways of thinking by deconstructively reflecting on our work. The question of whether a description is cognitively "real" or not becomes the question of which metaphor is the better (i.e., more useful) one. In a sense, this is liberating, and chimes well with the saying that "all models are wrong, but some are useful" (Box 1976). If we, as quantitative-empirical research generally does, assume that there is a measurable reality behind language, then the question is which metaphors are most useful in making understandable whatever it is that underlies them, whether these metaphors are real or not.

The advantage of the interrelatedness of these metaphors is that we can explain effects of measures of one perspective (e.g., the decompositional perspective) with measures from another perspective (e.g., the non-decompositional perspective). The problem is that, based on the effects themselves, there is often little "certainty" in which perspective offers the better explanation.

However, while some findings can be explained whether one believes in decomposition or not, some theories face more problems in explaining certain findings than others. For example, even if we cannot be certain what underlies morpho-phonetic effects, these effects do question several traditional theories on the morphology-phonology interaction and models of speech production. As explained in Section 2.1, these approaches (Roelofs & Ferreira 2019; Levelt et al. 1999; Dell 1986; Kiparsky 1982; Chomsky & Halle 1968) are largely unable to accommodate effects of morphological structure on the phonetic output. Many theories of morphology-phonology interaction assume that morphological boundaries are erased in the process of passing morphemic units on to phonological processing. And many models of speech production assume an articulator module that realizes phonemic representations with pre-programmed gesture templates independently of morphemic status. These approaches lack explanations for the fact that a word's morphological structure or semantics can cause differences in articulatory gestures, as they do not allow for a direct morphology-phonetics interaction. The present LDL study, however, suggests that meaning differences cause differences in articulation. In LDL, such interaction is expected and can be explained by its underlying theoretical principles of learning and experience. A stratification of the lexicon, as proposed by many decompositional approaches, may neither be required nor desirable.

If morphophonetic effects can be explained equally well or even better by LDL, then, on theoretical grounds, we might prefer LDL over decompositional models if we want to explain speech processing and linguistic memory. Other discussions have come to similar conclusions. Blevins et al. (2016) observe a growing consensus that decompositional analyses may not be able to explain even the most basic observations, and that the whole may indeed be more than its parts. LDL goes one step further in assuming that there are no parts, just associations between subsymbolic forms and meanings. However, while LDL does not commit to the morpheme, it can still operate with morphological functions like tense, mood, and derivational functions by associating them with a continuous form signal. Plag & Balling (2020) observe in their review that such a gradient view of association strengths is more compatible with previous evidence than approaches relying on signs and strict segmentation. Moreover, the idea that there is a stored lexicon across speakers of a language is seen increasingly critically (as explained in Sections 2.1.1 and 2.2.1). In addition, LDL brings along a few advantages for the modeling of linguistic representation. At the form level, LDL does not distinguish between elements of different morphological status. It can therefore handle elements that we would traditionally understand as "morphemes" and elements like phonaesthemes according to the same principles (Plag & Balling 2020). At the meaning level, due to its use of semantic vectors, LDL can model all kinds of meaning according to the same principles, too, as shown by the LDL studies on pseudowords (Schmitz et al. 2021b; Chuang et al. 2020). Computationally, in contrast to deep learning, LDL networks remain transparent (due to the two-layer structure) and linguistically realistic. It does not have to learn with more words than a speaker can actually be exposed to in their lifetime, and it goes through its data only once instead of thousands of times, i.e., the discriminative learner would be less resistant to variation when encountering another speaker (Baayen et al. 2019b). Finally, it operates on established learning rules that have been applied to all kinds of other, non-linguistic phenomena. Ultimately, a model that can explain not just linguistic effects, but many more effects in humans and even animals, may be more desirable (Pirrelli et al. 2020). All models are wrong and only some are useful, but it appears that LDL might be more useful than other models.

Of course, there are also still unsolved problems with discriminative approaches. At this point, the ontology of both lexomes and n-grams is still unclear, as is the nature of whatever it is that should replace the mental lexicon metaphor, i.e., the nature of the "network" (Plag & Balling 2020). It will be important and exciting to think about how we can understand these concepts. In addition, much more empirical research is necessary that models behavioral data with discriminative approaches. The validity of computational models can only ever be gauged by testing them against human, non-simulated data. Moreover, being in the process of abandoning the morpheme, we can also go further and ask which other units are necessary or unnecessary for linguistic theory. For example, what about the word? We may ask whether or when the word is necessary to understand larger structures like collocations, idioms, or even less frequent phrases. These questions are important especially for languages which may challenge Anglocentric intuitions about the definition of word, e.g., agglutinating or polysynthetic languages (see, e.g., Bickel & Zúñiga 2017). If speech is a continuous spectrum, like perhaps color, then the question according to which criteria one should divide this spectrum (if at all) is not trivial. Finally, as outlined above, discriminative learning claims some cognitive plausibility, which makes it vulnerable against insights from cognitive science and biology. For instance, Pirrelli et al. (2020) note that while error-driven learning is supported by evidence from neurobiology, biological neural networks are much more complicated than two-layer computational ones. Some questions about the ontology of the mental lexicon might only be answerable by doing brain research.

Considering the studies in the present book more generally, there are several more potential avenues for further research. There are many other correlates of morphological structure that can be explored, not just predictors, but also response variables. For instance, it would be interesting to see whether the results for acoustic duration are more reliable for other acoustic measures, like, e.g., pitch. But not just in speech production, also in speech comprehension can the measures examined in the present studies be investigated fruitfully, to explore whether or in how far decomposition could be a byproduct of recognition. In addition, experimental research can further test the mechanisms behind these effects, comparing the communicative account against the production ease account against the representational account (Jaeger & Buz 2017). Extending the present research to more languages and more types of speakers (to work against the WEIRD bias of primarily using data from Western, educated, industrialized, rich, and democratic societies, to which the present book contributes) is a must. In principle, the effects investigated in the present studies are not assumed to be language-specific, but general language production effects.

Finally, the potential advantages of a non-decompositional perspective compared to a decompositional perspective on language also have implications for non-linguistic research. I have illustrated how in discriminative learning models, the connection between form and meaning can be dynamic and relational, allowing morphological theory to reframe its semiotic legacy. It has been argued that since its discriminative underpinnings emphasize that language is a system of *différence*, discriminative learning elegantly carries the discipline back to its Saussurean heritage (Blevins 2016). However, disciplines that sometimes make use of structuralist ideas, like literary and cultural studies, often adopt the "sign" as a unit in semiotic analyses. Which implications would it have for these analyses if one were to reconceptualize both linguistic and non-linguistic meaning as being dissociated from linguistic and non-linguistic form – if all kinds of form-meaning relations were not organized into signs, but into an associative network? Does discriminative learning only tell us something about language, or does it also tell us something about our knowledge of the world, which we access and express with language? One of the ultimate tasks for understanding human cognition could be to create a unified model that relates all kinds of forms and meanings subsymbolically – linguistic, visual, musical – a unified model of meaning-making.

9 Conclusion

This book investigated two perspectives on speech processing: the decompositional perspective, which assumes words to be decomposed into smaller morphological units, and the non-decompositional perspective, which refrains from doing so. It explored the effects of several measures that are associated with these perspectives on the acoustic duration of English derived words. In doing so, it addressed two problems in morpho-phonetic research. The first one is an empirical problem: it is unclear in many cases how robust the effects of certain morpho-phonetic predictors really are. The second one is a theoretical problem: it is unclear where morpho-phonetic effects come from and which kinds of morphological structure they might reflect.

The empirical problem was addressed by conducting four exploratory corpus studies on a selection of some of the most important morphological, phonological, and semantic variables (three frequency measures including a measure of morphological segmentability, different prosodic categories, two informativeness measures, and several LDL-derived measures of articulatory certainty and semantic properties). The results for the traditional predictors (frequency, prosody, informativeness) showed that in large-scale studies, often across a high number of models, these predictors are far less robust than sometimes assumed. They mostly yielded null effects or patterns of effects that otherwise did not support the predictions derived from accounts taking a decompositional perspective (e.g., accounts based on boundary strength or on the storage of units in the lexicon). The results for the predictors derived from linear discriminative learning networks showed that some of them are predictive of acoustic duration – although they remain to be tested in a larger-scale modeling approach that is comparable to the present studies of traditional predictors. In addition, they offer interesting alternative explanations for mechanisms of speech processing.

The theoretical problem was addressed by critically discussing the two perspectives on speech processing and the interpretation of the measures associated with them. Effects of morphological or semantic properties on duration, for example those found in the LDL study, falsify models of speech production and theories of the morphology-phonology interaction that prohibit these properties to be reflected in articulation. Discriminative learning models, in which such effects are expected, thus have a theoretical advantage over decompositional, feed-forward models. However, this book also discussed the conceptual problems that arise due to the interrelatedness of many psycholinguistic predictors of both the decompositional and the non-decompositional perspective. It cautioned against taking for granted the intuitive explanations provided by the metaphors we use to describe their effects. If we take a more critical and deconstructive view on our research tools, including on the very language we use to describe what we measure, we open up the way to reconceptualize investigations of human language processing as a search for better metaphors, rather than as the search for some unobtainable, ontological truth. Models of discriminative learning might be an example of such better metaphors, and I think it would be worthwhile for future studies to consider them as alternative approaches in research on the morphology-phonology-phonetics interface.

So how do humans transmit thoughts from the mind of one person to the mind of another via sound? Unsurprisingly, the present book did not answer this question. However, we may have gotten a tiny bit closer to a more nuanced understanding of it. It will be exciting to see which new ideas and findings future research will contribute to our neverending quest to understand the structure and cognition of language.

References

Acquaviva, Paolo, Alessandro Lenci, Carita Paradis & Ida Raffaelli. 2020. Models of lexical meaning. In Vito Pirrelli, Ingo Plag & Wolfgang U. Dressler (eds.), *Word knowledge and word usage: A cross-disciplinary guide to the mental lexicon* (Trends in Linguistics: Studies and Monographs 337), 353–404. Berlin, Boston: De Gruyter Mouton. https://doi.org/10.1515/9783110440577-010.

Anderson, Stephen R. 1992. *A-morphous morphology*. Cambridge University Press. https://doi.org/10.1017/CBO9780511586262.

Arndt-Lappe, Sabine & Mirjam Ernestus. 2020. Morpho-phonological alternations: The role of lexical storage. In Vito Pirrelli, Ingo Plag & Wolfgang U. Dressler (eds.), *Word knowledge and word usage: A cross-disciplinary guide to the mental lexicon* (Trends in Linguistics: Studies and Monographs 337), 191–227. Berlin, Boston: De Gruyter Mouton. https://doi.org/10.1515/9783110440577-006.

Arnold, Denis, Fabian Tomaschek, Konstantin Sering, Florence Lopez & R. Harald Baayen. 2017. Words from spontaneous conversational speech can be recognized with human-like accuracy by an error-driven learning algorithm that discriminates between meanings straight from smart acoustic features, bypassing the phoneme as recognition unit. *PLoS ONE* 12(4). e0174623. https://doi.org/10.1371/journal.pone.0174623.

Arnold, Jennifer E. & Duane G. Watson. 2015. Synthesizing meaning and processing approaches to prosody: Performance matters. *Language, Cognition and Neuroscience* 30(1–2). 88–102. https://doi.org/10.1080/01690965.2013.840733.

Aronoff, Mark. 1976. *Word formation in generative grammar* (Linguistic Inquiry Monographs 1). Cambridge: MIT Press.

Auer, Peter. 2002. Die sogenannte Auslautverhärtung in ne[b]lig vs. lie[p]lich: Ein Phantom der deutschen Phonologie? In Michael Bommes, Christina Noack & Doris Tophinke (eds.), *Sprache als Form: Festschrift für Utz Maas zum 60. Geburtstag*, 74–86. Wiesbaden: Westdeutscher Verlag.

Aylett, Matthew & Alice Turk. 2004. The Smooth Signal Redundancy Hypothesis: A functional explanation for relationships between redundancy, prosodic prominence, and duration in spontaneous speech. *Language and Speech* 47(1). 31–56. https://doi.org/10.1177/00238309040470010201.

Aylett, Matthew & Alice Turk. 2006. Language redundancy predicts syllabic duration and the spectral characteristics of vocalic syllable nuclei. *The Journal of the Acoustical Society of America* 119(5.1). 3048–3058. https://doi.org/10.1121/1.2188331.

Baayen, R. Harald. 2007. Storage and computation in the mental lexicon. In Gonia Jarema & Gary Libben (eds.), *The mental lexicon: Core perspectives*, 81–104. Brill. https://doi.org/10.1163/9780080548692_006.

Baayen, R. Harald. 2008. *Analyzing linguistic data: A practical introduction to statistics using R*. Cambridge: Cambridge University Press. https://doi.org/10.1017/CBO9780511801686.

Baayen, R. Harald. 2011. Corpus linguistics and naive discriminative learning. *RBLA, Belo Horizonte* 11(2). 295–328. https://doi.org/10.1590/S1984-63982011000200003.

Baayen, R. Harald, Yu-Ying Chuang & James P. Blevins. 2018. Inflectional morphology with linear mappings. *The Mental Lexicon* 13(2). 230–268. https://doi.org/10.1075/ml.18010.baa.

Baayen, R. Harald, Yu-Ying Chuang & Maria Heitmeier. 2019a. *WpmWithLdl: Implementation of Word and Paradigm Morphology with Linear Discriminative Learning.* R package. Version 1.3.17.1. http://www.sfs.uni-tuebingen.de/~hbaayen/software.html.

Baayen, R. Harald, Yu-Ying Chuang, Elnaz Shafaei-Bajestan & James P. Blevins. 2019b. The discriminative lexicon: A unified computational model for the lexicon and lexical processing in comprehension and production grounded not in (de)composition but in linear discriminative learning. *Complexity* 2019. 1–39. https://doi.org/10.1155/2019/4895891.

Baayen, R. Harald, Ton Dijkstra & Robert Schreuder. 1997. Singulars and plurals in Dutch: Evidence for a Parallel dual-route model. *Journal of Memory and Language* 37(1). 94–117. https://doi.org/10.1006/jmla.1997.2509.

Baayen, R. Harald, Laurie B. Feldman & Robert Schreuder. 2006. Morphological influences on the recognition of monosyllabic monomorphemic words. *Journal of Memory and Language* 55(2). 290–313. https://doi.org/10.1016/j.jml.2006.03.008.

Baayen, R. Harald, Peter Hendrix & Michael Ramscar. 2013. Sidestepping the combinatorial explosion: An explanation of n-gram frequency effects based on naive discriminative learning. *Language and Speech* 56(3). 329–347. https://doi.org/10.1177/0023830913484896.

Baayen, R. Harald & Petar Milin. 2010. Analyzing reaction times. *International Journal of Psychological Research* 3(2). 12–28. https://doi.org/10.21500/20112084.807.

Baayen, R. Harald, Petar Milin, Dusica F. Đurđević, Peter Hendrix & Marco Marelli. 2011. An amorphous model for morphological processing in visual comprehension based on naive discriminative learning. *Psychological Review* 118(3). 438–481. https://doi.org/10.1037/a0023851.

Baayen, R. Harald, Petar Milin & Michael Ramscar. 2016. Frequency in lexical processing. *Aphasiology* 30(11). 1174–1220. https://doi.org/10.1080/02687038.2016.1147767.

Baayen, R. Harald, Richard Piepenbrock & Léon Gulikers. 1995. *The CELEX Lexical Database.* Philadelphia: Linguistic Data Consortium. https://doi.org/10.35111/gs6s-gm48.

Baayen, R. Harald, Lee H. Wurm & Joanna Aycock. 2007. Lexical dynamics for low-frequency complex words. *The Mental Lexicon* 2(3). 419–463. https://doi.org/10.1075/ML.2.3.06BAA.

Balling, Laura W. & R. Harald Baayen. 2008. Morphological effects in auditory word recognition: Evidence from Danish. *Language and Cognitive Processes* 23(7–8). 1159–1190. https://doi.org/10.1080/01690960802201010.

Bates, Douglas, Martin Mächler, Ben Bolker & Steve Walker. 2015. Fitting linear mixed-effects models using lme4. *Journal of Statistical Software* 67(1). 1–48. https://doi.org/10.18637/jss.v067.i01.

Bauer, Laurie, Rochelle Lieber & Ingo Plag. 2013. *The Oxford reference guide to English morphology.* Oxford: Oxford University Press. https://doi.org/10.1093/acprof:oso/9780198747062.001.0001.

Beard, Robert. 1995. *Lexeme-morpheme base morphology: A general theory of inflection and word formation* (SUNY Series in Linguistics). Albany: State University of New York.

Beckman, Mary E. & Janet B. Pierrehumbert. 1986. Intonational structure in Japanese and English. *Phonology Yearbook* 3. 255–309. https://doi.org/10.1017/S095267570000066X.

Bell, Alan, Jason M. Brenier, Michelle Gregory, Cynthia Girand & Daniel Jurafsky. 2009. Predictability effects on durations of content and function words in conversational English. *Journal of Memory and Language* 60(1). 92–111. https://doi.org/10.1016/j.jml.2008.06.003.

Bell, Alan, Daniel Jurafsky, Eric Fosler-Lussier, Cynthia Girand, Michelle Gregory & Daniel Gildea. 2003. Effects of disfluencies, predictability, and utterance position on word form variation in English conversation. *The Journal of the Acoustical Society of America* 113(2). 1001–1024. https://doi.org/10.1121/1.1534836.

Bell, Melanie J., Sonia Ben Hedia & Ingo Plag. 2020. How morphological structure affects phonetic realisation in English compound nouns. *Morphology*. 1–34. https://doi.org/10.1007/s11525-020-09346-6.

Ben Hedia, Sonia. 2019. *Gemination and degemination in English affixation: Investigating the interplay between morphology, phonology and phonetics* (Studies in Laboratory Phonology 8). Berlin: Language Science Press. https://doi.org/10.5281/zenodo.3232849.

Ben Hedia, Sonia & Ingo Plag. 2017. Gemination and degemination in English prefixation: Phonetic evidence for morphological organization. *Journal of Phonetics* 62. 34–49. https://doi.org/10.1016/j.wocn.2017.02.002.

Beręsewicz, Maciej. 2015. *calc.relip.mm: Variable importance for mixed models.* https://gist.github.com/BERENZ/e9b581a4b7160357934e.

Bergmann, Pia. 2018. *Morphologisch komplexe Wörter: Prosodische Struktur und phonetische Realisierung* (Studies in Laboratory Phonology 5). Berlin: Language Science Press. https://doi.org/10.5281/ZENODO.1346245.

Berkovits, Rochele. 1993a. Progressive utterance-final lengthening in syllables with final fricatives. *Language and Speech* 36(1). 89–98. https://doi.org/10.1177/002383099303600105.

Berkovits, Rochele. 1993b. Utterance-final lengthening and the duration of final-stop closures. *Journal of Phonetics* 21(4). 479–489. https://doi.org/10.1016/s0095-4470(19)30231-1.

Berkovits, Rochele. 1994. Durational effects in final lengthening, gapping, and contrastive stress. *Language and Speech* 37(3). 237–250. https://doi.org/10.1177/002383099403700302.

Bermúdez-Otero, Ricardo. 2018. Stratal Phonology. In Stephen J. Hannahs & Anna R. K. Bosch (eds.), *The Routledge handbook of phonological theory*, 100–143. London, New York: Routledge. https://doi.org/10.4324/9781315675428.

Bertram, Raymond, R. Harald Baayen & Robert Schreuder. 2000a. Effects of family size for complex words. *Journal of Memory and Language* 42(3). 390–405. https://doi.org/10.1006/jmla.1999.2681.

Bertram, Raymond, Matti Laine, R. Harald Baayen, Schreuder, Hyönä Robert & Jukka. 2000b. Affixal homonymy triggers full-form storage, even with inflected words, even in a morphologically rich language. *Cognition* 74(2). B13-B25. https://doi.org/10.1016/S0010-0277(99)00068-2.

Bertram, Raymond, Robert Schreuder & R. Harald Baayen. 2000c. The balance of storage and computation in morphological processing: The role of word formation type, affixal homonymy, and productivity. *Journal of Experimental Psychology: Learning, Memory, and Cognition* 26(2). 489–511. https://doi.org/10.1037/0278-7393.26.2.489.

Bickel, Balthasar & Fernando Zúñiga. 2017. The 'word' in polysynthetic languages: Phonological and syntactic challenges. In Michael Fortescue, Marianne Mithun & Nicholas Evans (eds.), *The Oxford handbook of polysynthesis*, 158–186. Oxford: Oxford University Press. https://doi.org/10.1093/oxfordhb/9780199683208.013.52.

Bien, Heidrun, R. Harald Baayen & Willem J. M. Levelt. 2011. Frequency effects in the production of Dutch deverbal adjectives and inflected verbs. *Language and Cognitive Processes* 26(4-6). 683–715. https://doi.org/10.1080/01690965.2010.511475.

Bien, Heidrun, Willem J. M. Levelt & R. Harald Baayen. 2005. Frequency effects in compound production. *Proceedings of the National Academy of Sciences of the United States of America* 102(49). 17876–17881. https://doi.org/10.1073/pnas.0508431102.

Blazej, Laura J. & Ariel M. Cohen-Goldberg. 2015. Can we hear morphological complexity before words are complex? *Journal of Eperimental Psychology: Human Perception and Performance* 41(1). 50–68. https://doi.org/10.1037/a0038509.

Blevins, James P. 2006. Word-based morphology. *Journal of Linguistics* 42(3). 531–573. https://doi.org/10.1017/S0022226706004191.

Blevins, James P. 2016. The minimal sign. In Andrew Hippisley & Gregory Stump (eds.), *The Cambridge handbook of morphology*, 50–69. Cambridge: Cambridge University Press. https://doi.org/10.1017/9781139814720.003.

Blevins, James P., Farrell Ackerman & Robert Malouf. 2016. Morphology as an adaptive discriminative system. In Daniel Siddiqi & Heidi Harley (eds.), *Morphological metatheory* (Linguistics Today 229), 271–302. Amsterdam: John Benjamins. https://doi.org/10.1075/la.229.10ble.

Boersma, Paul & David J. M. Weenik. 2001. *Praat: Doing phonetics by computer*. Version 5.4.04. http://www.praat.org/.

Booij, Geert E. 2010a. Compound construction: Schemas or analogy? In Sergio Scalise & Irene Vogel (eds.), *Cross-disciplinary issues in compounding* (Current Issues in Linguistic Theory 311), vol. 311, 93–108. Amsterdam: John Benjamins. https://doi.org/10.1075/cilt.311.09boo.

Booij, Geert E. 2010b. *Construction morphology* (Oxford Linguistics). Oxford: Oxford University Press.

Booij, Geert E. (ed.). 2018. *The construction of words: Advances in Construction Morphology* (Studies in Morphology 4). Cham: Springer. https://doi.org/10.1007/978-3-319-74394-3.

Bowden, Harriet W., Matthew P. Gelfand, Cristina Sanz & Michael T. Ullman. 2010. Verbal inflectional morphology in L1 and L2 Spanish: A frequency effects study examining storage versus composition. *Language Learning* 60(1). 44–87. https://doi.org/10.1111/j.1467-9922.2009.00551.x.

Box, George E. P. 1976. Science and statistics. *Journal of the American Statistical Association* 71(356). 791–799. https://doi.org/10.1080/01621459.1976.10480949.

Burani, Cristina & Alfonso Caramazza. 1987. Representation and processing of derived words. *Language and Cognitive Processes* 2(3-4). 217–227. https://doi.org/10.1080/01690968708406932.

Burnage, Gavin. 1990. *CELEX: A guide for users*. Nijmegen: Centre for Lexical Information.

Buschmeier, Hendrik & Marcin Włodarczak. 2013. TextGridTools: A TextGrid processing and analysis toolkit for Python. *Proceedings der 24. Konferenz zur Elektronischen Sprachsignalverarbeitung, Bielefeld, Germany*. https://pub.uni-bielefeld.de/record/2561620.

Butterworth, Brian. 1983. Lexical representation. In Brian Butterworth (ed.), *Language production, Vol. 2: Development, writing and other language processes*, 257–294. London: Academic Press.

Bybee, Joan. 2001. *Phonology and language use* (Cambridge Studies in Linguistics 94). Cambridge: Cambridge University Press. https://doi.org/10.1017/CBO9780511612886.

Bybee, Joan. 2002. Word frequency and context of use in the lexical diffusion of phonetically conditioned sound change. *Language Variation and Change* 14(3). 261–290. https://doi.org/10.1017/S0954394502143018.

Bybee, Joan. 2017. Grammatical and lexical factors in sound change: A usage-based approach. *Language Variation and Change* 29(3). 273–300. https://doi.org/10.1017/S0954394517000199.

Bybee, Joan L. 2000. The phonology of the lexicon: Evidence from lexical diffusion. In Michael Barlow & Suzanne Kemmer (eds.), *Usage-based models of language*, 65–85. Cambridge: Cambridge University Press.

Bybee, Joan L. 2007. *Frequency of use and the organization of language*. Oxford, New York: Oxford University Press. https://doi.org/10.1093/acprof:oso/9780195301571.001.0001.

Byrd, Dani, Jelena Krivokapić & Sungbok Lee. 2006. How far, how long: On the temporal scope of prosodic boundary effects. *The Journal of the Acoustical Society of America* 120(3). 1589–1599. https://doi.org/10.1121/1.2217135.

Cambier-Langeveld, Tina. 1997. The domain of final lengthening in the production of Dutch. *Linguistics in the Netherlands* 14. 13–24. https://doi.org/10.1075/avt.14.04cam.

Campbell, W. Nick. 1990. Evidence for a syllable-based model of speech timing. *Proceedings of the International Conference on Spoken Language Processing*. http://www.isca-speech.org/archive.

Caramazza, Alfonso. 1997. How many levels of processing are there in lexical access? *Cognitive Neuropsychology* 14(1). 177–208. https://doi.org/10.1080/026432997381664.

Caramazza, Alfonso, Albert Costa, Michele Miozzo & Yanchao Bi. 2001. The specific-word frequency effect: Implications for the representation of homophones in speech production. *Journal of Experimental Psychology: Learning, Memory, and Cognition* 27(6). 1430–1450. https://doi.org/10.1037/0278-7393.27.6.1430.

Caselli, Naomi K., Michael K. Caselli & Ariel M. Cohen-Goldberg. 2016. Inflected words in production: Evidence for a morphologically rich lexicon. *The Quarterly Journal of Experimental Psychology* 69(3). 432–454. https://doi.org/10.1080/17470218.2015.1054847.

Chatterjee, Samprit & Ali S. Hadi. 2006. *Regression analysis by example*, 4th edn. Hoboken: John Wiley & Sons. https://doi.org/10.1002/0470055464.

Chen, Jenn-Yeu & Train-Min Chen. 2006. Morphological encoding in the production of compound words in Mandarin Chinese. *Journal of Memory and Language* 54(4). 491–514. https://doi.org/10.1016/j.jml.2005.01.002.

Chen, Jenn-Yeu & Train-Min Chen. 2007. Form encoding in Chinese word production does not involve morphemes. *Language and Cognitive Processes* 22(7). 1001–1020. https://doi.org/10.1080/01690960701190249.

Cho, Taehong. 2001. Effects of morpheme boundaries on intergestural timing: Evidence from Korean. *Phonetica* 58. 129–162. https://doi.org/10.1159/000056196.

Chomsky, Noam & Morris Halle. 1968. *The sound pattern of English*. New York, Evanston, London: Harper and Row.

Chuang, Yu-Ying, Mihi Kang, Xuefeng Luo & R. Harald Baayen. 2021. Vector space morphology with linear discriminative learning. *Preprint*. arXiv:2107.03950.

Chuang, Yu-Ying, Marie L. Vollmer, Elnaz Shafaei-Bajestan, Susanne Gahl, Peter Hendrix & R. Harald Baayen. 2020. The processing of pseudoword form and meaning in production and comprehension: A computational modeling approach using linear discriminative learning. *Behavior Research Methods* 53. 945–976. https://doi.org/10.3758/s13428-020-01356-w.

Clahsen, Harald. 1999. Lexical entries and rules of language: A multidisciplinary study of German inflection. *Behavioral and Brain Sciences* 22(6). 991–1013. https://doi.org/10.1017/s0140525x99002228.

Clopper, Cynthia G. & Rory Turnbull. 2018. Exploring variation in phonetic reduction: Linguistic, social, and cognitive factors. In Francesco Cangemi, Meghan Clayards, Oliver Niebuhr, Barbara Schuppler & Margaret Zellers (eds.), *Rethinking reduction*, 25–72. Berlin, Boston: De Gruyter Mouton. https://doi.org/10.1515/9783110524178-002.

Cohen, Clara. 2014. Probabilistic reduction and probabilistic enhancement: Contextual and paradigmatic effects on morpheme pronunciation. *Morphology* 24. 291–323. https://doi.org/10.1007/s11525-014-9243-y.

Cohen, Clara. 2015. Context and paradigms. *The Mental Lexicon* 10(3). 313–338. https://doi.org/10.1075/ml.10.3.01coh.

Cohen-Goldberg, Ariel M. 2013. Towards a theory of multimorphemic word production: The heterogeneity of processing hypothesis. *Language and Cognitive Processes* 28(7). 1036–1064. https://doi.org/10.1080/01690965.2012.759241.

Coile, Bert van. 1987. A model of phoneme durations based on the analysis of a read Dutch text. *Proceedings of the European Conference on Speech Technology.* https://www.isca-speech.org/archive.

Cole, Pascale, Cécile Beauvillain & Juan Segui. 1989. On the representation and processing of prefixed and suffixed derived words: A differential frequency effect. *Journal of Memory and Language* 28(1). 1–13. https://doi.org/10.1016/0749-596X(89)90025-9.

Coleman, John, Ladan Baghai-Ravary, John Pybus & Sergio Grau. 2012. *Audio BNC: The audio edition of the Spoken British National Corpus.* University of Oxford. http://www.phon.ox.ac.uk/AudioBNC.

Côté, Marie-Hélène. 2013. Understanding cohesion in French liaison. *Language Sciences* 39. 156–166. https://doi.org/10.1016/j.langsci.2013.02.013.

Csardi, Gabor & Tamas Nepusz. 2006. The igraph software package for complex network research. *InterJournal, Complex Systems* 5. https://igraph.org.

Dąbrowska, Ewa. 2015. Individual differences in grammatical knowledge. In Ewa Dąbrowska & Dagmar Divjak (eds.), *Handbook of cognitive linguistics* (Handbooks of Linguistics and Communication Science 39), 650–668. Berlin, Boston: De Gruyter Mouton. https://doi.org/10.1515/9783110292022-033.

Davies, Mark. 2008. *The Corpus of Contemporary American English: 450 million words, 1990–present.* http://corpus.byu.edu/coca/.

Dell, Gary S. 1986. A spreading-activation theory of retrieval in sentence production. *Psychological Review* 93(3). 283–321. https://doi.org/10.1037/0033-295X.93.3.283.

Dell, Gary S. 1990. Effects of frequency and vocabulary type on phonological speech errors. *Language and Cognitive Processes* 5(4). 313–349. https://doi.org/10.1080/01690969008407066.

Di Sciullo, Anne-Marie & Edwin Williams. 1987. *On the definition of word* (Linguistic Inquiry Monographs 14). Cambridge: MIT Press.

Divjak, Dagmar. 2019. *Frequency in language: Memory, attention and learning.* Cambridge: Cambridge University Press. https://doi.org/10.1017/9781316084410.

Don, Jan. 1993. *Morphological conversion.* Utrecht: OTS, Rijksuniversiteit.

Edwards, Jan & Mary E. Beckman. 1988. Articulatory timing and the prosodic interpretation of syllable duration. *Phonetica* 45(2–4). 156–174. https://doi.org/10.1159/000261824.

Edwards, Jan, Mary E. Beckman & Benjamin Munson. 2004. The interaction between vocabulary size and phonotactic probability effects on children's production accuracy and fluency in nonword repetition. *Journal of Speech, Language, and Hearing Research* 47(2). 421–436. https://doi.org/10.1044/1092-4388(2004/034).

Engemann, Marie & Ingo Plag. 2021. Phonetic reduction and paradigm uniformity effects in spontaneous speech. *The Mental Lexicon* 16(1). 165–198. https://doi.org/10.1075/ml.20023.eng.

Ernestus, Mirjam, Mybeth Lahey, Femke Verhees & R. Harald Baayen. 2006. Lexical frequency and voice assimilation. *The Journal of the Acoustical Society of America* 120(2). 1040–1051. https://doi.org/10.1121/1.2211548.

Fábregas, Antonio & Martina Penke. 2020. Word storage and computation. In Vito Pirrelli, Ingo Plag & Wolfgang U. Dressler (eds.), *Word knowledge and word usage: A cross-disciplinary guide to the mental lexicon* (Trends in Linguistics: Studies and Monographs 337), 455–505. Berlin, Boston: De Gruyter Mouton. https://doi.org/10.1515/9783110440577-012.

Ferreira, Victor S. & Zenzi M. Griffin. 2003. Phonological influences on lexical (mis)selection. *Psychological Science* 14(1). 86–90. https://doi.org/10.1111/1467-9280.01424.

Filipović Đurđević, Dušica & Aleksandar Kostić. 2021. We probably sense sense probabilities. *Language, Cognition and Neuroscience*. 1–28. https://doi.org/10.1080/23273798.2021.1909083.

Firth, John R. 1957. A synopsis of linguistic theory, 1930–1955. In *Studies in linguistic analysis* (Special Volume of the Philological Society), 1–31. Oxford: Wiley-Blackwell.

Fox, John & Sanford Weisberg. 2011. *An R companion to applied regression,* 2nd edn. Thousand Oaks: SAGE.

Frazier, Melissa. 2006. Output-output faithfulness to moraic structure: Evidence from American English. In Christopher Davis, Amy R. Deal & Youri Zabbal (eds.), *Proceedings of the thirty-sixth annual meeting of the North East Linguistic Society*, 1–14. Amherst: Graduate Linguistic Student Association.

Fromont, Robert. 2003–2020. *LaBB-CAT*. University of Canterbury. https://labbcat.canterbury.ac.nz/.

Fromont, Robert & Jennifer Hay. 2012. LaBB-CAT: An annotation store. *Proceedings of the Australasian Language Technology Association Workshop* 10. 113–117.

Gahl, Susanne. 2008. *Thyme* and *time* are not homophones: The effect of lemma frequency on word durations in spontaneous speech. *Language* 84(3). 474–496. https://doi.org/10.1353/LAN.0.0035.

Gahl, Susanne & Ingo Plag. 2019. Spelling errors in English derivational suffixes reflect boundary strength. *The Mental Lexicon* 14(1). 1–36.

Gahl, Susanne, Yao Yao & Keith Johnson. 2012. Why reduce? Phonological neighborhood density and phonetic reduction in spontaneous speech. *Journal of Memory and Language* 66(4). 789–806. https://doi.org/10.1016/j.jml.2011.11.006.

Gahl, Susanne & Alan C. L. Yu. 2006. Introduction to the special issue on exemplar-based models in linguistics. *The Linguistic Review* 23(3). 213–216. https://doi.org/10.1515/TLR.2006.007.

Goldinger, Stephen D. 1998. Echoes of echoes? An episodic theory of lexical access. *Psychological Review* 105(2). 251–279. https://doi.org/10.1037/0033-295x.105.2.251.

Gordon, Elizabeth, Margaret Maclagan & Jennifer Hay. 2007. The ONZE corpus. In Joan C. Beal, Karen P. Corrigan & Hermann L. Moisl (eds.), *Creating and digitizing language corpora, Volume 2: Diachronic corpora*, 82–104. Basingstoke: Palgrave Macmillan. https://doi.org/10.1057/9780230223202_4.

Grömping, Ulrike. 2006. Relative Importance for Linear Regression in R: The Package relaimpo. *Journal of Statistical Software* 17(1). 1–27. https://doi.org/10.18637/jss.v017.i01.

Gussmann, Edmund. 1987. The lexicon of English de-adjectival verbs. In Edmund Gussmann (ed.), *Rules and the lexicon: Studies in word-formation*, 79–101. Lublin: Redakcja Wydawnictw Katolickiego Uniwersytetu Lubelskiego.

Guy, Gregory R. 1980. Variation in the group and the individual: The case of final stop deletion. In William Labov (ed.), *Locating language in time and space* (Quantitative Analyses of Linguistic Structure 1), 1–36. New York, London: Academic Press.

Guy, Gregory R. 1991. Explanation in variable phonology: An exponential model of morphological constraints. *Language Variation and Change* 3(1). 1–22. https://doi.org/10.1017/S0954394500000429.

Hall, John F. 1954. Learning as a function of word-frequency. *The American Journal of Psychology* 67(1). 138–140. https://doi.org/10.2307/1418080.

Hall, Tracy A. 1999. The phonological word: A review. In Tracy A. Hall & Ursula Kleinhenz (eds.), *Studies of the phonological word* (Current Issues in Linguistic Theory 174), 1–22. Amsterdam, Philadelphia: John Benjamins. https://doi.org/10.1075/cilt.174.02hal.

Halle, Morris. 1973. Prolegomena to a theory of word formation. *Linguistic Inquiry* 4(1). 3–16.

Halle, Morris & Alec Marantz. 1994. Some key features of Distributed Morphology. *MIT Working Papers in Linguistics* 21. 275–288.

Hanique, Iris & Mirjam Ernestus. 2012. The role of morphology in acoustic reduction. *Lingue e Linguaggio* 11. 147–164. https://doi.org/10.1418/38783.

Hanique, Iris, Mirjam Ernestus & Barbara Schuppler. 2013. Informal speech processes can be categorical in nature, even if they affect many different words. *The Journal of the Acoustical Society of America* 133. 1644–1655. https://doi.org/10.1121/1.4790352.

Harley, Heidi. 2012. Compounding in Distributed Morphology. In Rochelle Lieber & Pavol Štekauer (eds.), *The Oxford handbook of compounding*. Oxford University Press. https://doi.org/10.1093/oxfordhb/9780199695720.013.0017.

Harris, Zellig S. 1954. Distributional structure. *Word* 10(2–3). 146–162. https://doi.org/10.1080/00437956.1954.11659520.

Hay, Jennifer. 2001. Lexical frequency in morphology: Is everything relative? *Linguistics* 39(6). 1041–1070. https://doi.org/10.1515/ling.2001.041.

Hay, Jennifer. 2002. From speech perception to morphology: Affix ordering revisited. *Language* 78(3). 527–555. https://doi.org/10.1353/LAN.2002.0159.

Hay, Jennifer. 2003. *Causes and consequences of word structure*. New York, London: Routledge. https://doi.org/10.4324/9780203495131.

Hay, Jennifer. 2007. The phonetics of *un*. In Judith Munat (ed.), *Lexical creativity, texts and contexts* (Studies in Functional and Structural Linguistics 58), 39–57. Amsterdam, Philadelphia: John Benjamins. https://doi.org/10.1075/sfsl.58.09hay.

Hebb, Donald O. 1949. *The organization of behavior: A neuropsychological theory*. New York: Wiley.

Heitmeier, Maria & R. Harald Baayen. 2020. Simulating phonological and semantic impairment of English tense inflection with linear discriminative learning. *The Mental Lexicon* 15(3). 385–421. https://doi.org/10.1075/ml.20003.hei.

Heitmeier, Maria, Yu-Ying Chuang & R. Harald Baayen. 2021. Modeling morphology with linear discriminative learning: Considerations and design choices. *Frontiers in Psychology* 12. https://doi.org/10.3389/fpsyg.2021.720713.

Hildebrandt, Kristine A. 2015. The prosodic word. In John R. Taylor (ed.), *The Oxford handbook of the word*, 221–245. Oxford: Oxford University Press. https://doi.org/10.1093/oxfordhb/9780199641604.013.035.

Hockett, Charles F. 1954. Two models of grammatical description. *Word* 10(2–3). 210–234. https://doi.org/10.1080/00437956.1954.11659524.
Hoffmann, Sebastian & Sabine Arndt-Lappe. 2021. Better data for more researchers: Using the audio features of BNCweb. *ICAME Journal* 45(1). 125–154. https://doi.org/10.2478/icame-2021-0004.
Hoffmann, Sebastian & Stefan Evert. 2018. *BNCweb: CQP Edition*. Version 4.4. http://bncweb.lancs.ac.uk/.
Howes, Davis H. & R. L. Solomon. 1951. Visual duration threshold as a function of word-probability. *Journal of Experimental Psychology* 41(6). 401–410. https://doi.org/10.1037/h0056020.
Ivens, Stephen H. & Bertram L. Koslin. 1991. *Demands for reading literacy require new accountability measures*. Brewster: Touchstone Applied Science Associates.
Jaeger, T. Florian & Esteban Buz. 2017. Signal reduction and linguistic encoding. In Eva M. Fernández & Helen S. Cairns (eds.), *The handbook of psycholinguistics* (Blackwell Handbooks in Linguistics), 38–81. Chichester: Wiley-Blackwell.
Janssen, Niels, Yanchao Bi & Alfonso Caramazza. 2008. A tale of two frequencies: Determining the speed of lexical access for Mandarin Chinese and English compounds. *Language and Cognitive Processes* 23(7–8). 1191–1223. https://doi.org/10.1080/01690960802250900.
Jescheniak, Jörg D. & Willem J. M. Levelt. 1994. Word frequency effects in speech production: Retrieval of syntactic information and of phonological form. *Journal of Experimental Psychology: Learning, Memory, and Cognition* 20(4). 824–843. https://doi.org/10.1037/0278-7393.20.4.824.
Johnson, Keith. 2004. Massive reduction in conversational American English. In *Spontaneous speech: Data and analysis: The 1st Session of the 10th International Symposium*. 29–54. Tokyo.
Jurafsky, Daniel. 2003. Probabilistic modeling in psycholinguistics: Linguistic comprehension and production. In Rens Bod, Jennifer Hay & Stefanie Jannedy (eds.), *Probabilistic linguistics*, 39–95. Cambridge, London: MIT Press.
Jurafsky, Daniel, Alan Bell, Michelle Gregory & William D. Raymond. 2001. Probabilistic relations between words: Evidence from reduction in lexical production. In Joan Bybee & Paul J. Hopper (eds.), *Frequency and the emergence of linguistic structure* (Typological Studies in Language 45), 229–254. Amsterdam: John Benjamins. https://doi.org/10.1075/tsl.45.13jur.
Kawaletz, Lea. 2021. *The semantics of English -ment nominalizations*. PhD dissertation: Heinrich Heine University Düsseldorf.
Kiparsky, Paul. 1982. Lexical morphology and phonology. In In-Seok Yang (ed.), *Linguistics in the morning calm: Selected papers from SICOL*, 3–91. Seoul: Hanshin.
Klatt, Dennis H. 1975. Vowel lengthening is syntactically determined in a connected discourse. *Journal of Phonetics* 3(3). 129–140. https://doi.org/10.1016/S0095-4470(19)31360-9.
Kunter, Gero. 2016. *Coquery: A free corpus query tool*. www.coquery.org.
Kuperman, Victor, Mark Pluymaekers, Mirjam Ernestus & R. Harald Baayen. 2007. Morphological predictability and acoustic duration of interfixes in Dutch compounds. *The Journal of the Acoustical Society of America* 121(4). 2261–2271. https://doi.org/10.1121/1.2537393.
Kuznetsova, Alexandra, Per B. Brockhoff & Rune H. B. Christensen. 2016. *lmerTest: Tests in linear fixed effects models*. R package. Version 3.1.2. https://cran.r-project.org/web/packages/lmerTest/index.html.

Labov, William. 1989. The child as linguistic historian. *Language Variation and Change* 1(1). 85–97. https://doi.org/10.1017/S0954394500000120.

Ladefoged, Peter & Keith Johnson. 2011. *A course in phonetics*, 6th edn. Boston: Wadsworth Cengage Learning.

Landauer, Thomas K. & Susan T. Dumais. 1997. A solution to Plato's problem: The latent semantic analysis theory of acquisition, induction, and representation of knowledge. *Psychological Review* 104(2). 211–240. https://doi.org/10.1037/0033-295X.104.2.211.

Landauer, Thomas K., Peter W. Foltz & Darrell Laham. 1998. An introduction to Latent Semantic Analysis. *Discourse Processes* 25(2–3). 259–284. https://doi.org/10.1080/01638539809545028.

Langacker, Ronald. 2008. *Cognitive Grammar*. Oxford University Press. https://doi.org/10.1093/acprof:oso/9780195331967.001.0001.

Lapesa, Gabriella, Lea Kawaletz, Ingo Plag, Marios Andreou, Max Kisselew & Sebastian Padó. 2018. Disambiguation of newly derived nominalizations in context: A Distributional Semantics approach. *Word Structure* 11(3). 277–312. https://doi.org/10.3366/word.2018.0131.

Lee-Kim, Sang-Im, Lisa Davidson & Sangjin Hwang. 2013. Morphological effects on the darkness of English intervocalic /l/. *Laboratory Phonology* 4(2). 475–511. https://doi.org/10.1515/lp-2013-0015.

Lehiste, Ilse. 1972. The timing of utterances and linguistic boundaries. *The Journal of the Acoustical Society of America* 51(6B). 2018–2024. https://doi.org/10.1121/1.1913062.

Lehtonen, Minna, Helge Niska, Erling Wande, Jussi Niemi & Matti Laine. 2006. Recognition of inflected words in a morphologically limited language: Frequency effects in monolinguals and bilinguals. *Journal of Psycholinguistic Research* 35(2). 121–146. https://doi.org/10.1007/s10936-005-9008-1.

Levelt, William J. M., Ardi Roelofs & Antje S. Meyer. 1999. A theory of lexical access in speech production. *Behavioral and Brain Sciences* 22(1). 1–38. https://doi.org/10.1017/S0140525X99001776.

Lindblom, Björn. 1963. Spectrographic study of vowel reduction. *The Journal of the Acoustical Society of America* 35(11). 1773–1781. https://doi.org/10.1121/1.1918816.

Lindblom, Björn. 1990. Explaining phonetic variation: A sketch of the H&H theory. In William J. Hardcastle & Alain Marchal (eds.), *Speech production and speech modelling*, 403–439. Dordrecht: Springer Netherlands. https://doi.org/10.1007/978-94-009-2037-8_16.

Lindeman, Richard H., Peter F. Merenda & Ruth Z. Gold. 1980. *Introduction to bivariate and multivariate analysis*. Glenview, London: Scott, Foresman and Company.

Lohmann, Arne. 2018. Time and thyme are not homophones: A closer look at Gahl's work on the lemma-frequency effect, including a reanalysis. *Language* 94(2). e180–e190. https://doi.org/10.1353/lan.2018.0032.

Lohmann, Arne & Erin Conwell. 2020. Phonetic effects of grammatical category: How category-specific prosodic phrasing and lexical frequency impact the duration of nouns and verbs. *Journal of Phonetics* 78. 100939. https://doi.org/10.1016/j.wocn.2019.100939.

Lõo, Kaidi, Juhani Järvikivi, Fabian Tomaschek, Benjamin V. Tucker & R. Harald Baayen. 2018. Production of Estonian case-inflected nouns shows whole-word frequency and paradigmatic effects. *Morphology* 28. 71–97. https://doi.org/10.1007/s11525-017-9318-7.

Losiewicz, Beth L. 1995. Word frequency effects on the acoustic duration of morphemes. *The Journal of the Acoustical Society of America* 97(5). 3243. https://doi.org/10.1121/1.411745.

Machač, Pavel & Radek Skarnitzl. 2009. *Principles of phonetic segmentation*. Prague: Epocha Publishing House.

MacKay, Donald G. 1982. The problems of flexibility, fluency, and speed-accuracy trade-off in skilled behavior. *Psychological Review* 89(5). 483–506. https://doi.org/10.1037/0033-295X.89.5.483.

MacKenzie, Laurel & Meredith Tamminga. 2021. New and old puzzles in the morphological conditioning of coronal stop deletion. *Language Variation and Change* 33(2). 217–244. https://doi.org/10.1017/S0954394521000119.

Marantz, Alec. 2013. No escape from morphemes in morphological processing. *Language and Cognitive Processes* 28(7). 905–916. https://doi.org/10.1080/01690965.2013.779385.

Marcus, Gary F. 2001. *The algebraic mind: Integrating connectionism and cognitive science* (Learning, Development, and Conceptual Change). Cambridge: MIT Press.

Marslen-Wilson, William D. & Lorraine K. Tyler. 1997. Dissociating types of mental computation. *Nature* 387(6633). 592–594. https://doi.org/10.1038/42456.

Matthews, Peter H. 1991. *Morphology: An introduction to the theory of word structure*, 2nd edn. (Cambridge Textbooks in Linguistics). Cambridge: Cambridge University Press. https://doi.org/10.1017/CBO9781139166485.

Meunier, Fanny & Juan Segui. 1999. Frequency effects in auditory word recognition: The case of suffixed words. *Journal of Memory and Language* 41(3). 327–344. https://doi.org/10.1006/jmla.1999.2642.

Michel Lange, Violaine, Pauline P. Cheneval, Grégoire Python & Marina Laganaro. 2017. Contextual phonological errors and omission of obligatory liaison as a window into a reduced span of phonological encoding. *Aphasiology* 31(2). 201–220. https://doi.org/10.1080/02687038.2016.1176121.

Milin, Petar, Victor Kuperman, Aleksandar Kostić & R. Harald Baayen. 2009. Words and paradigms bit by bit: An information - theoretic approach to the processing of inflection and derivation. In James P. Blevins & Juliette Blevins (eds.), *Analogy in grammar: Form and acquisition*, 214–252. New York: Oxford University Press. https://doi.org/10.1093/acprof:oso/9780199547548.003.0010.

Moore, Eliakim H. 1920. On the reciprocal of the general algebraic matrix. *Bulletin of the American Mathematical Society* 26(9). 394–395.

Morton, John. 1969. Interaction of information in word recognition. *Psychological Review* 76(2). 165–178. https://doi.org/10.1037/h0027366.

Moscoso del Prado Martín, Fermín, Raymond Bertram, Tuomo Häikiö, Robert Schreuder & R. Harald Baayen. 2004. Morphological family size in a morphologically rich language: The case of Finnish compared with Dutch and Hebrew. *Journal of Experimental Psychology: Learning, Memory, and Cognition* 30(6). 1271–1278. https://doi.org/10.1037/0278-7393.30.6.1271.

Moscoso del Prado Martín, Fermín, Avital Deutsch, Ram Frost, Robert Schreuder, Nivja H. de Jong & R. Harald Baayen. 2005. Changing places: A cross-language perspective on frequency and family size in Dutch and Hebrew. *Journal of Memory and Language* 53(4). 496–512. https://doi.org/10.1016/j.jml.2005.07.003.

Munhall, Kevin, Carol Fowler, Sarah Hawkins & Elliot Saltzman. 1992. "Compensatory shortening" in monosyllables of spoken English. *Journal of Phonetics* 20(2). 225–239. https://doi.org/10.1016/S0095-4470(19)30624-2.

Munson, Benjamin. 2001. Phonological pattern frequency and speech production in adults and children. *Journal of Speech, Language, and Hearing Research* 44(4). 778–792. https://doi.org/10.1044/1092-4388(2001/061).

Nespor, Marina & Irene Vogel. 2007. *Prosodic phonology*. Berlin, New York: De Gruyter. https://doi.org/10.1515/9783110977790.

New, Boris, Marc Brysbaert, Juan Segui, Ludovic Ferrand & Kathleen Rastle. 2004. The processing of singular and plural nouns in French and English. *Journal of Memory and Language* 51(4). 568–585. https://doi.org/10.1016/j.jml.2004.06.010.

Nicenboim, Bruno, Timo B. Roettger & Shravan Vasishth. 2018. Using meta-analysis for evidence synthesis: The case of incomplete neutralization in German. *Journal of Phonetics* 70. 39–55. https://doi.org/10.1016/j.wocn.2018.06.001.

Nooteboom, Sieb G. 1972. *Production and perception of vowel duration: A study of the durational properties of vowels in Dutch*. Utrecht: University of Utrecht.

Oxford English Dictionary Online. 2020. Oxford University Press. www.oed.com.

Penrose, Roger. 1955. A generalized inverse for matrices. *Mathematical Proceedings of the Cambridge Philosophical Society* 51(3). 406–413. https://doi.org/10.1017/S0305004100030401.

Piantadosi, Steven T., Harry Tily & Edward Gibson. 2011. Word lengths are optimized for efficient communication. *Proceedings of the National Academy of Sciences of the United States of America* 108(9). 3526–3529. https://doi.org/10.1073/pnas.1012551108.

Pierrehumbert, Janet B. 2001. Exemplar dynamics: Word frequency, lenition and contrast. In Joan Bybee & Paul J. Hopper (eds.), *Frequency and the emergence of linguistic structure* (Typological Studies in Language 45), 137–158. Amsterdam: John Benjamins. https://doi.org/10.1075/tsl.45.08pie.

Pierrehumbert, Janet B. 2002. Word-specific phonetics. In Carlos Gussenhoven & Natasha Warner (eds.), *Laboratory Phonology 7* (Phonology and Phonetics 4), 101–140. Berlin, New York: De Gruyter Mouton. https://doi.org/10.1515/9783110197105.1.101.

Pinker, Steven. 1999. *Words and rules: The ingredients of language*. New York: Basic Books.

Pirrelli, Vito, Claudia Marzi, Marcello Ferro, Franco A. Cardillo, R. Harald Baayen & Petar Milin. 2020. Psycho-computational modelling of the mental lexicon: A discriminative learning perspective. In Vito Pirrelli, Ingo Plag & Wolfgang U. Dressler (eds.), *Word knowledge and word usage: A cross-disciplinary guide to the mental lexicon* (Trends in Linguistics: Studies and Monographs 337), 23–82. Berlin, Boston: De Gruyter Mouton. https://doi.org/10.1515/9783110440577-002.

Pisoni, David B. & Susannah V. Levi. 2007. Representations and representational specificity in speech perception and spoken word recognition. In M. Gareth Gaskell (ed.), *The Oxford handbook of psycholinguistics*, 2–18. Oxford: Oxford University Press. https://doi.org/10.1093/oxfordhb/9780198568971.013.0001.

Plag, Ingo. 2018. *Word-formation in English*, 2nd edn. Cambridge: Cambridge University Press. https://doi.org/10.1017/9781316771402.

Plag, Ingo & R. Harald Baayen. 2009. Suffix ordering and morphological processing. *Language* 85(1). 109–152. https://doi.org/10.1353/lan.0.0087.

Plag, Ingo & Laura W. Balling. 2020. Derivational morphology: An integrative perspective on some fundamental questions. In Vito Pirrelli, Ingo Plag & Wolfgang U. Dressler (eds.), *Word knowledge and word usage: A cross-disciplinary guide to the mental lexicon* (Trends in Linguistics: Studies and Monographs 337), 295–335. Berlin, Boston: De Gruyter Mouton. https://doi.org/10.1515/9783110440577-008.

Plag, Ingo & Sonia Ben Hedia. 2018. The phonetics of newly derived words: Testing the effect of morphological segmentability on affix duration. In Sabine Arndt-Lappe, Angelika Braun, Claudine Moulin & Esme Winter-Froemel (eds.), *Expanding the lexicon: Linguistic innovation, morphological productivity, and ludicity*, 93–116. Berlin, Boston: De Gruyter Mouton. https://doi.org/10.1515/9783110501933-095.

Plag, Ingo, Christiane Dalton-Puffer & R. Harald Baayen. 1999. Morphological productivity across speech and writing. *English Language and Linguistics* 3(2). 209–228. https://doi.org/10.1017/S1360674399000222.

Plag, Ingo, Julia Homann & Gero Kunter. 2017. Homophony and morphology: The acoustics of word-final S in English. *Journal of Linguistics* 53(1). 181–216. https://doi.org/10.1017/S0022226715000183.

Plag, Ingo, Arne Lohmann, Sonia Ben Hedia & Julia Zimmermann. 2020. An <s> is an <s'>, or is it? Plural and genitive-plural are not homophonous. In Lívia Körtvélyessy & Pavol Štekauer (eds.), *Complex words: Advances in morphology*, 260–292. Cambridge: Cambridge University Press. https://doi.org/10.1017/9781108780643.015.

Pluymaekers, Mark, Mirjam Ernestus & R. Harald Baayen. 2005a. Articulatory planning is continuous and sensitive to informational redundancy. *Phonetica* 62(2–4). 146–159. https://doi.org/10.1159/000090095.

Pluymaekers, Mark, Mirjam Ernestus & R. Harald Baayen. 2005b. Lexical frequency and acoustic reduction in spoken Dutch. *The Journal of the Acoustical Society of America* 118(4). 2561–2569. https://doi.org/10.1121/1.2011150.

Pluymaekers, Mark, Mirjam Ernestus & R. Harald Baayen. 2006. Effects of word frequency on the acoustic durations of affixes. In *Proceedings of Interspeech 2006 and 9th International Conference on Spoken Language Processing*. 953–956. https://doi.org/10.21437/Interspeech.2006.

Pluymaekers, Mark, Mirjam Ernestus, R. Harald Baayen & Geert E. Booij. 2010. Morphological effects on fine phonetic detail: The case of Dutch *-igheid*. In Aditi Lahiri, Cécile Fougeron, Barbara Kühnert, Mariapaola D'Imperio & Nathalie Vallée (eds.), *Laboratory Phonology 10* (Phonology and Phonetics), 511–531. Berlin, New York: De Gruyter Mouton. https://doi.org/10.1515/9783110224917.5.511.

Poplack, Shana. 1980. The notion of the plural in Puerto Rican Spanish: Competing constraints on (s) deletion. In William Labov (ed.), *Locating language in time and space* (Quantitative Analyses of Linguistic Structure 1), 55–67. New York, London: Academic Press.

Prasada, Sandeep & Steven Pinker. 1993. Generalization of regular and irregular morphological patterns. *Language and Cognitive Processes* 8(1). 1–56. https://doi.org/10.1080/01690969308406948.

R Core Team. 2022. *R: A language and environment for statistical computing*. Version 4.2.1. Vienna: R Foundation for Statistical Computing. http://www.R-project.org/.

Raffelsiefen, Renate. 1999. Diagnostics for prosodic words revisited: The case of historically prefixed words in English. In Tracy A. Hall & Ursula Kleinhenz (eds.), *Studies of the phonological word* (Current Issues in Linguistic Theory 174), 133–201. Amsterdam, Philadelphia: John Benjamins. https://doi.org/10.1075/cilt.174.07raf.

Raffelsiefen, Renate. 2007. Morphological word structure in English and Swedish: The evidence from prosody. In Geert E. Booij, Luca Ducceschi, Bernard Fradin, Ernesto Guevara, Angela Ralli & Sergio Scalise (eds.), *Online Proceedings of the Fifth Mediterranean Morphology Meeting (MMM5)*. 209–268. Fréjus.

Raftery, Adrian E. 1995. Bayesian model selection in social research. *Sociological Methodology* 25. 111–163. https://doi.org/10.2307/271063.

Ramón y Cajal, Santiago. 1894. The Croonian lecture: La fine structure des centres nerveux. *Proceedings of the Royal Society of London* 55(331–335). 444–468. https://doi.org/10.1098/rspl.1894.0063.

Ramscar, Michael & Daniel Yarlett. 2007. Linguistic self-correction in the absence of feedback: A new approach to the logical problem of language acquisition. *Cognitive Science* 31(6). 927–960. https://doi.org/10.1080/03640210701703576.

Ramscar, Michael, Daniel Yarlett, Melody Dye, Katie Denny & Kirsten Thorpe. 2010. The effects of feature-label-order and their implications for symbolic learning. *Cognitive Science* 34(6). 909–957. https://doi.org/10.1111/j.1551-6709.2009.01092.x.

Roelofs, Ardi & Victor S. Ferreira. 2019. The architecture of speaking. In Peter Hagoort (ed.), *Human language: From genes and brains to behavior*, 35–50. Cambridge, Massachusetts: MIT Press.

Roettger, Timo B. 2019. Researcher degrees of freedom in phonetic research. *Laboratory Phonology* 10(1). 1–27. https://doi.org/10.5334/labphon.147.

Roettger, Timo B., Bodo Winter & R. Harald Baayen. 2019. Emergent data analysis in phonetic sciences: Towards pluralism and reproducibility. *Journal of Phonetics* 73. 1–7. https://doi.org/10.1016/j.wocn.2018.12.001.

Rumelhart, David E. & James L. McClelland. 1986. *Parallel distributed processing: Explorations in the microstructure of cognition*. Cambridge: MIT Press. https://doi.org/10.7551/mitpress/5236.001.0001.

Saussure, Ferdinand de. 1916. *Cours de linguistique générale*. Edited by Charles Bally and Albert Sechehaye. Paris: Payot.

Schmitz, Dominic, Dinah Baer-Henney & Ingo Plag. 2021a. The duration of word-final /s/ differs across morphological categories in English: evidence from pseudowords. *Phonetica*. https://doi.org/10.1515/phon-2021-2013.

Schmitz, Dominic, Ingo Plag, Dinah Baer-Henney & Simon D. Stein. 2021b. Durational differences of word-final /s/ emerge from the lexicon: Modelling morpho-phonetic effects in pseudowords with linear discriminative learning. *Frontiers in Psychology* 12. 680889. https://doi.org/10.3389/fpsyg.2021.680889.

Schreuder, Robert & R. Harald Baayen. 1997. How complex simplex words can be. *Journal of Memory and Language* 37. 118–139. https://doi.org/10.1006/jmla.1997.2510.

Schuppler, Barbara, Wim A. van Dommelen, Jacques Koreman & Mirjam Ernestus. 2012. How linguistic and probabilistic properties of a word affect the realization of its final /t/: Studies at the phonemic and sub-phonemic level. *Journal of Phonetics* 40(4). 595–607. https://doi.org/10.1016/j.wocn.2012.05.004.

Selkirk, Elisabeth O. 1982. *The syntax of words* (Linguistic Inquiry Monographs 7). Cambridge, London: MIT Press.

Seyfarth, Scott. 2014. Word informativity influences acoustic duration: Effects of contextual predictability on lexical representation. *Cognition* 133(1). 140–155. https://doi.org/10.1016/j.cognition.2014.06.013.

Seyfarth, Scott, Marc Garellek, Gwendolyn Gillingham, Farrell Ackerman & Robert Malouf. 2017. Acoustic differences in morphologically-distinct homophones. *Language, Cognition and Neuroscience* 33(1). 32–49. https://doi.org/10.1080/23273798.2017.1359634.

Shafaei-Bajestan, Elnaz, Masoumeh Moradipour-Tari, Peter Uhrig & R. Harald Baayen. 2020. LDL-AURIS: Error-driven learning in modeling spoken word recognition. *PsyArXiv*. 1–36. https://doi.org/10.31234/osf.io/v6cu4.

Shattuck-Hufnagel, Stefanie & Alice Turk. 1998. The domain of phrase – final lengthening in English. *The Journal of the Acoustical Society of America* 103(5). 2889. https://doi.org/10.1121/1.421798.

Solomyak, Olla & Alec Marantz. 2010. Evidence for early morphological decomposition in visual word recognition. *Journal of Cognitive Neuroscience* 22(9). 2042–2057. https://doi.org/10.1162/jocn.2009.21296.

Sóskuthy, Márton & Jennifer Hay. 2017. Changing word usage predicts changing word durations in New Zealand English. *Cognition* 166. 298–313. https://doi.org/10.1016/j.cognition.2017.05.032.

Sproat, Richard & Osamu Fujimura. 1993. Allophonic variation in English /l/ and its implications for phonetic implementation. *Journal of Phonetics* 21(3). 291–311. https://doi.org/10.1016/S0095-4470(19)31340-3.

Stein, Simon D. & Ingo Plag. 2021. Morpho-phonetic effects in speech production: Modeling the acoustic duration of English derived words with linear discriminative learning. *Frontiers in Psychology* 12. 678712. https://doi.org/10.3389/fpsyg.2021.678712.

Stein, Simon D. & Ingo Plag. 2022. How relative frequency and prosodic structure affect the acoustic duration of English derivatives. *Laboratory Phonology* 13(1). https://doi.org/10.16995/labphon.6445.

Sternke, Katharina. 2021. Eye tracking evidence for homophone disambiguation based on frequency. Paper presented at *Workshop of the DFG Research Unit FOR2373*, 19 March, Düsseldorf.

Sugahara, Mariko & Alice Turk. 2009. Durational correlates of English sublexical constituent structure. *Phonology* 26. 477–524. https://doi.org/10.1017/S0952675709990248.

Szymanek, Bogdan. 1985. *English and Polish adjectives: A study in lexicalist word-formation*. Lublin: Redakcja Wydawnictw Katolickiego Uniwersytetu Lubelskiego.

Tabak, Wieke, Robert Schreuder & R. Harald Baayen. 2010. Producing inflected verbs. *The Mental Lexicon* 5(1). 22–46. https://doi.org/10.1075/ml.5.1.02tab.

Taft, Marcus & Kenneth I. Forster. 1975. Lexical storage and retrieval of prefixed words. *Journal of Verbal Learning and Verbal Behavior* 14(6). 638–647. https://doi.org/10.1016/S0022-5371(75)80051-X.

Tomaschek, Fabian, Peter Hendrix & R. Harald Baayen. 2018. Strategies for addressing collinearity in multivariate linguistic data. *Journal of Phonetics* 71. 249–267. https://doi.org/10.1016/j.wocn.2018.09.004.

Tomaschek, Fabian, Ingo Plag, Mirjam Ernestus & R. Harald Baayen. 2019. Phonetic effects of morphology and context: Modeling the duration of word-final S in English with naïve discriminative learning. *Journal of Linguistics* 57(1). 1–39. https://doi.org/10.1017/S0022226719000203.

Tomaschek, Fabian, Benjamin V. Tucker, Michael Ramscar & R. Harald Baayen. 2021. Paradigmatic enhancement of stem vowels in regular English inflected verb forms. *Morphology* 31(2). 171–199. https://doi.org/10.1007/s11525-021-09374-w.

Torreira, Francisco & Mirjam Ernestus. 2009. Probabilistic effects on French [t] duration. *Interspeech*. 448–451. https://doi.org/10.21437/Interspeech.2009.

Tucker, Benjamin, Michelle Sims & R. Harald Baayen. 2019a. Opposing forces on acoustic duration. Preprint submitted to Elsevier. *PsyArXiv*. 1–38. https://doi.org/10.31234/osf.io/jc97w.

Tucker, Benjamin V., Daniel Brenner, D. K. Danielson, Matthew C. Kelley, Filip Nenadić & Michelle Sims. 2019b. The Massive Auditory Lexical Decision (MALD) database. *Behavior Research Methods* 51(3). 1187–1204. https://doi.org/10.3758/s13428-018-1056-1.

Tucker, Benjamin V. & Mirjam Ernestus. 2016. Why we need to investigate casual speech to truly understand language production, processing and the mental lexicon. *The Mental Lexicon* 11(3). 375–400. https://doi.org/10.1075/ml.11.3.03tuc.

Turk, Alice & Stefanie Shattuck-Hufnagel. 2020. *Speech timing: Implications for theories of phonology, speech production, and speech motor control*. New York: Oxford University Press. https://doi.org/10.1093/oso/9780198795421.001.0001.

Turnbull, Rory. 2018. Patterns of probabilistic segment deletion/reduction in English and Japanese. *Linguistics Vanguard* 4(s2). https://doi.org/10.1515/lingvan-2017-0033.

Umeda, Noriko. 1977. Consonant duration in American English. *The Journal of the Acoustical Society of America* 61(3). 846–858. https://doi.org/10.1121/1.381374.

Vaan, Laura de, Mirjam Ernestus & Robert Schreuder. 2011. The lifespan of lexical traces for novel morphologically complex words. *The Mental Lexicon* 6(3). 374–392. https://doi.org/10.1075/ml.6.3.02dev.

Vaan, Laura de, Robert Schreuder & R. Harald Baayen. 2007. Regular morphologically complex neologisms leave detectable traces in the mental lexicon. *The Mental Lexicon* 2(1). 1–23. https://doi.org/10.1075/ml.2.1.02vaa.

Vaissière, Jacqueline. 1983. Language-independent prosodic features. In Anne Cutler & D. Robert Ladd (eds.), *Prosody: Models and measurements* (Springer Series in Language and Communication 14), 53–66. Berlin, Heidelberg: Springer. https://doi.org/10.1007/978-3-642-69103-4_5.

Vannest, Jennifer, Raymond Bertram, Juhani Järvikivi & Jussi Niemi. 2002. Counterintuitive cross-linguistic differences: More morphological computation in English than in Finnish. *Journal of Psycholinguistic Research* 31(2). 83–106. https://doi.org/10.1023/A:1014934915952.

Vitevitch, Michael S. & Paul A. Luce. 2004. A web-based interface to calculate phonotactic probability for words and nonwords in English. *Behavior Research Methods, Instruments, and Computers* 36(3). 481–487. https://doi.org/10.3758/BF03195594.

Wagenmakers, Eric-Jan. 2007. A practical solution to the pervasive problems of p values. *Psychonomic Bulletin & Review* 14(5). 779–804. https://doi.org/10.3758/BF03194105.

Walsh, Liam, Jennifer Hay, Bent Derek, Liz Grant, Jeanette King, Paul Millar, Viktoria Papp & Kevin Watson. 2013. The UC QuakeBox Project: Creation of a community-focused research archive. *New Zealand English Journal* 27. 20–32. https://doi.org/10.26021/2.

Wasserstein, Ronald L., Allen L. Schirm & Nicole A. Lazar. 2019. Moving to a world beyond "p < 0.05". *The American Statistician* 73(1). 1–19. https://doi.org/10.1080/00031305.2019.1583913.

Wicherts, Jelte M., Coosje L. S. Veldkamp, Hilde E. M. Augusteijn, Marjan Bakker, Robbie C. M. van Aert & Marcel A. L. M. van Assen. 2016. Degrees of freedom in planning, running, analyzing, and reporting psychological studies: A checklist to avoid p-hacking. *Frontiers in Psychology* 7. 1832. https://doi.org/10.3389/fpsyg.2016.01832.

Widrow, Bernard & Marcian E. Hoff. 1960. Adaptive switching circuits. *IRE WESCON Convention Record Part IV*. 96–104. https://doi.org/10.21236/AD02.

Wightman, Colin W., Stefanie Shattuck-Hufnagel, Mari Ostendorf & Patti Price. 1992. Segmental durations in the vicinity of prosodic phrase boundaries. *The Journal of the Acoustical Society of America* 91(3). 1707–1717. https://doi.org/10.1121/1.402450.

Wittgenstein, Ludwig. 2009 [1953]. *Philosophical investigations,* 4th edn. Chichester: Wiley-Blackwell.

Wunderlich, Dieter. 1996. A minimalist model of inflectional morphology. In Chris Wilder, Hans-Martin Gärtner & Manfred Bierwisch (eds.), *The role of economy principles in linguistic theory* (Studia Grammatica 40), 267–298. Berlin: Akademie Verlag. https://doi.org/10.1515/9783050072173-011.

Xu, Yi. 2010. In defense of lab speech. *Journal of Phonetics* 38(3). 329–336. https://doi.org/10.1016/j.wocn.2010.04.003.

Zhou, Xiaolin & William Marslen-Wilson. 1994. Words, morphemes and syllables in the Chinese mental lexicon. *Language and Cognitive Processes* 9(3). 393–422. https://doi.org/10.1080/01690969408402125.

Zimmerer, Frank, Mathias Scharinger & Henning Reetz. 2014. Phonological and morphological constraints on German /t/-deletions. *Journal of Phonetics* 45. 64–75. https://doi.org/10.1016/j.wocn.2014.03.006.

Zimmermann, Julia. 2016. Morphological status and acoustic realization: Findings from New Zealand English. In Christopher Carignan & Michael D. Tyler (eds.), *Proceedings of the Sixteenth Australasian International Conference on Speech Science and Technology*. 201–204. Parramatta, Australia.

Zuraw, Kie, Isabelle Lin, Meng Yang & Sharon Peperkamp. 2020. Competition between whole-word and decomposed representations of English prefixed words. *Morphology* 31. 201–237. https://doi.org/10.1007/s11525-020-09354-6.

Index

Bold page numbers indicate figures; *italics* indicate tables.

activation diversity 4, 57, 169, 181, 182, 187, 189, 190
affirming the consequent fallacy 197
affix probability. *see* probability (conditional)
alignment. *see* phonetic segmentation
A-Morphous Morphology 22, 49
articulation 14, 15, 22, 27, 39, 53, 199
articulatory path 167, 179, 180, 185, 186
articulatory reduction. *see* reduction
attention 101

baseline activation 22
Bayesian statistics 108
biology 53, 198, 203
Bloomfieldian linguistics 9, 12, 13
boundary
– morphological 10, 14, 25, 26, 27, 31, 102, 103, 153, 188
– prosodic **34**, 33–39, 117, 119, 120, 121, 122, 123, 124, 154, 155, 199
– strength 10, 25, 35, 48, 117, 120, 199, 205
bracket erasure 14, 53, 54

certainty 4, 29, 53, 54, 57, 80, 102, 168, 169, 179, 186, 200, 201
cognitive fallacy 13, 21, 50, 55, 156, 197, 201, 203
cognitive reality. *see* cognitive fallacy
collinearity 74, 82–83, 85, 97, 103, 133, 138, 150, 200
communicative account 27, 39, 46, 118, 153, 154
computation 2, 3, 9, 17, 22, 23, 27, 48, 49, 189
conditional affix probability. *see* probability (conditional)
connectionist approaches 50, 199
conversational speech 17, 66, 67, 97, 121, 189
corpus data 66–68, 68, *72*, 82

decomposability. *see* segmentability
decompositional perspective 2, 8–9, **10**, 9–17, 19, 20, 21, 24, 25, 43, 52, 53, 58–59, 63, 192, 196, 198, 202, 204, 205
derivational function 63
discriminative learning 51–58, 157–191, 192, 195, 196, 197, 204, 206
Distributed Morphology 11
distributional semantics 55, 197
dual-route models 20, 21, 27
duration
– baseline **75**, 73–76, 193
– difference **75**, 74–76
– effects on 1, 3–4, 22–24, 28–30, 33, 34–36, 36, **89**, **90**, **91**, *94*, *96*, *109*, *111*, **112**, **114**, *117*, *131*, *134*, *135*, *136*, **137**, *138*, *139*, *140*, **141**, *142*, *143*, *144*, **145**, *146*, *147*, *148*, **149**, *173*, *175*, **177**, **178**, 201
– observed 73, 74, **75**

entrenchment 18
etymology 69
exemplar models 49
exploratory research 62, 193
exponent 12, 196

feed-forward models 2, 13, 14, 15, 16, 47, 205
frequency 3, 5, 17–18, 22–23, 43, 55, 66, 76, 97–101, 152, 199–200, 200
– base 3, 18, 19, 23, 24, 59, 78, 97, 98
– bigram 79
– effects of **89**, **90**, **91**, *94*, *96*, 97, *109*, *111*, **112**, *175*, 194
– lemma 69, 77, 99
– relative 3, 25–26, 24–31, 36, 41, 69, 78, 101–104, 108, 110, 117, 118, 153, 154
– string. *see* probability (joint)
– word 19, 21, 23, 24, 76–78, 97, 98–99
full-listing models 22, 48, 99

gemination 40

generativism 9, 13, 14, 47, 55
gesture 13, 14, 15, 16, 22, 199
GP-alignment 33

heterogeneity of processing hypothesis 26, 27
homophones 77, 100

inflection 20, 48
information density. *see* informativeness
informativeness 4, 39–47, 101, 150–156, 199, 200
informativity. *see* informativeness
item-and-arrangement theories 10

lexical access. *see* lexical storage
Lexical Phonology 14
lexical storage 2, 3, 11, 13, 17, 18, 19, 20, 21, 22, 27, 48–51, 53, 100, 189, 198
lexical stratum 14
lexicalist view 11
lexome 159, 162
linear discriminative learning. *see* discriminative learning
linear regression 81–84, 170, 200

mean word support 167–168, *173*, **177**, **178**, **179**, 180, 186
memory 12, 22, 27, 50, 51, 52, 100, 197, 198, 201, 202
mental lexicon 12, 13, 15, 18, 21, 27, 48, 50, 203, 204
Minimalist Morphology 20
morpheme 1, 2, **10**–13, 13, 14, 19, 20, 26, 33, 40, 47, **52**, 53, 54, 63, 100, 159, 196, 197, 198, 203
morphological category 63
morphological function 63
morphological paradigm 40, 47, 49, 102
morphological productivity 64, 126
morphology-phonology interface 14, 16, 53, 59, 206
motor practice 22, 77, 80, 99
mutual information 42

naïve discriminative learning 55, 56, 161
neural networks 51, 199, 203

non-decompositional perspective 2, 8–9, 22, 43, 47–51, 52, 53, 58–59, 63, 162–164, 192, 196, 198, 202, 204, 205
null hypothesis significance testing 72, 86, 108, 193

ontological reality. *see* cognitive fallacy

Paradigmatic Signal Enhancement Hypothesis 102
path entropies 168, *173*, **177**, **178**, **179**, 180, 186
p-hacking 193
phonaesthemes 53, 203
phoneme 15, 26, 53, 196
phonetic segmentation 67, **70**, **71**, 70–71
phonological foot 32, **34**
phonological word. *see* prosodic word
polysemy 11, 169, 190
postlexical level 2, 9, 15, 16, 26, 53
pre-boundary lengthening 31, 34–36, 121
predictability. *see* probability
probability 40–42, 200
– biphone 79–80
– conditional 41, 44, *45*, 46, 125 *126*, *131*, *133*, *134*, *135*, *136*, **137**, *138*, *139*, *140*, 130–141, **141**, 150, 152, 199
– joint 41, 44
– paradigmatic 40, 43, 102, 187
– prior 41, 44
– syntagmatic 41, 43, 152
– transitional 103, 124, 153, 154, 155, 165, 167, 199
production ease account 27, 43, 118, 153
prosodic hierarchy **32**, 121
Prosodic Phonology 32
prosodic word 3, 14, 31–39, 63, 119–124
pword. *see* prosodic word

reduction 16, 17, 22–24, 26–28, 31, 36, 39, 46, 79, 85, 86, 104, 105, 110, 120, 125, 132, 150, 151, 152, 180, 187, 189, 190, 199, 201
redundancy
– in storage 13, 19, 21, 48, 49
– measure 40, 42, 44
representation strength 18

representational account 28
rules 9, 13, 14, 20, 21, 48–49, 54

Saussurean sign 1, **10**, 11, 12, 20, **52**, 163, 196, 204
segmentability 1, 3, 24–31, 35, 101–104, 112, 118, 119, 153–154, 188–189, 199
semantic density 169, *173*, **177**, **179**, 181, 187–189
semantic information load 42, 45, 46, 126–128, *142*, *143*, *144*, **145**, *146*, *147*, *148*, **149**, 142–150, 151, 152
semantic neighbors 169, *183*, **185**, 183–185
semantic opacity. *see* semantic transparency
semantic transparency 25, 45, 126, 169, 188, 190, 199
semantic vector length 168–169, *173*, **178**, **179**, 181–182, 189–190
semantic vectors 55–56, 160–164, 195
semiotic hierarchy 9, 14
separationist view 11, 12, 19, 196
Smooth Signal Redundancy Hypothesis 154

speech processing 1, 2, 6, 8, 9, 10, 13, 17, 18, 46, 47, 54, 100, 189, 192, 194, 201, 202, 205
speech production models 10, 13, 15, 20, 53
speech rate 66, 78
Stratal Optimality Theory 15
Stratal Phonology 15, 16, 20, 27
stress 32, 34, 64, 65, 122
structuralism 9, 14, 47, 55, 56, 204
surprisal. *see* informativeness
syntagmatic and paradigmatic axis 9, 47
syntax 9, 12, 14, 47, 122

target correlation 169

uncertainty. *see* certainty
usage-based perspective 18, 44, 155

WEIRD bias 204
whole-word storage 19, 20, 21, 24, 27, 48, 99, 100, 194
Word and Paradigm Morphology 22, 47, 48, 55

www.ingramcontent.com/pod-product-compliance
Lightning Source LLC
Chambersburg PA
CBHW050523170426
43201CB00013B/2062